Lawyers for People of Moderate Means

some problems
of availability of
legal services

Barlow F. Christensen

American Bar Foundation

Library of Congress Catalog Number: 70-124879

AMERICAN BAR FOUNDATION
1970

Summary of Contents

Contents

Preface

In the summer of 1965, an American Bar Association Special Committee began the task of studying availability of legal services and making recommendations to the Association's House of Delegates. Subsequently, an American Bar Foundation research project was undertaken to provide the Committee with research support. This book is made up of papers written as a part of that project.

These papers do not describe empirical studies, at least in the nose-counting sense. Portions—most notably the treatment of lawyer referral services—are based on fairly extensive and systematic observation, but none of the studies described is empirical in the sense of being either a field study or an examination of a collection of statistical data. Rather, the studies are largely analytical and polemical.

Field research or statistical studies would be of obvious value in relation to many of the questions involved, of course. But the breadth of the subject to be covered, together with serious limitations of time and resources, precluded extensive field research, and reliable data were not readily available for statistical analysis. Superficial field studies and generalization from inadequate data were rejected as probably fruitless and possibly misleading.

Neither is this book a synthesis of everything written on the subject, nor even an exhaustive treatment of the few topics selected for examination. While a vast amount of material is tangentially relevant to the subject of availability of legal services, relatively little of it is directly in point. A synthesis of the existing literature would therefore be either too short and general to be of value or, if exhaustive, nothing less than a complete treatise on law practice, the legal profession, and the entire law.

A modest analytical task has therefore been undertaken: The task of isolating and probing tentatively a few of the fundamental issues involved in the problem of availability of legal services. The objective has been to look at these issues from a point of view that is perhaps a bit different from the usual perspective. No claim is made that this perspective is the only one, but it may produce some helpful insights. And if the legal profession, by utilizing this perspective, can come to understand itself better and to apply this understanding to the essential problem of making lawyers' services available to more people, the purposes of this work will have been fulfilled.

Acknowledgments

The customary acknowledgments are inadequate to express the debt owed to others for help in the completion of this study. Recognition must nevertheless be given to many people for contributions they have made.

Professor Elliott E. Cheatham has been a source of inspiration and direction. Geoffrey C. Hazard, Jr., Executive Director of the American Bar Foundation, has given encouragement, stimulation, ideas, and invaluable criticism. So, too, has F. B. MacKinnon, of the Foundation staff. Indeed, nearly all members of the ABF professional staff have at one time or another contributed helpful ideas and suggestions. Olavi Maru, Reference Librarian of the Cromwell Library, has been of special assistance. Portions of the manuscript were read by Sheldon Roodman, Esquire, and his suggestions have been most helpful.

Particular mention should be made of those who were members of the American Bar Association Special Committee on Availability of Legal Services during the development of this work: Chairman F. William McCalpin, William H. Avery, Paul Carrington, Robert J. Kutak, Richard W. Nahstoll, Chesterfield Smith, and Theodore Voorhees. Their provocative discussions, wise counsel, and usually gentle but always perceptive criticisms have been of inestimable value. In addition, many other ABA Committees and a great many lawyers from all over the country have offered helpful comments.

Finally, the money to finance this study has come from the American Bar Endowment. The author is deeply grateful to the Endowment, and through it to all members of the American Bar Association, for this vital support.

The assistance rendered by these people and many others has contributed immeasurably to the study here reported. It is surely better than it could ever have been without such help. Defects that have persisted, however, are solely the responsibility of the author.

Notes

General Note

As this work was being prepared in final form for publication, the American Bar Association House of Delegates adopted a new Code of Professional Responsibility to replace the old Canons of Professional Ethics. A problem thus arose with respect to the many references herein to the old Canons and to ethics committee opinions and court decisions interpreting them.

These references will remain unchanged, with no attempt to translate or cross-reference to provisions of the newly adopted Code. One reason is the formidable nature of the task. Finding the applicable Code provisions for every reference to the Canons or opinions is apt to be a long, tedious, and somewhat speculative process, unlikely to be worth the effort. The new Code will not become effective in regulating the conduct of lawyers until adopted in the several states, and securing its adoption may take some time. The old Canons will thus continue in force in the immediate future. Moreover, while the new Code does make some substantive changes and additions to the old Canons, it represents primarily a reformulation of the old principles and concepts. And although no one can be sure how the new Code will be interpreted, the interpretations heretofore made in ethics committee opinions and court decisions are likely to be used as guides to interpretation of the new Code. The discussion of ethical principles here in terms of the old Canons, opinions, and decisions therefore appears both useful and expedient.

**A Note
on the
Citations**

The style of citation in this volume marks a departure from the usual law review system. Rather than burden each page with a heavy ballast of footnotes, the author and the editors have chosen to import a method of citation from the social sciences which places all works referred to at the back of the book (see pp. 297-313). These are referred to by boldface number in the text. For example, (**63**) will be found in "Works Cited" in its proper numerical position. Specific page references are made thus: (**63**:184). Commentary or explanatory material, however, is kept at the bottom of the page, adjacent to the text to which it applies.

Lawyers for
People of
Moderate
Means

I

The Problem
in Perspective

The rule of law is today being tested as seldom before in the history of the republic. Citizens who are aggrieved and frustrated at what they regard as the failure of the legal, economic, and social systems to fulfill their expectations of equal justice and opportunity are resorting increasingly to violence and disorder in preference to orderly processes of change. To those who believe that law is the only foundation of true liberty, justice, and equality of opportunity, this growing rejection of the rule of law is a source of acute distress. Perhaps even more distressing—and frightening—is the cynical conclusion of a tiny but highly vocal and active minority that the American dream is ended and that social justice can be built only upon the ruins of the democratic system.

The present crisis seems to be at least partly a result of a sort of polarization that causes things to be seen quite differently by different observers. Those who believe in the democratic system and the rule of law tend to see—and perhaps for too long have seen—only the achievements of the system and not its failures. The dissenters overlook the system's very real accomplishments and see only that it thus far seems to have failed in matters they deem to be of vital importance.

Unfortunately, a movement toward rejection of the rule of law cannot be reversed merely by the mouthing of platitudes about how far the democratic system has come or by the proliferation of promises about what the system may in due time accomplish. The man whose frustrations lead him to reject the rule of law may no longer be willing to wait for "due time," and he is apt to see the system's achievements largely in terms of protecting one man's property at the expense of another man's spirit—or even his life. A point seems to have been reached in the nation's development, therefore, where those who still cherish the American dream have but one real alternative, and that perhaps for only a very little while longer: *to make the democratic system really work to achieve genuine social justice for all Americans.*

Making the system work seems to a large degree to be a matter of relevance. Those areas where the system has thus far failed seem to be areas where the system's answers are not entirely relevant to society's essential problems. For example, the realization has finally come to most authorities that tearing down slum buildings—the old approach to urban renewal—is not really responsive to the problems of urban poverty. Another example is in the field of racial discrimination, where it is becoming apparent that equal employment opportunity laws are relatively meaningless without genuinely equal access to education and training opportunities, and that, in turn, the efficacy of education and training is severely limited by the social and psychic disruptions produced by poverty and the environment of the urban ghetto. Still another example is in the field of automobile accident reparations, where deficiencies and inequities are beginning to generate serious doubt about the real relevance of the fault principle and the litigative process to the social problem of automobile accidents.

The question of relevance has, or should have, special poignancy for lawyers, as failure to examine lawyers' functions against the background of today's problems and to adjust them accordingly is a sure path to professional obsolescence. The custom drafting of instruments for transactions that no longer really require custom-drafted paper, for example, may mean an occasional fee for a lawyer, but it may also mean that the public will grow tired of paying for work that does not need doing and begin to take all such transactions—including those aspects that do require a lawyer's attention—to the lawyer's lay competitors. What may be worse, the dissipation of lawyers' efforts on tasks not requiring lawyers' skills diverts them from more productive utilization. For lawyers, then, whose particular concern is the rule of law, the task of making the system work requires consideration of the relevance of law, legal institutions, and lawyers' services to the serious social problems of the age.

But what has all this to do with availability of legal services? Availability can be looked at as a fairly simple problem of distribution—a matter of finding methods of making "legal services" more readily "available" to people who "need" them. But in a very real sense, availability of legal services is also a problem of relevance.

For one thing, "legal services" may not be as readily determinable a commodity as the term itself would seem to suggest, and any careful attempt to define it must come eventually to questions about the kinds of problems people have and about the appropriateness of lawyers' skills to the solution of such problems. Similarly, the "availability" of those services to the public may involve not only the obvious factor of their physical accessibility, but also their price and even their suitability to the problems to which they are to be applied. And "need" is nothing more than someone's estimate of the importance or urgency of particular problems. Thus, availability of legal services is very much a matter of the relevance of lawyers to society's essential problems; the ultimate answers to the questions of availability will therefore be determined in large part by the answers given to the question of the relevance of lawyers and lawyers' services to today's problems. And the answers to this latter question are in turn largely determined by the even more basic question of the relevance of law and legal institutions to the crucial problems of contemporary society.

A modest study of availability of legal services is an obviously inappropriate vehicle for an inquiry into a subject as vast as the role of law in society, however pertinent and enticing such an inquiry might be. But availability of legal services is, in a sense, a question of relevance even when viewed as essentially a problem of distribution. Even laws and legal institutions that are genuinely responsive to essential problems may nevertheless be irrelevant to those problems if the legal services necessary to make them operative are not readily obtainable by those who might benefit from them. Assuming, then, that lawyers and the services they are able to provide have, and will continue to have, some relevance to society's essential problems, it is appropriate that consideration be given to methods of making lawyers' services more readily obtainable by segments of the public that do not now make fullest beneficial use of them. And here, the pertinent and significant questions are those that simply ask how lawyers produce and distribute their services.

From within this more narrow framework, the focus of inquiry should probably be limited still further. The problems of furnishing legal services to the poor[*][1] are being studied intensively in other American Bar Foundation projects and will not be treated here.[2] It may be, of course, that the insights and answers developed in these other studies will have application to the problems of furnishing legal services to non-indigent segments of the population. But this inquiry will not attempt to explore the special problems involved in distributing legal services to the poor.

The furnishing of legal services to property and commercial clients[3] will likewise be excluded, mainly because most of the problems of distribution have been solved satisfactorily in practice. Large efficient law firms have developed as a response to the needs — and ability to pay — of the more affluent segments of society. And the large firms seem to be serving these clients well. For purposes of this study, then, the rendition of legal services to business and property clients will be of interest primarily for the contributions that experience in that field might make to solution of the problems of distributing legal services to the rest of the public.

Two other limitations may also be advisable. The problems of furnishing representation in criminal matters will not be treated. Those problems deserve far more attention than they could be given in this modest study, and, indeed, far transcend any inquiry that would be feasible within the bounds of the concept of "availability" as it is above defined. The furnishing of representation in unpopular causes has also been excluded for the same reason.

The objective of this study, then, will be to examine some of the problems involved in the production and distribution of

---

[*]Citations in boldface type refer the reader to the numbered "Works Cited" at 297–313; where numbers immediately follow the boldface reference, the reader is referred to specific pages in that work.

1. As used here, the term "the poor" is intended to mean people who would be eligible for free legal services from legal aid or legal service agencies. Standards of eligibility are different from place to place, however, and a precise definition is thus impossible.

2. American Bar Foundation projects studying legal services for the poor have thus far resulted in the following publications: **279**; **280**; **282**; **285**. These projects, under the direction of Barbara A. Curran, are now nearing completion.

3. The terms "property and commercial clients" and "property and business clients" are meant here to refer to those who either operate some form of business enterprise or who possess sufficient money or property to have serious concern about finding ways of protecting it.

legal services in civil matters to people of moderate means.[4] It will be premised on the assumptions that lawyers have and will continue to have at least some relevance to society's essential problems, that questions about the production and distribution of lawyers' services are therefore pertinent, that those questions should be answered by the legal profession itself, and that they can be answered through the difficult but sometimes unpleasant processes of self-examination, self-criticism, and self-improvement.

Self-examination and self-criticism tend to be made especially difficult by a marked heterogeneity within the bar. Indeed, the legal profession appears in many ways to be a coalition of several different groups with quite dissimilar characteristics and, in some instances, with conflicting interests. Generally speaking, the lawyer in the large firm, with a predominantly business clientele, is clearly different from either the big-city solo practitioner or the member of a small urban firm with predominantly low- and middle-income individuals as clients. So, too, salaried government lawyers seem to have some distinctive characteristics and problems, as do corporation house counsel and labor union lawyers. The general practitioner in the small community is different still from all these. The point is not to define the categories, but rather to suggest something of the diversity of practice, and consequently of both interest and need, among the various segments of the bar.

Recognition of this diversity does not yet seem to be general within the profession. Many lawyers continue to insist on the homogeneity and fungibility of members of the bar, an in-

4. The terms "people of moderate means" and "moderate-income people" will be used interchangeably to denote that segment of the population above the poverty level but below the level described in note 3 *supra* as "property and commercial clients." Obviously, these categories cannot be delimited precisely; indeed, the three levels overlap to some extent. As a rough characterization, however, "people of moderate means" might be thought of usefully, in terms of income, as those earning between $5,000 and $15,000 a year. There are two striking points to be noted about this segment of the public. The first is its size. In 1963, 60 percent of the nation's families—a total of approximately 28 million family units—had annual family incomes of more than $5,000 but less than $15,000 (317:36, 333). The second significant point is the relatively small amount of legal service that now seems to be provided to this large group of people, except in such fields as personal injury, divorce, and criminal law—and perhaps probate, to some extent, and real estate, at least in some sections of the country. This statement cannot be documented; there have been no meaningful studies of the clientele of lawyers, and the few attempts that have thus far been made to study the public's use and potential use of lawyers are quite unsatisfactory (300:14). They do at least suggest, however, that the use of lawyers by people of moderate means may be far from optimal (302:4, 5; see also 99:60-62).

creasingly unreal but persistent view founded upon traditional premises that seem no longer to be entirely in accord with the facts.

The setting for the traditional view—the small town with a settled and homogeneous population, where everyone knew everyone else—is no longer typical of America. The nation's population is instead now predominantly urban, anonymous, heterogeneous, rootless, and mobile.

So too, with the archetype of the traditional lawyer—the small-town solo practitioner. He built his practice slowly but solidly on an acquired reputation for integrity and competence. He gave gratuitous service to the poor and earned an ample but well-deserved living from the rest. One of the few literate men in town, he became the trusted and honored counselor of all. And, of course, he was the only available expert on the law.

But the traditional small-town lawyer is becoming increasingly atypical of the legal profession.[5] Today's lawyer may be a member of a large legal staff, either for a big corporation or for a government agency. He may be employed by a labor union, either on salary or on full-time retainer. He may engage in a specialized practice, either as a member of a large general-practice firm with predominantly business clients, or as a member of a firm that handles only one kind of legal business. Even the lawyer who does draw his clients primarily from the general public is usually no more to today's constantly changing urban population than a name in the classified section of the telephone book or on a building directory. His literacy is, by itself, no longer of special value to a generally literate public, nor is his once-unique expertise in the law now always either truly expert or exclusive. The lawyer may, indeed, still have something unique to offer the public, but it is offered in a variety of remarkably diverse circumstances.

5. As of 1966, a majority (53.3 percent) of the lawyers in private practice were still individual practitioners, but their numbers have been declining gradually over the past fifteen years. What is more important, the percentage of lawyers in private practice who are solo practitioners has declined from 68.6 percent to 53.3 percent over the past twenty years. Moreover, the percentage of all lawyers who are solo practitioners has dropped dramatically from 61.2 percent in 1948 to only 39.1 percent in 1966. The corollary, of course, is that the number of lawyers employed by private concerns has risen in the same period from 5,555 (3.2 percent of all lawyers) to 33,222 (11.5 percent of all lawyers), and the number employed by government has risen from 21,273 (12.4 percent of the total number of lawyers) to 40,992 (14.2 percent). Thus, nearly two-thirds of all lawyers today are engaged in activities other than the individual private practice of law, as compared with just over one-third in 1948 (57:18–21).

Diversity within the legal profession may have implications at many different levels. It will no doubt affect the nature — and perhaps the quality — of the professional services rendered by lawyers in different practice situations. It will probably also affect the compensation to be earned from professional services performed in different contexts. Diversity tends to multiply the number of different kinds of services offered by the bar, as well as the conditions under which they are offered. It may also affect the extent to which different lawyers are able to perceive the problems of availability of legal services or to appreciate the nature of those problems. It will surely result in variations in the degree to which different lawyers will be affected by such problems and by various possible solutions to them. And finally, it may exert a controlling influence upon the willingness of various segments of the bar to accept appropriate solutions.

The matter may be complicated even more by the fact that large firm lawyers, who are probably least affected by the problems of making legal services available to people of moderate means, seem to dominate the positions of power in the larger and more influential bar associations and thus have much to do with determining policy for the profession. On the other hand, solo practitioners and small firm lawyers, who would seem to be most affected by those problems, are probably closer to the state legislatures and perhaps are thus able to exert a greater influence on legislation. It is clear, then, that efforts at self-examination, self-criticism, and self-improvement by the legal profession should take into consideration the many differences in characteristics, attitudes, interests, and needs of the various elements of the bar.

Much of the largely exploratory examination that follows will be cast in what are essentially economic terms. Self-examination and self-criticism often tend to be inhibited by traditional rhetoric, and the formulation of issues in new and different terms may help to encourage freer thought. More importantly, the problems involved in the distribution of legal services to people of moderate means, particularly in civil matters, seem, to a significant extent, to be economic problems. The discussion will therefore be divided into three parts: first, an examination of the product itself — lawyers' services; second, an appraisal of the demand for the product — the client's point of view; and third, a look at some of the factors that seem to affect the market for the product — its price and quality, its accessibility, public knowledge and attitudes, and the availability of competitive products.

A
The Product:
Lawyers' Services

In talking about the product to be distributed, the term "lawyers' services" would perhaps be a more useful one than "legal services." As suggested earlier, "legal services" may not be as readily determinable a commodity as the term would seem to suggest. Indeed, no single substantive definition appears to exist—at least none that is satisfactory for the purposes of this discussion.

The term has been most often considered in contexts where the issues have been narrow and substantially unrelated to the problems of concern here. Most come from unauthorized practice cases and opinions, where the issue is whether a particular activity is one that should be restricted exclusively to lawyers.[6] They thus tend to define "legal services" in terms of the functions lawyers have traditionally performed. They do so, of course, for the purpose of placing limits upon the activities of laymen, and not to describe the almost infinite variety of things lawyers may do.

As so defined, the term "legal services" seems manifestly unsuitable. At this point in history, the legal profession can ill afford to spend time ruminating about the things that lawyers have traditionally done, and even less to become involved in intensive examination of what a particular court or unauthorized practice committee may have once characterized as the "unlawful practice of law" for purposes of curtailing the activities of laymen. Instead, the focus must be upon the things *lawyers* can and should do for people in an increasingly complex age. The legal profession's concern should be the more effective, more productive, more beneficial, and more rewarding employment of lawyers' unique abilities—in short, the development of the profession to meet the demands of the time.

6. For cases and opinions dealing with what constitutes "the practice of law," see Bass (**70**:5–6, 67–68).

The term "lawyers' services" has therefore been chosen as part of a general working concept, with the intention that it be used here to denote those functions, whether traditional or not, that lawyers appear especially well qualified to perform and that make the most productive and beneficial use of lawyers' special skills and attributes. And what unique qualities or abilities do lawyers have to offer to the public?

The training of lawyers — including both the formal training of law school and the informal on-the-job training acquired in the first years of practice — does provide them with significant attributes. The first is skill in the difficult but highly valuable technique of disciplined analysis leading to the use of legal principles in the solution of individual problems. This analytical problem-solving skill appears to be the very essence of "lawyering." The second is a commitment to ethical principles, or at least a "professional outlook" embracing the important concepts of the lawyer's independence in the exercise of his professional judgment and his duty of loyalty to his client. The third is a degree of familiarity with the law and with techniques for finding the law. The fourth attribute of the lawyer is possession of practice skills, most of which are acquired through experience. Among these are the skills of advocacy, counseling, drafting, and negotiation.

If these are lawyers' special skills and attributes, what kinds of services make the most productive use of them? What kinds of things do lawyers — as lawyers — do? What kinds of things do their skills equip them to do?

An exhaustive catalogue of the things lawyers do would be difficult to compile, although such a catalogue might be of interest and value. Here, however, an attempt will be made only to suggest some of the broad categories into which lawyers' many services would seem to fall, and to point out some relationships between these classifications and the basic issue of this discussion — how better to produce and distribute the lawyer's product to people of moderate means.

Different analytical approaches may give rise to different classification systems. For the purposes of this inquiry, four have been selected for at least passing comment. These four systems of classification slice through different cross-sections of the knot of related issues:

1. Classification according to the objective of the service

2. Classification according to the functional characteristics of the service

3. Classification on the basis of the context or legal setting in which the service is performed

4. Classification by degree of special skill required for performance of the service

From an over-all standpoint, two preliminary observations appear to be worth mentioning. First, the activities that might properly be included in any one classification are varied and shade with minute gradations into those typical of other categories. And second, the solving of most legal problems usually involves the performance of several different kinds of service at once.

1
*The Objective
of the Service*

Lawyers' services can be viewed as having two basic objectives: They may be remedial, directed toward getting the client out of a particular legal difficulty; or they may be preventive, directed toward keeping the client out of legal difficulty.

Sometimes this dichotomy is put in terms of offensive and defensive strategy, although the two analytical approaches are not entirely parallel. Remedial legal services are usually, although not always, defensive in nature. But in preventing legal problems, the strategy may be either offensive or defensive. Counseling a client about the steps he must take to comply with applicable law is essentially defensive, though preventive; seeking to alter the applicable law through lobbying is the employment of an offensive strategy for a preventive purpose. Test case litigation may have both preventive and remedial elements and may involve both offensive and defensive strategy.

Preventive legal work involves highly creative use of lawyers' skills, but so far its most effective application has been limited to the affairs of government, large organizations, and business and property clients. Legal aid agencies have long tried to practice preventive law on behalf of the poor, but in the past their efforts have been seriously hampered by the gross inadequacy of funds, facilities, and staff. Today, however, offensive strategy for preventive purposes is coming more and more to be used in behalf of the poor, most notably in the federally funded legal service programs (see 165:99, 100).

Some group legal service plans[7] have sought to provide people of moderate means with preventive legal services. Among the best examples, perhaps, are the automobile clubs, which have not only endeavored to furnish members with information about their rights and obligations as motorists, and thus help them avoid legal problems, but also to protect the common interests of their members by bringing test cases and by lobbying to change unfavorable laws.

The great bulk of the legal work performed by private lawyers for persons of moderate means, however, remains remedial in nature, despite the bar's efforts in recent years, through programs like the Annual Legal Check-up (see 78:33), to encourage public use of lawyers' services for preventive purposes. The middle-class public would seem to offer a vast potential for expanded use of lawyers' services in the creative field of preventive law. The big problem, of course, is how to provide preventive legal services at fees middle-class people can, and will be willing to, pay.

2
Functional
Characteristics

Classifying lawyers' services according to their functional characteristics has resulted in the customary and familiar division of activities into the three categories of counseling, drafting, and representation. This is a useful system of classification, but it does not appear to cover all the things lawyers do. Title work, for example, though it typically results in counseling and some drafting, also involves, as a substantial ingredient, research and analysis. When using this functional approach, therefore, perhaps it would be well to think in terms of these three classes as "ultimate functions," supported, in turn, by another important

7. See chapter 7 *infra.*

group of operational activities, including: research, interviewing, investigation (perhaps "fact-gathering" would be better), analysis, and administration. Perhaps there are others as well.

3
The Contexts or Legal Settings
in Which the Services
Are Performed

Another possible way of looking at lawyers' services is to examine the contexts or legal settings in which a particular function is performed. Thus, a lawyer's service for a client, whether counseling, drafting, or representation, or whether undertaken to prevent or cure legal problems, may be performed in the context of formal judicial proceedings. Or it may be performed in connection with administrative proceedings, or in arbitration. The lawyer may also do his work in a variety of informal contexts, such as those in which he usually performs negotiating and lobbying functions.

a
Services performed
in connection with
judicial proceedings

This is the traditional setting for lawyers' activities, and it puts to good use most of the special skills lawyers possess. It is also a field of activity that is still left pretty much to lawyers. There are exceptions, however. Nonlawyers practice before the U.S. Tax Court, for instance. And lawyers never appear, or appear infrequently, before certain other judicial tribunals. Examples are the small claims court, from which lawyers are frequently excluded; the traffic court, where lawyers appear with some frequency only in cases involving serious offenses; and the juvenile court, where, until very recently, theory has seemed to militate against extensive representation in either delinquency or neglect cases.

b
Services performed
in connection with
administrative proceedings

Administrative agencies, unlike the courts, have never been
the exclusive province of lawyers. In fact, lawyers' special qualifications for representing the public in administrative proceedings have only recently been given official recognition by legislation exempting lawyers from special requirements for practice
before federal administrative agencies (**429**).

The theory of administrative law is that many kinds of problems can be handled most expeditiously by tribunals with specialized expertise, making it possible to dispense with many of
the cumbersome trappings of judicial procedure and lawyers.
Experience has shown, however, particularly in fields like workmen's compensation, that although the administrative approach
may have certain advantages, simply calling a decision-maker
"administrator" instead of "judge" works no special magic. As
long as decision-making involves the resolution of disputes of
fact, interpretation of law, and application of law to fact, and as
long as decisions affect the rights of individuals, the special
abilities of lawyers are likely to be called for, even though they
may be exercised in the context of a specialized kind of tribunal.
Thus, the continuing growth of the administrative structure at all
levels of government will surely create an ever-increasing need,
especially in the atypical case, for the functions lawyers can so
well perform, even though this development may also result in
the diminished use of lawyers on routine cases.

c
Services performed
with respect to
arbitration and negotiation

This category covers a fairly broad range of activity, in terms
both of the context in which a particular function is performed
and of the degree to which lawyers' special skills are utilized. It
may range all the way from formal arbitration of a complex labor

dispute, through negotiation with an insurance company on be-half of a claimant, to talking informally with a client's neighbor about a mean dog. At one level or another, most lawyers spend a substantial amount of time performing functions in these con-texts, and, depending upon the subject to which their efforts are applied, they probably do much of their most creative legal work in these areas. It should be mentioned, of course, that nonlaw-yers also work extensively in these fields, even to the point of occupying the dominant position in certain of them.[8]

d
**Services performed
in connection with
legislative proceedings**

A growing field for the employment of lawyers' skills in behalf of clients is that of lobbying—seeking to influence legislation. It is probably no accident that so many of the statements given before legislative hearings are given by lawyers. It is probably also significant that such statements are rarely given in behalf of individuals of moderate means.

4
*The Extent to Which
the Services To Be Performed
Require Lawyers' Special Skills*

A method of classification that would appear to be most directly useful for this study would differentiate among lawyers' services on the basis of the extent to which they require lawyers' special abilities for their satisfactory performance—a classifica-tion that quite obviously relates back to the nature of the client's problem.

The first difficulty encountered with such a classification sys-tem is that of deciding who is to determine whether lawyers' special abilities are required. One method of making the deci-sion would be for the bar alone to determine what is good for the

8. E.g., commercial arbitration.

public and to decide what the public should have. The other would be to rely solely upon the public's evaluation of what services require lawyers' special abilities.

The first approach has been the one used traditionally in the unauthorized practice field. It does have a certain rational validity: The lawyer is clearly better qualified than anyone else — including even the public itself — to determine how and where their special expertise might be used most productively. A lawyer's decision that a particular function deserves, or does not deserve, his attention is one that only he can make intelligently.

The approach is not without hazards, however, as it offers an ever-present temptation to allow self-interest to exert undue influence on the decision, even though the profession is committed to the ideal of public service as the controlling consideration in such determinations. And even where the bar is careful to base its decision upon public interest, the result cannot avoid some coloration from the fact that lawyers see things through lawyers' eyes. Moreover, although public interest may really require that a particular function be performed only by lawyers, a problem can arise in getting the public to accept this fact.

As will be discussed later, questions about what services are to be offered, who is to provide them, and on what terms, are questions that must ultimately be determined by demand. The decisions are therefore made in the end by the public, both through the legislative process and in the marketplace. Thus, to suggest that lawyers alone have the right to decide what services people will get, who will provide them, and on what terms, is not only unduly authoritarian but also somewhat naive.

For purposes of analysis, however, there would appear to be some utility in having at least a tentative initial determination made from the viewpoint of the lawyer. The following attempt at classification will be made, therefore, essentially from the profession's point of view, with the knowledge that the public will ultimately decide whether or not the classification makes sense.

There appear to be three levels of service, as classified on the basis of the extent to which lawyers' special skills are required. First, there are services relating to problems that require individual, careful, and extensive application of lawyers' skills.

These services, which include most of those rendered in relation to what might be called "legal catastrophes," could perhaps be termed "custom services." Second, there are services relating to problems that may be appropriate for the application of lawyers' skills but that might be given some sort of standardized treatment. Included in this category of "routine services" are those that should, for one reason or another, nevertheless be performed by lawyers; those that might be performed by laymen under the supervision of lawyers; and those that could be performed by laymen without the supervision of lawyers. And third, there are some services performed by some lawyers that relate to problems that are not at all appropriate for the application of lawyers' skills and that would perhaps be better left to nonlawyers.

Legal drafting may serve to illustrate these three categories of service. Custom drafting is the kind of individualized service required by unique or complex transactions, problems, or situations. The lawyer fashions an original instrument or document precisely to fit the requirements of the particular case. Custom services are performed, for instance, in drafting instruments to effect complex corporate mergers. Such one-of-a-kind drafting calls for highly creative use of lawyers' special capabilities.

Routine drafting, on the other hand, would be the kind of individually done but essentially "ready-made" service appropriate to frequently encountered transactions, problems, or situations that have become rather common and more or less standardized. Drafting for modern routine residential real estate transactions would appear to be in this category, with the effectuating instruments tending to be fairly well standardized, even when drafted by lawyers on an individual basis. Generally speaking, such drafting requires the lawyer's special legal ability to a comparatively lesser extent than does custom drafting. Indeed, there are those who contend that routine drafting for residential real estate transactions could be done adequately by laymen.

One example of the third category is the drafting of bank checks. Once drafted by lawyers on a custom basis, checks are now drafted by nearly everyone and handled by the billions through computers. Clearly, this service no longer requires lawyers' special skills and is now better performed by the lay agency than by lawyers.

Generally, custom services are—and perhaps should continue to be—the subject of proscriptive rules that permit them to be performed only by lawyers. The situation with respect to routine services is more complicated, however.

The category of routine services covers a broad area, in some of which lawyers share with laymen both the benefits and the obligations of service to the public. There are probably some routine services that should be reserved to lawyers because they nevertheless require lawyers' special skills. Perhaps there are others that could be performed adequately by laymen but that should be reserved to lawyers for some other reason. The argument is often made, for example, that drafting in routine residential real estate transactions should be reserved to lawyers in order to encourage and facilitate the obtaining of lawyers' advice by the parties to such transactions. In addition, there may be some things not *requiring* lawyers' abilities that could be done by laymen but that should be done by lawyers because lawyers can do them better. And here, it is appropriate for the profession to encourage the use of lawyers, even though the services involved do not belong within the bar's monopoly. Perhaps other functions might be performed adequately, and to the benefit of the public, by laymen acting under the supervision of lawyers. Where this is so, the profession would seem to have a duty not merely to permit but also to encourage the public to use properly supervised laymen.

Services not requiring lawyers' skills seem generally to be the province of marginal lawyers, who for economic reasons must do for clients whatever the clients need to have done. Such unproductive use of lawyers' skills is in the interest of neither the public nor the profession. This is not to say that a well-run law office might not provide nonlegal services—performed by nonlawyers—as an incidental service for the accommodation of clients. But lawyers themselves should not be wasting their abilities in activities not requiring their skills.

Three observations are suggested by the foregoing. First, the problems, transactions, and situations to which lawyers' skills might appropriately be applied seem to be changing constantly. The complex and unique custom transactions of one generation often become the routine of the next, while new problems arise, calling for new custom treatment. Second, when the public become convinced that a particular kind of problem or transaction

is—or ought to be—routine, they may not have unlimited pa-
tience with the efforts of the legal profession to retain the problem in the custom category. Third, even though the services
required for routine transactions in individual cases may not call
for the exercise of a high degree of legal skill, truly creative
performance of legal functions with respect to such routine
transactions may nevertheless take place at a different level. An
example of this is the drafting of master or standard forms for
repeated use in a great number of routine transactions—e.g.,
standard real estate documents, standard contracts of insurance,
and standard consumer credit instruments. The preparation and
use of such instruments constitutes an effective offensive strategy on behalf of the institutions for whose benefit they are
drafted. Unfortunately, methods have not yet been found to
enable lawyers to perform the same kind of creative function
extensively on behalf of people of moderate means.

The product for which improved methods of production and
distribution are sought, then, is "lawyers' services"—a complex
bundle of functions so difficult of definition as to require classification and analysis on a number of different planes. Increased
utilization by people of moderate means is the goal. Attention
will now be turned to the factors that appear to affect public
utilization of lawyers' services.

B
Potential Demand: The Public's Needs

Do people of moderate means really need more legal services
than they are now getting? This is one of the first questions to be
encountered in a study of availability of legal services; it is not
necessarily the first to be answered, however. Indeed, as will be
seen in a moment, it probably does not require an answer. More
significantly, perhaps it is unanswerable.

1
Need or Demand?

Need, like beauty, is in the eyes of the beholder. It is an
essentially subjective concept, the evaluation of which depends

upon who is doing the evaluating, for what purposes, and under what conditions. One of the many dictionary definitions of "need," for example, is "a pressing lack of something essential" (340:564). But who is to determine whether something is essential, and how is that determination to be made? And how pressing is "pressing"? Only the person who lacks something can evaluate how essential it is to him or how pressing may be its lack. It is sometimes suggested, of course, that people can have needs of which they are unaware. But this means only that they do not perceive their lack of something someone else deems to be essential, do not consider it to be essential for themselves, or do not feel that the lack of it is pressing.

In considering availability of legal services, then, perhaps it would be more meaningful to think in terms of what is sometimes spoken of as "felt need" — a pressing lack of something perceived as essential *by the person who lacks it.* But this still goes only part of the way. Felt need is a subjective thing, unobservable and unmeasurable except as expressed in some manner. And the ultimate measure of how pressing a lack of something is felt to be by the man who lacks it is the action he will take — what he will do, what he will pay, or what he will forego — in order to obtain it. If someone who lacks something takes no action to obtain it, he is probably unaware that he lacks it, does not know how to obtain it, or, from his own point of view and under the particular conditions then existing, does not regard it as so essential or its lack so pressing as to justify his taking the action that appears to him to be necessary to get it. And, conversely, action implies perception of the lack, knowledge of how to remedy it, and a decision that the thing lacked is so essential as to justify the action.

This decision is not made in a vacuum; most people have "felt needs" for a wide variety of things at once. Thus, when a person who is aware that he could make use of lawyers' services either takes some action or refrains from acting to obtain them, he is also expressing his conclusion as to which of his "felt needs" have priority in the allocation of his limited resources.

And this, of course, is "demand," a good utilitarian concept that has been defined as "an expressed desire for ownership; willingness and ability to purchase a commodity or service; or the quantity of a commodity or service wanted at a specified price and time" (340:564). Demand is, after all, the crucial phe-

nomenon, not some subjective and abstract "need" and not what
lawyers think people should have, but rather the *action* people
may be expected to take, under any given set of conditions, to
obtain lawyers' services. The problem of the legal profession is
not, therefore, to decide for the public what it is that they
"need," but to try to learn something about the conditions under
which there may be some demand for lawyers to do what they
are equipped to do.

2
A Possible Theory
of Demand

In thinking about the problems of availability of lawyers'
services to people of moderate means, lawyers tend to be drawn
toward one or the other of two different theories of demand. The
one simply denies that there is any "unmet need for legal services" among people of moderate means, i.e., that there is any
demand or potential demand for lawyers' services that is not
presently being met through traditional patterns of law practice.
The other theory admits the possibility that people of moderate
means may harbor a potential demand for lawyers' services beyond the service that the bar is presently furnishing to them, but
it calls for studies of the market survey type to quantify such
demand.

The first theory is all too familiar to those who have been
engaged in the legal aid movement over the years. The development of adequate organized programs for supplying legal assistance to the poor has always been hampered by the notion
that the "need for legal services" was merely a function of
property ownership, that therefore the poor had little "need" for
such services, and that the "needs" that they did have were
already being filled adequately through the informal rendering
of gratuitous services by private lawyers.[9] This notion has per-

9. Shortly before this went to press, the results of a revealing study were published
(242:309). The study was designed to learn something of how the organization of the legal
system and of people's affairs affect the definition of problems as "legal" and the seeking
of help from lawyers. It found that certain factors—most notably the individual's income
and location in the social structure—do affect the use of lawyers' services by affecting the
legal resources available to different segments of the population and the kinds of problems encountered by different segments. It further concluded that all segments of society

sisted, despite the fact that wherever organized legal aid offices have been set up, they have attracted clients in numbers far beyond the service capacity provided by severely limited resources. This phenomenon has been demonstrated even more dramatically by the new federally funded legal services programs. The sudden availability of greatly increased resources with which to provide legal services to the poor, together with the introduction of new and better arrangements and techniques for reaching those poor people who have problems, caused the demand to rise far beyond available resources.[10] Clearly, a latent or potential demand awaited only the availability of legal assistance under the right conditions to be translated into actual demand far in excess of supply. No one yet knows how much legal service the poor might be able to use; for immediate practical purposes, however, the demand can probably be regarded as virtually limitless.

One should be cautious about generalizing too extensively from the legal aid experience, of course. The fact that the demand of the poor for free legal services may be virtually limitless under "no cost" conditions does not mean necessarily that the potential demand among people of moderate means is also limitless—or even that it is greater than the apparent actual demand. But the same spirit of caution should also warn against too hasty a rejection of the legal aid experience as an analogy. Indeed, chances appear to be pretty good that the demand for lawyers' services among people of moderate means will be found to have a similar kind of elasticity.

Those who hold the other theory of demand acknowledge that people of moderate means probably could use lawyers' services to a far greater extent than they now do, but they hesitate to take

---

have untreated problems that might appropriately be characterized as legal and become the subjects of lawyers' services, and that one segment or another might be said to have fewer legal problems only in the narrow sense that they have fewer of the business and property problems that the legal profession has traditionally been organized to serve (212:317).

10. Half a million cases were handled by OEO Legal Services units in 1968 (321; 165:100). The demand that produced these cases was generally unrecognized—or at least unacknowledged—by the legal profession prior to the inauguration of the OEO Legal Services program. Many lawyers argued that there was no "need" on the part of the poor for legal services beyond those being rendered by traditional legal aid agencies. But when the services were in fact made available, half a million cases a year turned up. Moreover, even half a million cases are probably but a fraction of the potential demand. Legal services offices appear to be swamped with clients, and it has been estimated that the legal services program would have to be ten times its present size to provide legal services to all the poor who might benefit from them (164:1, 3).

action to meet the potential demand until it has been measured
by means of market survey studies. This approach has much to
recommend it. Certainly, knowledge about the magnitude of the
potential demand would be most helpful. More importantly,
knowledge about the extent and nature of the problems people
encounter is essential if rational answers are ever to be given to
the basic question of the relevance of lawyers' services to the
problems of society. Such knowledge can be obtained only
through well-conceived and well-executed studies of the public
itself. But such studies are long and expensive when done right
and would far exceed the time and resource limitations of a
modest project such as this. Moreover, quantification is not an
absolute precondition of a study of demand, or even of a rational
approach to the problem of meeting it. After all, what did anyone
know about the probable demand for automatic transmissions
before they were developed and produced?

A third theory of demand for lawyers' services has therefore
been utilized here. Put simply, the theory assumes that demand
for lawyers' services is highly elastic, a product of many variable
factors. It concludes that demand can therefore be studied profitably in terms of the factors that seem to produce it. Knowledge
about the factors that appear to produce demand for lawyers'
services may then suggest something about the measures that
might be taken to make lawyers' services more readily available
to people of moderate means.

3
Factors
Affecting Demand

What factors, then, appear to affect or determine the demand
for lawyers' services? Several come readily to mind. People from
different segments of society seem not only to encounter
different kinds of legal problems with varying frequency but also
to be affected by them in different ways and to different degrees.
Consumer credit problems, for example, may sometimes be encountered by upper middle-income people, but such problems
have much greater impact upon people of small or moderate
means. This is, of course, because people of moderate means

probably use consumer credit more than do those who are more affluent, because they are less likely than are the affluent to possess the knowledge and sophistication required to understand fully the nature of the obligation incurred or to negotiate more advantageous terms, and because they are particularly vulnerable to such collection procedures as wage garnishment. This variable — the nature of the public itself — has been used here primarily to define the scope of the inquiry. Because the problems of availability may be different for different segments of society, the focus of this study has been limited to people of moderate means, with emphasis on the urban setting.

There is also considerable variation in the seriousness or urgency of various kinds of problems. Indictment on a felony charge is far more apt to give rise to a demand for lawyers' services than the possibility of one's property rights being slightly affected by a proposed zoning change, whatever the segment of society involved.

While the nature and seriousness of problems are factors that help to determine demand for lawyers' services, they are factors not easily altered. Moreover, they are factors that go primarily to the basic issue of the relevance of law, legal institutions, and lawyers' services to the public's fundamental problems. As this study of availability of legal services is concerned with only a small part of the question of relevance — the adequacy of present methods of producing and distributing lawyers' services — it will not dwell upon the seriousness or urgency of different problems but will examine yet another group of factors affecting demand for lawyers' services. These are the possibly alterable factors that relate specifically to the production and distribution of the services that lawyers presently offer. There appear to be four of these factors: (1) The quality of the service offered, (2) the cost to the client (the price, from his point of view), (3) the accessibility of the service, and (4) public knowledge and attitudes about law, lawyers, and lawyers' services.

There is still another set of factors affecting demand for lawyers' services. The demand for a particular service may vary according to the number and nature of alternative solutions available to people with problems. A potential client may, for instance, be willing to seek counsel from a lawyer in a situation where he would regard litigation, particularly of the offensive strategy type, as completely unacceptable. Perhaps even more importantly, he may prefer still a different solution obtainable from some nonlawyer source as more desirable than either of the lawyer-provided services. This factor is in some ways another side of the relevance question, of course; lawyers' services may become irrelevant to the problems of the public because of changes in either the problems or in the number and character of solutions available. Thus, a complete answer must include measures that will make lawyers' services more responsive to people's problems. But at least part of the answer may lie in the improvement of the production and distribution of lawyers' services, so that they become more attractive in comparison with other alternatives. Consideration of the quality of lawyers' services should therefore include consideration of the quality of possible nonlawyer alternatives; the price of lawyers' services has meaning only in relation to the price of alternative solutions to the problems; the accessibility of lawyers should be evaluated in the light of the accessibility of nonlawyer sources of assistance; examination of public knowledge and attitudes about lawyers should be made against the background of the public's knowledge and attitudes about alternative sources of solutions to problems.

To summarize, the theory of demand used in this analysis regards the demand for lawyers' services as highly elastic. When a particular service obtainable from a lawyer is responsive to the problem of a potential client, the demand for that service will depend upon the potential client's knowledge about law, lawyers, and legal services and upon the quality, price, and accessibility of the service—as compared with alternative solutions to the problem. Proposals for making lawyers' services more readily available will be evaluated on the basis of these factors.

A few general observations may be in order with respect to the apparent extent of the present and potential demand for lawyers' services. As suggested earlier, some segments of the public have long recognized the value of lawyers' skills and are utilizing lawyers on an ever-increasing scale. These segments include business and property clients as well as large institutions, both governmental and private. It might also be noted that changes now taking place in the field of legal services for the poor indicate a demand for lawyers' services that will, for a good while into the future, exceed the resources society is willing to devote to it (**164**:1, 3).

There is no reason to suppose that the potential demand for lawyers' services among people of moderate means is significantly smaller than it is among the other segments of society. Indeed, there is every reason to believe that it is relatively as great (**212**:317). While people of moderate means may not have the same problems as the affluent with respect to the preservation of wealth and property, they probably have more problems than the wealthy in such fields as consumer credit and landlord-tenant. At the same time, their lack of resources probably forecloses them from some of the alternative solutions available to the wealthy, so that if they get satisfactory solutions to their problems at all they must do so through the law and lawyers' services. Similarly, while people of moderate means may not have many problems arising out of welfare law, they are more likely than are the poor to have problems having to do with property ownership.

Reason suggests, then, that the level of potential demand for lawyers' services is probably comparable in all segments of society, with only the nature of the problems different from one segment to another (**212**:317). Potential demand has already been largely translated into actual demand among property and business clients, by virtue of the ability of such clients to pay for the services offered by good lawyers and law firms. The offering of competent services without cost through legal aid and the newer federally financed legal service programs is likewise translating potential demand into actual demand among the poor. Is it not reasonable to believe that a largely untapped potential demand for lawyers' services similarly exists among people of moderate means, awaiting only the availability of services on acceptable terms to be translated into an actual demand of substantial proportions?[11] Moreover, as society in-

11. The bar-sponsored Lawyer Referral Service program gives some hint of a vast potential demand for lawyers' services among people of moderate means. In 1966, for the first time in the history of the program, the total number of cases referred to lawyers exceeded one hundred thousand (**45**). And if just those referral services now in operation were as effective as the best among them, the total would be two million new cases a year (**104**:1, 7). Moreover, because lawyer referral services have not been established in all the communities where they are needed, and because even the best among existing referral services appear to be realizing only part of their potential, this estimate of two million new cases a year should probably be thought of as merely scratching the surface of the potential demand for lawyers' services among people of moderate means.

creases in complexity, and as the individual citizen's life becomes more and more bound up with regulations, restraints, and controls — both governmental and private — the demand for the kinds of functions lawyers are peculiarly well equipped to perform will surely also continue to expand.

This line of thought leads to an interesting paradox. Although the number of law graduates seems to be increasing (see 153:197-211; 55:19, 20), the supply of lawyers expected to be available in the immediate future may well be inadequate to handle even a slight over-all increase in the middle-class public's use of lawyers' services, just as it seems already to be inadequate to supply the demand being uncovered by the legal services programs for the poor (see 176:169). Measures taken to make lawyers' services more readily available to people of moderate means may therefore result in a demand beyond the capacity of the present legal profession to supply.

This prospect presents the profession with a three-fold challenge. First, the lawyer's obligation as a professional requires that he do everything he can to enable all segments of society to make the fullest beneficial use of legal services. Second, because such efforts may cause the demand to increase beyond the present supply, ways must be found to apply lawyers' efforts to the performance of those functions that will best utilize their special abilities and be most beneficial to the public. This means the development of measures to better equip lawyers to perform those functions efficiently. And third, the profession must create — or at least permit the creation of — safe, reliable, and effective mechanisms for supplying to the public those law-related services that lawyers themselves may no longer be able to perform.

C
Meeting Demand —
A Market
Viewpoint

The problem of providing legal services to people of moderate means seems, to a significant extent, to be one of competition. The practice of law is a service enterprise. As such, it must compete directly with an array of nonlegal commodities and services, for the consumer's attention as well as for his dollar. Not only must law-related services compete with other kinds of goods and services, but the lawyer himself must also vie with both other lawyers and nonlawyers for the opportunity of supplying them. Reluctance to accept this fact and failure to deal adequately with it appear to lie at the heart of many of the legal profession's present problems.

"Competition" has always been a dirty word to the legal profession, raising, as it does, images of "commercialization," "solicitation," "exploitation," and "turning an honorable profession into a mere trade or business." But to invoke these images is not to dispel the truth that lawyers who seek to provide legal services to people of moderate means must exist and function in an increasingly difficult competitive environment (see **147:31**).

The problem of solicitation may be a good example of an apparent divergence between myth and fact with respect to competition. The invective directed at "improper solicitation of legal business" — and incidentally, much of the opposition to the *Brotherhood of Railroad Trainmen* decision (hereinafter called *BRT*) (**364**) — is generally cast in terms of a claimed threat to the lawyer's professionalism and image from activities that would "commercialize" the legal profession.

But does the concern stem wholly from fear for professionalism and the professional image? Lawyers at the top of the economic heap and no longer caught in the competitive squeeze — at least partly because their own successful forms of solicitation have come to be regarded as proper — may be motivated primarily by a desire to preserve professionalism and the professional image. But one might be pardoned for harboring at least some suspicion that some of those who talk loudest about "professionalism" are really worried about something far different — the *competitive advantage* that "improper" solicitation gives to lawyers who engage in it. Indeed, running through almost every argument about the *BRT* scheme is the objection that it gives to some lawyers preferential access to lucrative industrial injury cases. Similarly, not even the disfavor with which the profession views "ambulance-chasing" lawyers appears attributable solely to the fact that they are unprofessional — although they are — or that they impair the profession's image — and they do — or that they "commercialize" the profession — as they do. At least part of the profession's dislike for the

"ambulance-chasing" lawyer seems to stem from the simple fact
that he gets what is regarded as an unfair share of the available
personal injury business.[12]

One reason for the inability of many lawyers to compete
effectively in serving people of moderate means may be that the
profession has been unable or unwilling to find ways of equipping them to compete within ethically acceptable limits, pre-
ferring instead to try to stifle outside competition. This is not to
say, necessarily, that proscriptive laws are wrong, but only that
such laws can preserve neither the profession's monopoly nor its
status unless lawyers are in fact meeting public demands and
expectations.

The profession has long recognized the existence of the competition problem in its handling of unauthorized practice, but
solutions directed toward either meeting competition or absorb-
ing it—approaches that are commonly used in the commercial
world—have usually been rejected in favor of proscribing it by
restrictive laws. This latter course is not unknown in the commercial world, incidentally—state licensing of public carriers for
exclusive operation over designated routines being an example.
But because restrictive rules are generally inconsistent with the
basic competitive theory of our economic system, the success of
such proscriptive laws in the commercial world appears to rest at
least in part on how well they fit public needs, public desires,
and public expectations. Thus, much of the work of public utilities commissions is directed toward the adjustment of the restrictions to public needs and expectations, both through the
promulgation of general regulations and through the deciding of
individual cases, not toward the suppression of unauthorized or
illicit activities.

But no really effective adjustment mechanism has operated to
keep the legal service monopoly in tune with public demands.
And in pressing its attack against unauthorized practice in fields
where the public seems to demand something different from
what the lawyer monopoly is providing, the bar may run the risk
of having the public rise up and cast the lawyers out—either

12. In passing, it might be suggested that the success of "ambulance-chasing" lawyers
as competitors could perhaps be related, at least in part, to a degree of social utility in
their activities. They do get timely legal help to people who need it. While this may not
justify such activities, it does point up the desirability of the profession's undertaking to
find ethically acceptable ways of performing the socially useful functions now being
performed unethically by "ambulance chasers."

overtly, through the democratic process,[13] or less directly in the market place.

Perhaps it should be pointed out that these observations are not meant as a suggestion that lawyers abandon the essential elements of their professionalism in favor of self-interest. Quite the contrary. Many of those lawyers most highly respected as professionals do compete successfully, and with comparatively little help from the unauthorized practice rules. At the same time, many of those who appear to be somewhat less respected as professionals seem also to be ineffective competitors.[14] Thus, the point is simply that effective competition by lawyers is not only consistent with high professional ideals but also essential to their realization. Lawyers can fully discharge their duties to clients, courts, and society only if they are truly competitive in providing their services to the public.

How, then, are lawyers to compete? What elements constitute effective competition? And how might these elements help lawyers to provide services to people of moderate means?

The elements of effective competition are the same as those factors previously referred to in the discussion of demand, but looked at from a somewhat different point of view — that of the "market" rather than that of individual clients. Given a particular segment of the public and a specific problem, the competitive effectiveness of any particular service that might be offered by a lawyer will usually depend upon: (1) the quality of the service; (2) its price; (3) its accessibility to the public; (4) public knowledge and attitudes about it and about its supplier; and (5) the quality, price, accessibility of, and public knowledge about practical nonlawyer-supplied alternatives.

1
Quality

The quality of the service offered by a lawyer is in large part a question of his professional competence, a complex and difficult subject. Among the elements that affect it are: the quality of

13. E.g., the Arizona constitutional amendment permitting realtors to draft real estate instruments (**420**; see also **406**; **4**:188; **71**:169; **263**:1).

14. There are exceptions, of course. Lawyers who "chase ambulances" are usually regarded as unprofessional, even though many of them are very effective competitors.

applicants for admission to law school and their pre-law school
training; the level of law school admission standards; the nature
and quality of law school training; the nature and administration
of requirements for admission to practice; the institutional settings in which lawyers practice; the degree of specialization in
law practice; the extent and nature of continuing legal education; and the bar's diligence in policing and disciplining itself.

Unfortunately, there seem to be deficiencies in present methods of dealing with all of these crucial elements. At least part of
the reason may lie in the profession's divergence into dissimilar
and more or less isolated segments, a division that lawyers seem
unduly reluctant to recognize. To put it bluntly, the bar persists
in regarding all lawyers as equal, when in fact some are "more
equal than others." Blindness to this fundamental and pervasive
fission inhibits effective action with respect to the problems of
lawyers' competence.

This division exists as an essential fact in each of the
above-described "elements affecting professional competence."
Take, as an example, the quality of prospective law students,
their pre-law school training, and law school admission requirements. While the nation's top law schools receive an
ever-increasing flow of outstanding applicants and admit only
the best of these, some other schools admit almost anyone who
can raise the tuition. Even among reputable law schools, the
range—in terms of amount, kind, and quality—of permissible
pre-law school preparation must seem rather strange to anyone
familiar with the stringent standards and pre-professional training requirements of some other disciplines. And even the best
law schools seem none too sure about the characteristics they
should look for in prospective law students or about the best
methods of discovering these characteristics.

And what of the quality and nature of legal training itself?
Perhaps one indication of the varied quality is the fact that, as of
the fall term of 1968, thirty-two law schools, with a combined
enrollment of over five thousand, were not on the approved list
of the American Bar Association. Moreover, only seven of these
thirty-two had taken even the beginning step toward meeting
the ABA's minimal standards by applying for provisional approval (**55:16-18**).[15] Variation also appears in the content of legal

15. These unapproved schools conferred over eight hundred law degrees in the
1967–1968 academic year (**55:25-26**).

education, which ranges all the way from the highly provincial "three year local law cram courses," which are offered by some of the substandard schools, to the varied and demanding curricula of better schools. And again, even the better schools seem unsure about what they should be teaching and why.

Bar admission procedures constitute another weak link in the chain, in some instances perhaps even accentuating rather than alleviating the extreme variance in competence among lawyers. At best, bar admissions requirements and procedures seem to do a somewhat less than ideal job of screening out those whose deficiencies of character or ability make them unfit to practice law. At worst—and this is particularly so with restrictive residence requirements and rules for admission of lawyers licensed in other states—they sometimes seem to be used as mere instruments of provincial self-interest.

One of the most important elements affecting competence and integrity in law practice is the institutional setting in which lawyers practice.[16] And here, perhaps, is where the bar's division into dissimilar segments has its most dramatic effect. The top students from the better law schools go into the larger law firms, where they are exposed to the high ethical attitudes and behavior and the excellent professional performance of successful colleagues. They are often given more or less formalized on-the-job training. And, perhaps most important, their practice is commonly concentrated in the higher levels of the judicial structure and the administrative system, where the pressures for excellence and integrity are high and where opportunity and temptation to "cut corners" are minimal. It is not surprising, then, that they tend to develop into honest and highly competent lawyers.

But take the mediocre fellow who manages to grind his way through a substandard law school. He has no chance of landing a job with a big firm, so he ends up hanging out his shingle in front of a second-floor walk-up office in a neighborhood where the rents are low. There he learns to practice law by practicing—usually at the expense of both his clients and himself. Economic pressures provide a compelling incentive to "cut corners." And his ambit is not the Federal District Court or the Securities and Exchange Commission, but the magistrate's court

16. This seems to be the fundamental point made by Jerome Carlin in his study of the professional attitudes and behavior of urban lawyers (91).

and the local health department or zoning commission where opportunity to "cut corners" is likely to be more than ample. Moreover, his colleagues and associates in that segment of the bar are likely to offer him only the kind of example that would encourage "corner-cutting." Is it surprising that he often develops into a cut-rate, "corner-cutting" lawyer?

This is not meant to suggest that all graduates of substandard law schools are incompetent. Obviously they are not; some great lawyers are graduates of substandard law schools. But the shyster is too common a phenomenon to be ignored, and the evidence seems to indicate that he is primarily a product of this unhealthy combination of inadequate selectivity by law schools in admission of students and by state authorities in admission of lawyers to practice, inadequate training, and a corruptive practice environment.

Specialization is also related to professional competence. Perhaps the field of taxation would provide a helpful illustration. The bar has long had tax specialists, of course, but their services have been primarily for business and property clients; they have never been available to people of moderate means to any significant extent. In fact, professional restrictions have prevented lawyers from offering special tax skills to the general public in any effective manner.[17] As a result, accountants have moved solidly into tax practice, and the bar has resorted to a running battle with accountants to try to maintain a line of some kind between tax accounting and tax law practice. Whatever else this approach to the regulation of professional conduct may have accomplished, one effect has clearly been the practical unavailability to people of moderate means of the kind of highly competent tax advice and service available to business and property clients.

Much might also be said about other factors relating to the quality of legal services available to the moderate-income

17. Opinion No. 260 of the American Bar Association Ethics Committee prohibits lawyers from holding themselves out as possessing special qualifications in the field of tax law (13:581). [The foregoing citation refers to a page number in the published volume of ABA Ethics Committee Opinions (13). References to specific opinions in the volume will hereinafter carry only the opinion number. Thus, formal opinions of the ABA Committee on Professional Ethics will be referred to as "ABA Eth. Ops." Informal Opinions of the same committee will be referred to as "ABA Inf. Eth. Ops."] Neither are lawyers permitted to associate themselves with accountants and still hold themselves out as lawyers (6:Canon No. 33; ABA Eth. Ops., Nos. 239, 269). And a lawyer who is also an accountant may not let the public know of his qualifications in both fields, even though the combination of skills may be of special value to the public in tax matters (ABA Eth. Ops., No. 297).

group — such things as the profession's permissive and casual attitude toward continuing legal education,[18] as well as what appears to be a "live and let live" philosophy of professional discipline.[19] Combined, these and other factors tend to perpetuate disparities in the quality of lawyers' services that should be totally unacceptable to a profession. Clearly, if lawyers are to compete effectively, much needs to be done to make sure that the services available to all segments of the public are of high quality.

2
Price

Price is probably the most important element of competition and must be given special consideration. Quality and price are, of course, interconnected. Inept advocacy and bad advice are probably too dear at any price, however low, while some services are bargains even though the price appears high. When services are of acceptable quality, however, the two critical points with respect to competition become the price in relation to the value of the matter in issue and the price in relation to the client's ability to pay.

If the price a client must pay for a given lawyer's service is unduly large in relation to the value of the matter in issue, he may decide to seek a solution in some other way. He may go "lawyer-shopping" to find a cheaper lawyer. He may seek some kind of nonlawyer help, such as the opinion of a broker instead of the advice of a lawyer in a real estate transaction. He may resort to self-help — drafting his own will, for example. Or he may simply forego his cause as not worth the expenditure.

Even in those instances where the matter in issue is important and well worth the price of the legal service required to assert it,

18. The increasing attention being given continuing legal education at all levels of the organized bar affords some hope that the program will become a significant factor in developing and maintaining competence.

19. The appointment by the American Bar Association of a Special Committee on Evaluation of Disciplinary Enforcement is an encouraging sign, and the work of that Committee promises to be a good first step toward development of really effective disciplinary procedures (see 37). That this effort is being made none too soon is evidenced by the movement in Michigan to remove the licensing and discipline of attorneys from the Supreme Court and the integrated state bar and to turn those tasks over to state administrative boards (see 9).

a prospective client who is in fact unable to pay the price may be forced to resort to one or the other of these same alternatives. Some way of dealing with the price problem must therefore be a central theme in any discussion of availability of legal services.

There appear to be two main ways of handling the price problem. Measures may be taken to reduce the unit price of the service, or methods may be found to help the consumer pay the price. Industrial mass production is the ultimate example of the first approach; installment credit exemplifies the second.

In seeking ways to reduce the unit price of lawyers' services, one soon encounters a substantial obstacle in the very nature of those services. Almost by definition—and certainly by tradition—lawyers' services are individual and custom-produced. They are not easily standardized or made routine, and in many instances the attempt would be dangerous as well as foolish. But at the same time, there may be functions that could safely and conveniently be standardized, either for more expeditious handling by the lawyer himself or for delegation to properly qualified and supervised sub-professional personnel. Better law office management may help to reduce the price of lawyers' services, as may computerized research. Specialization as a means of reducing the unit price of services is a major element of many group legal service plans, as well as of low cost legal service bureau proposals. Improvement of legal institutions, of judicial and administrative procedures, and of substantive law would also no doubt help to reduce the cost of handling legal problems for persons of moderate means.

To the extent that the price of lawyers' services cannot be brought within the purchasing ability of middle-class people, ways must be found to help finance them. Again, a number of possibilities appear.

Perhaps the most obvious is installment credit of the kind used to finance other consumer purchases. Another possibility is the insurance principle—meant here to include the entire concept of risk-spreading. This principle is an element of group legal service plans, of prepaid legal expense insurance proposals, of some low-cost legal service bureau proposals, and of governmental subsidies like the English Legal Aid and Advice Schemes. Even where individual lawyers seek to solve the cost problem by providing services at unprofitable fees, the burden is being spread among the bar. These different approaches raise a variety of problems, both economic and political. They do promise at least partial answers to the problem of the price of legal services, however, and pressure for some kind of risk-distributing arrangement will probably continue to grow. The legal profession has the obligation of making sure that the ultimate responses are sound and in the public interest.

3
Accessibility

Many lawyers find it hard to accept the fact that lawyers' accessibility may be a problem. Their doors are open to anyone who wants to walk in; their names are in the phone book; they are accessible.

But in the field of legal services as in few others, accessibility means more than just being open for business. Many middle-class people do not know a lawyer personally, and choosing an unknown lawyer "cold," either from the Yellow Pages or by walking into a random office, may be an impossibly forbidding prospect. In a very real sense, the big city lawyer in his downtown office is inaccessible to most people of moderate means. And even the small town lawyer might be surprised at the barriers that exist between himself and prospective moderate-income clients. People do not really want lawyers' services, even when they recognize that they have legal problems. Surely, this diffidence, reinforced by traditional fears and suspicions, is a major deterrent to a great many people of moderate means.

Accessibility has another aspect as well. To the person who has a legal problem, "availability of legal services" does not mean accessibility of *a* lawyer. It means accessibility of someone able to provide the particular services that the client's problem requires and someone in whom the client has confidence. Thus, the selection of a lawyer also presents serious difficulties to people of moderate means who often do not have and cannot obtain the knowledge essential to intelligent selection.

Three devices are often urged as methods of enhancing the accessibility of lawyers' services to these people: lawyer referral services, group legal service programs, and special low-cost legal service bureaus or clinics. All appear to address themselves to the problems of accessibility, and all will be given extended consideration in later chapters of this report.

4
Public Knowledge
and Attitudes

Finally, there is the question of public knowledge and attitudes as an element of competition in the purveying of lawyers' services. This element has to do, of course, with the profession's public relations, probed so interestingly by the Missouri Bar Survey (220). But it involves much more than just public relations. Basically, it is a matter of the public's knowledge of, and attitudes about, law, legal institutions, and lawyers as sources of solutions to problems. Obviously, educating the public about law and legal rights, teaching them to recognize legal problems, attempting to dispel their fears and antagonisms toward the law and lawyers, and letting them know about available sources of legal help, would all seem to be important elements in any effort to improve the availability of lawyers' services.

Perhaps another aspect of the matter deserves note as well. Many of the private lawyer's competitors for the legal service business of people of moderate means — bankers, insurance agents, trust company attorneys, lawyers for labor unions and other groups — enjoy the benefit of enhanced public confidence derived from the public's confidence in the institutions with which these competing sources of service are associated. Affiliation with a respected and trusted institution carries with it not only the implied — and sometimes explicit — endorsement of the institution, but also the implication, whether true or not, that the institution will stand behind its representative and make good in the event of error. Professor Cheatham has put it this way: "It is no accident that the largest area of unauthorized practice of law is the middle classes. Laymen go to unauthorized practitioners who are accessible, whose charges they do not fear, and whose dependability they rely on because of connections with familiar institutions they trust" (99:63-64).

It may also be worthwhile to look at the problem of public

knowledge and attitudes from still another viewpoint. One basic reason for the legal profession's apparent position of competitive disadvantage, as compared with other possible alternatives for the solution of problems, appears to be the failure of lawyers to maintain, at least in the eyes of people of moderate means, what might be called an "image of competence."

The medical profession might again provide a useful analogy. Most of us who are old enough to remember the old-fashioned general medical practitioner no doubt still harbor some feelings of nostalgia about him. He was the wise, skilled healer. Kind, gentle, and unhurried, he was friend and counselor as well as doctor. And, of course, he made house calls.

But where is he today? And, what is more important, how many of us would really have him back — *if* we had to give up today's highly trained medical specialists in return? When a pediatrician refuses to come to the house at midnight to see a child with a slight fever, we might think we would prefer the old generalist. But would we really choose him rather than a competent radiologist to examine an X-ray for tubercular lesions? And who would trade open heart surgery and corneal transplants for the old-time doctor's bedside manner?

The point, obviously, is that by honestly admitting, primarily through the training and certification of specialists, that the field of medicine is too vast for complete mastery by any one doctor, and by elevating the standards of all medical training and practice, the medical profession has developed and offers real and unmistakable competence to the public. Doctors have thus created an "image of competence" based on actual competence that effectively disposes of most of their competition problems. The modern doctor, be he generalist or specialist, may be cold or aloof. He may be somewhat inaccessible. He may appear expensive, though he is not necessarily overpriced in relation to the value of the service he performs. But he has no real competition; not because of proscriptive laws — although, of course, they exist — but because most people today simply would not think of going elsewhere to obtain the sophisticated services he offers. As one result, the medical profession's unauthorized practice program has quite a different character from that of the bar.

But what about the legal profession? When the person of moderate means thinks about competent assistance with tax problems, does he think about lawyers? Almost surely not; he is more apt to think about one of the commercial income tax services or about the Certified Public Accountant. When the man of moderate means thinks about planning for his family in the event of his death, will he not be likely to turn to his life insurance agent or his bank rather than to a lawyer? When he buys a house, will the thought of consulting a lawyer even enter his mind, or will he rely unquestioningly upon his realtor and the title insurance company?

To be sure, lawyers who serve property and business clients probably have an "image of competence" in the eyes of their clients. And people probably still think first of lawyers when the talk is of law suits; lawyers generally may thus be said to have maintained something of an "image of competence" with regard to litigation. But in many of the other areas in which lawyers' services might be so beneficial, many people of moderate means probably do not regard lawyers as feasible or even appropriate sources of help.

The analogy is imperfect of course. The picture is overdrawn and there are important differences between the legal and medical professions. Furthermore, the medical profession's specialization system is certainly not without its problems (see **106**). The problem of retaining for the public the benefits heretofore provided through traditional general practice—particularly diagnostic services, emergency services, and continuing comprehensive care—is especially difficult. But the point made earlier still stands. An "image of competence," based upon unmistakable and publicly known actual competence, could be the professional's most effective competitive weapon.

D
Conclusions

The foregoing analysis may be summed up rather simply. Demand for, and use of, lawyers' services by people of moderate means are both highly elastic. They are determined by certain elements of competition, including: the quality of the service; its price; its accessibility; and public knowledge and attitudes about law, lawyers, and lawyers' services. All of these elements must be evaluated against the background of the quality, price, accessibility, and knowledge and attitudes about competitive solutions to people's problems. Availability of legal services for people of moderate means is thus essentially a marketing problem. The task of the profession should be to find ways to help lawyers—honorably but effectively—to develop and maintain a healthy market for services that will be of value to clients and of benefit to society.

The Cost of
Legal Services

The problem of making legal services more readily available to the public—and particularly to people of moderate means—is, then, in large part an economic problem. This is not to say that lawyers' fees are universally too high or that people of moderate means cannot generally "afford" legal services—although this may in fact be true with respect to some fees and some people. Instead, this acknowledgment of the importance of the economic element in the problem of availability of legal services is meant primarily as a recognition that cost has much to do with the extent to which people actually do utilize lawyers' services in the solution of problems.

Being able to afford something and actually purchasing it are quite different matters. A man may genuinely be able to afford the price of a will, a lawyer's fee for representation in a real estate transaction, or the cost of legal services in one of the many other situations in which people could beneficially make more frequent use of lawyers' knowledge and skills. But at the same time, he may choose to spend his limited means for something else, either because this "something else" is more pressing or desirable than lawyers' services, or because he regards the "something else" as a better value for his money. If the cost of legal service in relation to the anticipated benefit from it seems excessive in comparison with the cost and value of other possible purchases, then, unless the legal service is seen as an absolute imperative, the potential client will probably forgo the legal service in favor of the thing that to him seems the better immediate value—landscaping in preference to estate planning, perhaps. It is appropriate, then, to examine the question of cost and to evaluate possible methods of reducing the adverse effects of cost upon the use of lawyers' services by people of moderate means.

The problem has two main elements. One has to do with the price of the lawyer's work product and the cost factors in producing it. The other has to do with the client's ability to pay a fair price for the services he requires.

A
Price
and the Cost of
Production*1

If inability or unwillingness to pay reasonable fees for some of the services offered by lawyers does in fact keep many people of moderate means from making the fullest possible use of those services, then it is proper that production costs be examined to see if they might somehow be reduced, thus making possible some reduction in the price. At the outset, however, it must be acknowledged that the possibilities for such reduction appear limited. Because of the very nature of the American legal system, the services of lawyers usually must be custom products. A client's specific legal difficulty must be evaluated in the light of a complex accretion of law, and the solving of a particular problem typically requires prediction of how a changing body of law will develop. Preventive or remedial measures must also be tailored to fit both the facts and the applicable law. The lawyer is thus required to choose carefully among complex alternatives at almost every step. This is an inherently costly procedure, and there seem to be few ethically acceptable methods of reducing the cost of doing it.

1
Lower Quality
Services

One solution that lawyers would no doubt unanimously regard as unethical and improper would be to reduce the price of legal services available to people of moderate means by lower-

---

*Citations in boldface type refer the reader to the numbered "Works Cited" at 297–313; where numbers immediately follow the boldface reference, the reader is referred to specific pages in that work.

1. An excellent and much more extensive treatment of many of the ideas summarized below may be found in Johnstone & Hopson (**166**:77-159, 329-54, 536-49).

ing the quality of those services. Unhappily, however, this solution may be more common in practice, at least among some lawyers, than the profession would like to believe.

Many of the legal problems of people of moderate means are rather small in monetary value, and as a rule small cases are not highly remunerative in relation to the time and effort their proper handling often calls for. The lawyer who has a large number of such cases is frequently in the position of the merchant who sells his goods at a loss but tries to make it up in volume. As a result, the temptation may be great, especially where economic pressures are very strong, to give small matters the least possible amount of attention and to concentrate instead on the few lucrative cases that do come along.

Much of the delay for which lawyers are sometimes criticized may also stem from this same kind of pressure. Some lawyers who are reluctant to lower the quality of their professional performance may instead yield to economic pressure by putting matters of small economic importance aside for later attention. Client dissatisfaction is the predictable result. Unfortunately, delay itself may impair the quality of the services rendered. Furthermore, the pressures of time may cause the postponed matters ultimately to be dealt with hurriedly, despite the lawyer's good intentions, so that the services turn out to be poor in quality as well as slow.

Lowering the quality of legal services is an unattractive method of reducing their cost, but there is another facet to the matter. Lawyers sometimes are accused of making legal mountains out of molehill problems—even of manufacturing expensive law suits out of minor disputes or transactions. The great bulk of this criticism is surely unjustified; it no doubt arises from the failure of many clients to appreciate the real complexity of apparently simple problems or to understand that seemingly over-elaborate remedies may actually be essential to the client's own best interests. Indeed, the number of lawyers who would deliberately inflate the services they perform beyond the necessities of the case at hand, whether for larger fees or for any other reason, is probably very small.

On the other hand, clients may be somewhat justified in at least wondering whether some lawyers, in their zeal to fashion the best preventive or remedial measures they can for their clients, do not sometimes tend inadvertently to forget the limited means of their clients or the modest economic value of their clients' problems. Perhaps the choice offered to clients of moderate means is too frequently limited to an election between a remedy that costs more than the client's claim is worth and no remedy at all.

These observations are not meant as a suggestion that clients of moderate means and clients with small problems should be given poor quality legal services. The client of moderate means, no less than the rich man, should have access to legal services of an extent and quality commensurate with his problems. But neither the rich man nor the man of moderate means should be forced to pay high fees for elaborate remedies to problems that might just as well be solved by simpler and less costly measures. The hundred thousand dollar racing car, admirable though it may be for the purpose to which it is put, is not usually a suitable answer to the personal transportation needs of either the rich or the poor. Perhaps there is a need for lawyers to devote more attention than they have thus far to the development of effective but economically justifiable legal solutions to small problems. Whatever the possibilities in this regard, however, the simple expedient of rendering inferior or poor quality services in small cases is not an acceptable method of reducing the cost of legal services to the public.

2
Devaluing
the Lawyer's Time
and Skills

A possible alternative solution is for the lawyer to reduce the price of his services without regard to the cost of producing them, thus devaluing his own time and skill. There are no doubt those among the public who would endorse this approach, on the ground that lawyers make too much money anyway. Studies suggest, however, that the lawyers who have high incomes are not generally those whose practices consist mainly of clients of moderate means (see **92:116**). Indeed, the time and skill of

lawyers serving moderate-income clients seem already to have
been devalued about as far as possible (see **92**:116). Yet the
prices of many of the services they offer still seem to be higher
than people of moderate means are able or willing to pay. It
would seem unrealistic, therefore, to think of further devalua-
tion.

3
*Increasing
the Efficiency
of Lawyers*

Measures taken to increase lawyers' efficiency may offer
some promise of reducing the cost of legal services to people of
moderate means. If greater efficiency and more productive use
of time will enable the lawyer to produce a greater quantity of
his custom product at the same or lower cost, then he may be
able to sustain a reasonable valuation on his time and skills
while lowering the price of his services to his clients.

a
**Specialization and
routinization of
functions**

One reason the lawyer sometimes has trouble producing his
product at a price people of moderate means can pay would
seem to be that he too often seeks to offer a range of services
broader than his functional capabilities. The law has expanded
far beyond the capacity of any one man even to be aware of it all.
When a lawyer ignores this fact by attempting to handle every
kind of problem that comes to him, the result may be poor
quality services, higher fees than are justifiable, or both. On the
other hand, the lawyer who concentrates his efforts in a field of
law practice of manageable proportions has at least some chance
of developing sufficient expertise and efficiency to perform his
specialized services at prices reasonably related to their value to
clients. Thus specialization in law practice, discussed at length

in the following chapter, may do a great deal to reduce the cost of producing legal service.

One valuable result of specialization in law practice might be the development of an ability to handle a greater number of problems as a matter of routine rather than on a custom basis. Every lawyer is able to do a certain amount of "practicing off the top of his head." This means only that his training and experience have produced a sufficient working knowledge of a given field of practice to enable him both to handle the less difficult problems in it without extensive research or study and to recognize those problems that do require more elaborate attention.

The bar has not always fully appreciated this rather important fact, all too frequently becoming disturbed at the thought that specialization might result in the rendition of legal services "as a mere matter of routine."[2] In truth, however, this ability to see and to take advantage of opportunities for the routine handling of legal problems appropriate for routine treatment is a help rather than a hindrance to genuine professionalism. It is this ability that enables the senior partner in the large firm not only to use his own expensive time more effectively, but also to determine what things might be done just as well and more economically by a younger partner, an associate, or even a lay employee. Indeed, it is also this ability which enables even the solo general practitioner to utilize the skills of his trusted secretary in the performance of many routine — but sometimes clearly legal — functions in his office.

Obviously, a specialist is able to give this kind of desirable routine treatment to a greater number of problems in his field of expertise than can a generalist undertaking to serve clients in the same field of practice. At the same time, it appears likely that even the generalist could, if he analyzed his practice, find areas where routine procedures could be developed. Greater "routinization" of appropriate legal functions, particularly in the context of specialized practice, is undoubtedly one important measure that might be taken to reduce the cost of producing legal services.

2. For an extreme statement of the argument against the "routine" handling of legal problems see 305:483. This article takes the unusual position that experience is irrelevant to legal problem-solving and even incompatible with legal reasoning. See also Teschner (304).

b
More effective use
of nonlawyer
personnel

The use of nonlawyers to perform functions usually performed by lawyers is closely connected with both specialization and routinization of functions. This approach seeks to substitute inexpensive labor for expensive wherever possible in the production of lawyers' services. Stated this way, the idea may sound a bit radical, at least as applied to law practice. But in fact, lawyers have been doing it for years. Large firms generally maintain more or less formalized systems for utilizing different kinds of nonlawyer personnel in the production of legal services, and it is the rare solo practitioner who does not delegate at least some legal functions to his secretary.

Unfortunately, knowledge about the functions lawyers perform and about the procedures and techniques they utilize in performing them is not yet sufficiently detailed or extensive to furnish a complete picture of all the possible uses of nonlawyer personnel in the production of legal services. Some of the possibilities were explored in one of the reports of the American Bar Association Special Committee on Availability of Legal Services (29:529), and recent studies are adding to available knowledge on the subject.[3] The concept will no doubt be further developed by the work of the new ABA Special Committee on Lay Assistants for Lawyers (29:352-53, 529). Moreover, at least one training program for legal paraprofessionals is now under way (110).[4] Thus, it would probably be safe to generalize that much of the time-consuming routine labor of law practice might well be done adequately by properly trained laymen acting under the supervision of lawyers.

In considering this method of lowering the cost of lawyers' services, perhaps it would be helpful to consider the functions that might be performed by nonlawyers in three categories. First there are those functions that are clearly nonlegal in char-

3. A study directed specifically at the use of nonlawyers in federally funded projects providing legal services to the poor has been done by the University Research Corporation under a grant from the federal Office of Economic Opportunity (346).

4. The project described is being conducted by Columbia Law School in conjunction with the national Talent Corps and the Neighborhood Law Offices program of the Legal Aid Society. It is funded by the Columbia Urban Center, the New World Foundation, and the Aaron E. Norman Fund.

acter but that are nevertheless often performed by lawyers. Among them would be many clerical functions — as when a lawyer spends his own valuable time looking for a file that could and should be located for him by a file clerk or secretary. Purely administrative and housekeeping functions would also be included; so also might certain nonlegal activities that are somewhat more closely connected with actual legal work, such as going to the courthouse to file papers. Such nonlegal activities probably occupy significant amounts of the valuable time of many lawyers.

The second category consists of genuine legal functions that can be broken down into component steps, some of which are capable of being performed by properly trained lay technicians. The use of lay investigators for fact-gathering in litigation is one fairly common example. Other legal service components that might possibly be entrusted to trained technicians functioning under lawyers' direction include: obtaining issuance and service of subpoenas; preparing routine pleadings; "shepardizing" decisions; abstracting depositions, interrogatory replies, and data from files; interviewing and taking statements from clients and others; preparing inventories and doing other routine work connected with probate proceedings; preparing articles of incorporation, by-laws, and corporation minutes; and doing other similar routine work in connection with foreclosures, bankruptcies, and many other matters.

Most lawyers are probably in full agreement with the concept of using trained nonlawyer technicians in such limited capacities and under their own supervision. A legal function performed under the lawyer's control and supervision and for which the lawyer assumes complete responsibility is the lawyer's service, even though nonlawyers may have performed some of the steps in the procedure. Legal services so performed retain their custom character and are professional in every sense.

A third category presents somewhat more difficulty, however. It consists of functions legal in nature but capable of being performed in their entirety by properly trained laymen. In essence, the concept underlying this category contemplates that laymen would actually function as lawyers in limited fields of practice. For example, proposals have been made that laymen be used to provide legal services to the poor, both as advisors and as advocates (**86**; see also **175**:65-66). A notable example of the practical application of the concept in some jurisdictions is the appearance of law students in court under certain limited circumstances to represent indigent criminal defendants (**290**; **188**; see also **213**; cf. **203**). Conveyancing is another possible function for properly trained lay technicians, and there may be others.

A number of problems are presented by the proposal that some legal services might be performed in their entirety by what might be termed "paralegal" personnel. One such problem arises out of the difficulty of developing criteria for determining which matters may be handled by such paralegal personnel, and which must be given the full professional attention of lawyers.

The client's economic resources do not provide a reasonable basis for such a determination. Indeed, no one would now seriously urge that poor people, or people of moderate means, should get their legal services from nonlawyers just because their means are limited, while the rich are served by fully trained lawyers. Of course, legal services provided by a trained nonlawyer might be preferable to none at all, but the client's means ought not be the sole factor determining which level of service he gets.

The economic value of the matter involved is not much better as a ground for determining whether a trained nonlawyer should be allowed to handle it. Some cases might possibly be differentiated on the basis of the economic value of the interest involved, with the so-called small claims handled by paralawyers and the large ones by full-fledged lawyers. But even small claims may involve extremely difficult legal questions, and the resolution of such questions may be far more important to the poor person or the person of moderate means than the actual economic value of the case. Furthermore, many claims and legal problems are really immeasurable in economic terms—most notably, criminal cases, civil rights cases, and many family law matters.

Perhaps the question to be answered in determining whether a problem should be handled by a lawyer or by a trained paraprofessional is really two-fold: First, would a paralawyer be capable of handling it adequately? And second, what level of service is economically justified by the matter in issue? The first question is properly for the lawyer; the second should perhaps be for the client. If a lawyer determines that a matter is one which could be handled adequately by a paraprofessional, then maybe the client should have the option of either having it handled on that less expensive basis or—if he is willing and able to pay the price and thinks the expenditure justified—of having it given the full professional treatment by the lawyer.

Thus far it has been presumed that the use of nonlawyers either as technicians or as paralawyers to reduce the cost of producing legal services would be limited to lawyers' offices, where such personnel would function under the direct supervision of lawyers. Some proposals, however, contemplate that they would operate independently, or nearly so. This, of course, raises still further problems, as well as some interesting possibilities. Again, the main problem has to do with determining which problems are to be handled by the nonlawyer personnel and which by lawyers.

There would appear to be two possible approaches to making such determinations where the supportive nonlawyer personnel were functioning independently or semi-independently. In the first, they would be used much as doctors now use independent pharmacists and clinical laboratories, and as dentists now use independent dental laboratories.[5] Legal technicians and paralawyers, functioning independently, would be permitted to perform their limited services only upon the "prescription" of a lawyer.[6] This would, of course, leave with the lawyer the decision as to what matters were within the capabilities of particular nonlawyer personnel. It would also give the small firm lawyer and his client access to a greater range of supplementary services than would be possible were this kind of assistance available only through full-time employment within law firms.

The main disadvantage with this approach seems to be the duplication of fees that may result in cases where clients already know the kind of services needed, know that they can be adequately performed by paralawyers, and know which paralawyers to consult. In those cases, the client would have the unnecessary burden of paying a lawyer's fee in addition to the fee paid to the

5. A series of Idaho cases provides an interesting example of some of the problems that have arisen in the regulation of independent dental laboratories. The Idaho Supreme Court began by holding that dental laboratories had a constitutionally protected right to provide their services directly to the public (362). This holding was grounded on what appears to have been an erroneous finding that dental laboratories had traditionally performed their functions directly for the public (see 416:1247, 1256). This holding caused extreme difficulty in subsequent attempts to define just what functions such laboratories should be permitted to perform directly for the public (360; 361; 359).

6. The idea of a "lawyer's prescription" appears to have originated with Louis M. Brown, of the California Bar (see 81).

nonlawyer for the actual performance of the service. In the vast majority of cases, however, clients of moderate means probably do not know all this and need to have their problems diagnosed and the remedies prescribed by a lawyer. Thus, in most cases there would be no duplication. The client would pay the lawyer a fee for his crucial services in diagnosing the problem and prescribing a remedy; he would pay the legal technician or paralawyer for performance of the prescribed services. The important point is that he would be able to obtain these latter services at a lower price than would have been the case had they all been performed by the lawyer.

In the other approach, the decision as to which matters would be handled by lawyers and which by nonlawyers would be made prospectively through legislation, or perhaps rules of court, specifying in detail the things that legal technicians or paralawyers might and might not do. Perhaps the best example is again in the field of medicine, where optometrists are permitted to perform certain diagnostic and treatment functions quite independent of physicians (e.g., **422**).

This approach would, of course, eliminate the duplication problem just mentioned, but it would at the same time create the reverse problem—clients going first to legal technicians or paralawyers and then having to be sent to lawyers. More seriously, it would present a substantially greater danger that supportive legal personnel might tend to go beyond the limits of their capabilities and perform services that they were not competent to perform. It is one thing to authorize trained nonlawyers to perform limited legal functions when, and as, instructed to do so by lawyers. It is quite another to authorize them to do so when, and as, they themselves determine, limited only by the restrictions in their licenses.[7]

It may also be noteworthy that one consequence of this approach would probably be a somewhat narrower range of services available to the public through legal technicians and paralawyers. This is because the services they would be permitted to

7. One observer has commented that the absence of any significant problem with respect to the giving of legal advice by the lay personnel of the English Citizens' Advice Bureaus rests in large part upon a "proper attitude of humility" on the part of the lay people who operate the Bureaus. (Letter to the author from Seton Pollock, Secretary, Contentious Business, The Law Society [May 8, 1968]). Whether a "proper attitude of humility" could be expected to be an adequate limitation or safeguard upon the conduct of paraprofessional legal personnel in the American context is questionable.

offer would probably have to be more narrowly and strictly limited than would be the case were they to function under the instructions of lawyers. At the same time, this approach would no doubt make those services much more readily available to the public.

An orthodox response to the question of how legal assistants ought to be used would probably restrict them to functioning under the direction of lawyers, either in lawyers' offices or through "lawyers' prescriptions." Such a response would be grounded on the profession's traditional concern for the interests of clients. It might also be encouraged, however, by a sort of Gresham's Law of law practice—cheap services would tend to drive out the more expensive, and lawyers might ultimately lose those functions that independent supportive personnel were permitted to perform for the public. But if some of the functions now being performed by lawyers who have had seven years of college and law school education can in fact be performed adequately and at lower cost by nonlawyers who have had two years of technical legal training, can the exclusive retention of those functions by lawyers be justified? As always, the answer must be determined by what is good for the public.

The essential issue with respect to the use of nonlawyers in the rendition of legal services, whether under lawyers' supervision or independently, is that of finding some acceptable accommodation between the demands of economic necessity and those of professional integrity. Were it possible, in terms of expense as well as in terms of the supply of lawyers, the ideal would perhaps be to have all legal problems, large or small, given the full custom treatment by a top quality lawyer. But it is not possible. Legal services are supplied in the context of the economic structure, and their distribution must therefore be responsive to the demands of that structure. There are just not enough lawyers to give all problems that kind of treatment, and even if there were, clients could not afford it.

The medical profession has encountered and continues to encounter the same kind of problem. A great many functions that were once performed exclusively by doctors are now performed by laymen. This has come about because it is not feasible—either economically or in terms of the number of doctors available—to have all medical procedures performed by doctors.

The doctor who utilizes the services of a nurse to perform many routine treatment procedures and who has access to technicians for the performance of many diagnostic procedures is able to serve his patients for fees that patients are generally willing and able to pay. Were he to perform all of these functions himself, as doctors once did, the result would probably be one of two things. Either his fees would be elevated beyond the reach of most people, with a consequent reduction in the use of medical care by the public, or doctors' incomes would be depressed, with a consequent reduction in the number of young men willing to undergo the lengthy and arduous training to become doctors. And this would probably be so even with medical insurance, as the increased cost would still be passed on to the patient through higher insurance premiums.

An even more suggestive accommodation of the medical profession to the conflicting demands of economics and public health is the use of nurses and other personnel to conduct mass immunization programs. Here, one doctor may supervise many nurses — or even technicians — in the administration of immunization procedures to the public on a mass basis. Still another example is the screening of school children for vision and hearing defects. Here the entire procedure may be conducted entirely without a doctor. Such screening tests are typically supervised only by a registered nurse and administered by laymen who may have had only limited training.

Admittedly, it would be ideal if all school children could be examined regularly for vision and hearing defects by licensed ophthalmologists and otolaryngologists. But they cannot, because there are not enough of these specialists to do such a mass job, and because the cost would surely be prohibitive. Thus the alternatives are really not examinations by trained doctors on the one hand, and screening by laymen under the direction of registered nurses on the other; rather the choice is between having the screening done by supervised laymen and not having it done at all. While the results may sometimes be less than completely satisfactory, they are nevertheless sufficiently beneficial to justify providing those kinds of service to the public. Of course, it is significant that parents who wish to do so always have the option of having their children examined regularly by ophthalmologists and otolaryngologists. It may also be significant that few appear to do so even when they can afford it, except where vision and hearing problems become so severe as to noticeably impair the child's ability to function.

Much the same kind of problem is involved in the matter of making lawyers' services available to people of moderate means, and perhaps much the same kind of accommodation might one day be made. Most lawyers would probably be horrified at the thought of "dime-store type" legal services being dispensed to people of moderate means by laymen, even though such laymen might be trained as technicians or paraprofessionals. But when the matter is looked at from the viewpoint of vision and hearing screening in the schools, mass public immunization programs, and utilization of nurses and technicians in regular private medical practice, it may not appear so shocking. Perhaps it will be possible for the legal profession to develop similarly effective, yet professionally justifiable, methods of providing people of moderate means with the legal services they need.

c
Other measures
for increasing lawyers'
efficiency

Other possible methods of reducing the cost of producing legal services may include better use of the services of other professions, the possible future use of computers and other technological innovations, better management of the housekeeping details of law practice, and the organization of lawyers into more efficient units for the practice of law.

Legal problems do not ordinarily occur in isolation. They usually contain elements that go beyond the strictly legal, and they are frequently bound up closely—in both causative and derivative relationships—with other human problems. Lawyers are coming more and more to realize, therefore, that definitive solutions often call for the knowledge and skill of other disciplines, sometimes as integral parts of legal solutions and at other times as supplemental or co-equal remedies.

The use of engineers, physicians, accountants, psychologists, and others in the solution of clients' problems may be expected to have much the same effect upon the cost problem as does specialization among lawyers themselves. An engineer's time, for example, may be as expensive as that of a lawyer. But when the client's problem calls for the services of an engineer, those services will undoubtedly be better and less expensively performed by a professional engineer whose expertise enables him to perform them expeditiously than by a lawyer who attempts to educate himself in engineering and to act as an engineer at his client's expense.

The use of computers to perform functions now performed by lawyers, particularly the mechanical search and retrieval functions of legal research, is also a possible method of reducing the expense of legal services (see **182**; see also **189**). Of course, computers do not yet appear to offer significant cost advantages, although they do now seem to be entering the realm of commercial feasibility. Ultimately, they would seem to promise research services that are both better and cheaper.

Conceptually, the use of computers in law practice is much the same as the use of trained lay technicians and paraprofessionals, and it raises the same questions—although it does not necessarily produce the same answers. How much of the lawyer's function can be given over to computers? How much should be given over? And, to what extent should the public be given direct access to computerized legal services?

The capabilities of lay technicians and paraprofessionals constitute the appropriate limits to their use. Lawyers are probably safe in using such personnel to provide legal services to clients to the extent that the capabilities of such lay assistants permit.

But what are the limits on the capabilities of computers? "Brave New World" thinking envisions computers as replacements for lawyers, and even for courts.[8] If there is any limit, perhaps it is in the present difficulty—and tremendous expense—of developing and programming computer systems to do anything more than the essentially mechanical search and retrieval functions (see **182**:733). But it is a bold man indeed who would now even dare to guess at the ultimate limits.

The question of the ultimate limits can probably be left for future solution, however. For now, computers do seem to promise greater efficiency in the search and retrieval operations of legal research. To the extent that they thus offer better service at acceptable cost, or professionally acceptable service at lower cost, lawyers should use them in serving their clients.

8. For a satirical exposition of this point of view see Rohner (**266**).

But what about the other main question—the extent to which the public is to be given direct access to computerized legal services independently of lawyers? (See **198**; cf. **135**; **197**; **112**.) This, of course, is the same problem that arises with respect to the use of nonlawyer assistants. One danger implicit in the utilization of independent paraprofessionals would not arise with respect to computerized legal services, however. While a person with limited training in the law might on occasion attempt to answer questions or perform services beyond his capabilities, a computer would be unlikely ever to do so. The other difficulty, clients' lack of understanding of their problems, would affect the rendition of legal services by both independent paraprofessionals and computers. Put simply, people of moderate means probably would not know what questions to ask. There would thus still seem to be need for the services of lawyers in connection with most computer-rendered legal services.

All this is rather speculative, of course, and perhaps not necessary to the simple observation that as computer technology develops, lawyers should be alert to the possible use of computers wherever they might improve lawyers' services and reduce their cost to clients.

Still another facet of the problem of efficiency in law practice is the matter of better management of the nonlegal aspects of law office operation. The bar is doing some good work here, mainly through the Economics of Law Practice program of the American Bar Association (see especially **36**). This program has dealt with such subjects as: better use of space and equipment; better forms of law office organization; better accounting and record keeping—including the keeping of time records; and better methods of recruiting and training personnel. Although in the past the program has concentrated on the use of these methods to raise lawyers' incomes, it may be hoped that in the future the program might also help to reduce the cost of lawyers' services to people of moderate means.

Closely related to the concepts thus far discussed is the idea that lawyers should organize themselves into firms or other law practice units of sufficient size to make optimum use of these varied methods of attaining efficiency in law practice. It is not a foregone conclusion, of course, that large firms are essential to the effective use of these methods. There are instances in which comparatively small firms have developed highly efficient operations. And, of course, pooling arrangements for both equipment and personnel might make many of these efficiencies available to solo and small firm lawyers. Experience in the providing of legal services to business clients, however, would seem to suggest that large firms are more likely than the small to achieve the end objective of really efficient law practice. Certainly, the statistics on lawyers' incomes indicate that this is so (108), and some of the same principles that cause lawyers practicing as partners to earn more than those practicing alone would also seem to be the operative principles with respect to the cost of lawyers' services to people of moderate means. Indeed, from the standpoint of availability and cost, it is difficult to overstate the importance of the joining together of lawyers in larger practice units (see 169).

4
Minimum Fee Schedules
and the Price of
Lawyers' Services

It might at first appear that what has been said about reducing the price of lawyers' services is in direct conflict with the concept of the recommended minimum fee schedule, a concept that has long been promulgated by the organized bar. There may indeed be some legitimate questions to be asked about the minimum fee schedule idea,[9] but those questions are not necessarily raised by proposals to reduce the price of lawyers' services by increasing efficiency in law practice.

The theory underlying minimum fee schedules seems to run essentially as follows: (1) The existence of an economically healthy legal profession as a source of independent counsel and representation for all is in the public interest; (2) for any given legal service there is a minimum expenditure of time and effort beneath which a professionally acceptable performance of the service is impossible; (3) at the same time, there is a minimum

---

9. Such questions might range all the way from doubts about the basic rationale of the minimum fee schedule to inquiries about the appropriateness of particular minimum fees and may include examination of the factual assumptions upon which minimum fee determinations are based and even speculation about problems of price fixing and restraint of trade.

rate of return for a lawyer's efforts, below which it is impossible for him to maintain the sound economic condition that is in the public interest;[10] and (4) the product of these two minimum elements — time and effort, and rate of return — is thus the lowest ethically acceptable fee for a given service.[11]

Obviously, if this theory is sound, and if the bar has correctly assessed the minimum acceptable expenditure of time and effort for a given service and the minimum rate of return necessary for economic solvency, then any reduction in the price of a lawyer's service below the recommended minimum fee would inevitably mean either professionally unacceptable performance or impairment of the lawyer's economic situation. But if, in fact, adoption of measures designed to improve efficiency should enable lawyers to render professionally acceptable services in a given kind of case at production costs below those that have heretofore been possible, then the same theory would seem to call for a reduced minimum fee.

Whether minimum fee schedules would ever actually be modified to make allowance for reductions in the cost of producing lawyers' services is quite another question, however. In theory they should be so modified, but in practice they might prove to be unresponsive to changes in production cost. Thus, while the concept of minimum fee schedules is not challenged by the suggestion of efficiency measures to reduce the price of lawyers' services, the administration of fee schedules might well be drawn into question. The proposal of efficiency measures as methods of reducing price thus does present the bar with a

10. Of course, this minimum rate of return is based on a number of assumptions. The proposition that an economically healthy bar requires a certain minimum rate of return, for example, presumes something about the desirable or necessary standard of living for lawyers. It also presumes that the appropriate model for determination of the minimum rate of return is the lawyer who relies wholly upon his law practice for his economic support and whose time is fully employed in law practice. There may be lawyers who are underemployed and whose economic situations would be enhanced rather than impaired by small fees, even though they were to give their cases the time and effort necessary for professionally acceptable performance. Similarly, there may be lawyers with other sources of financial support who would render professionally acceptable services at low fees without impairing their own economic situations. But these have been rejected as models, apparently on the ground that if such lawyers were permitted to charge low fees, other lawyers would have to meet their prices, and most would have to do it either by rendering professionally unacceptable services or by impairing their own economic positions.

11. While this appears to be the rationale used to justify minimum fee schedules, it is not usually articulated so explicitly (see 35:1). Neither does this rationale describe how minimum fees are actually determined. In most instances, recommended minimum fees appear to be based on the fees customarily charged for the various legal services by lawyers in the locality covered by the particular schedule (35:8-11).

challenge to reexamine fee schedules from time to time in light
of changes in the manner in which lawyers' services are produced.

5
Conclusions on Price
and the Cost of
Production

The measures discussed above for reducing the price of lawyers' services are neither new nor original. Most have been
urged many times before, and efforts are presently being made
to put some of them into effect. Perhaps this review of them will
have served a purpose, however, if it does no more than remind
the legal profession of the importance of economic factors in the
matter of availability of legal services and encourage lawyers to
give a bit more attention to the economic problem of handling
the legal problems of people of moderate means.

B
Aids in
Meeting Legal Expenses

While measures designed to increase lawyers' efficiency
might result in some reduction in the price of legal services and
thus have some effect on the use of those services by people of
moderate means, such measures are not a complete answer. The
resolution of difficult legal problems will probably always be
expensive, no matter how efficient lawyers are or may become.
And, although more efficient law practice may enable lawyers to
offer routine services at lower fees, an optimum use of even
modestly priced routine services may nevertheless cause serious
budgetary problems for many people of moderate means. Thus,
attention should also be given to various possibilities for assisting people to meet the expense of legal services. Among such
possibilities are four methods of spreading or reallocating expense.

First, there is the proposal that a successful litigant should be
able to recover his attorney's fee from the unsuccessful party as a

cost of litigation, a measure that would shift entirely to the losing litigant a burden that now falls on both parties. Next, there are the legal service financing programs, which seek to relieve the economic burden of legal services by spreading the expense out over the client's own future earnings through loans or other time payment arrangements. Third are the legal service insurance and prepayment arrangements. Prepayment arrangements, included in most legal service insurance proposals but not technically insurance, would do much the same thing as the loan plans but would spread the expense over an earning period before the services were used. Genuine insurance for legal services would attempt to deal with major expenses occasioned by the fortuitous occurrence of legal catastrophes to some individuals among a larger group by spreading such occasional major expenses of the few among the entire group. And fourth, there are legal service subsidies which would spread the expense, or a part of it, among the taxpayers or some other subsidizing group.

1
Recovery of
Attorneys' Fees as a
Cost of Litigation

A number of writers have discussed this subject (e.g., **126**; **178**; **297**; **125**; **231**; but see **349**). Generally they make the following points: (a) It is unjust to impose upon the party who is "in the right" the economic burden of asserting or defending his rights against the wrongdoer. (b) While allowing prevailing parties in law suits to recover their attorneys' fees from the losers might inhibit the bringing of frivolous claims or the raising of frivolous defenses, it would probably not deter people with legitimate claims from bringing actions nor would it deter people with legitimate defenses from defending them. The risk of having to pay an opponent's legal fees would be but a minor uncertainty added to the much greater uncertainties of litigation. (c) The allowance of attorneys' fees might even encourage the bringing of legitimate claims and the raising of legitimate defenses by assuring the litigant who is confident of his case that he will be made entirely whole if he wins. (d) Many other countries, including both England and Canada, allow the prevailing party to a lawsuit to recover his attorneys' fees from the loser. (e) Attorneys' fees were at one time generally allowed as a cost of litigation in this country. The discontinuance of this practice has been attributed variously to "historical accident," to the public's distrust of and hostility to the legal profession in earlier days, or to the individualism of early America and the "sporting theory of justice." (f) Recovery of attorneys' fees is presently allowed in this country under certain limited circumstances – e.g., in divorce proceedings, workmen's compensation cases, and eminent domain proceedings. (g) The awarding of attorneys' fees as a cost of litigation encourages the settlement of disputes by compromise and adjustment rather than by litigation. (h) The awarding of attorneys' fees as a cost of litigation might obviate the contingent fee, with its attendant evils. Here, attention will be focused on only the second and third of these points.

With respect to availability of legal services, the primary consideration in determining the proper allocation of the burden of attorneys' fees between parties to litigation is the effect a given allocation will have upon the public's use of the litigative process and, as a consequence, upon the public's use of lawyers' services. As is the case in so many other fields of concern to the legal profession, the data are inadequate to support any kind of precise determination as to the effect of a particular allocation in either encouraging or discouraging litigation. But there are a few pertinent facts that appear to possess some inferential value.

To begin with, the present American system, which generally denies to the successful litigant any recovery of the attorneys' fees required for the vindication of his rights, does in fact seem to inhibit the assertion of some legitimate claims – particularly small ones.[12] Of course, no one knows how many. In addition, the practice of European countries in generally allowing a successful litigant to recover his attorneys' fees from the losing party apparently produces satisfactory results (see **34**; **65**; **273**; **66**; **136**; **329**:1223-24). Furthermore, allowing recovery of attorneys' fees in certain kinds of cases appears to have been reasonably successful even in this country (**329**:1226-30).

Any attempt to determine how a rule allowing recovery of attorneys' fees as a cost of litigation would affect the public's use

12. Professor Ehrenzweig gives a classic example from his own experience (**125**).

of lawyers and the litigative process requires examination of a number of relevant factors. Such variable factors as the size or importance of the matter at issue, the probable cost of litigation, and the strength of the respective parties' cases appear to be especially significant. Indeed, the deterrent effect of the allocation of the burden of attorneys' fees between the parties to litigation appears to be essentially a function of these three factors.

Where the probable cost of litigation is small in comparison with the value or importance of the matter to be litigated, then the allocation of the burden of attorneys' fees would seem to have little to do with whether or not the action would be brought. And this would seem to be so regardless of whether the parties' cases were strong or weak. Obviously, a plaintiff with a strong case would bring his action even though he thereby risked the loss of an amount that included not only his own attorneys' fees but also those of his opponent. Similarly, the defendant with a strong case would make his defense rather than settle, regardless of the allocation of a relatively small burden of attorneys' fees between the parties.

Nor would the allocation of attorneys' fees seem to be determinative in even weak cases where the probable cost of litigation is small in comparison with the value of importance of the matter in issue. If a party's case were strong enough to justify risking his own attorney's fees, he would probably be willing to risk the burden of paying his opponent's legal expenses as well, as long as the value of the matter far outweighed the probable cost. There may be a narrow field where the allocation of attorneys' fees might have some effect, but it would seem to be extremely small.

The allocation of the burden of attorneys' fees may have a great deal to do with encouraging or discouraging litigation, however, where the probable cost of litigation is large in comparison with the value or importance of the matter in issue. For when the cost of prosecuting or defending an action is as great as the value of the matter involved, even the winning party loses. This is so, for example, with virtually all of the great mass of so-called small cases. It may also be so with some large ones.

Significantly, the effect of the allocation in these circumstances probably depends largely upon the strength of the cases of the respective parties. The plaintiff with a weak case may very well be deterred from bringing his action, or the defendant with a weak case may be induced to settle rather than to defend, by the prospect of incurring a double dose of litigation costs that are already comparatively high. Thus, where litigation promises to be expensive in relation to the value or importance of the matter in issue, a rule allowing successful litigants to recover their own attorney's fees from their unsuccessful opponents doubtless would deter the bringing and defending of many weak cases. The result may well be just the opposite, however, with well-founded cases. Who knows how many small but entirely legitimate claims presently go unasserted because the cost of litigating them is prohibitively expensive or thought to be so? Who knows how many people — people with sound, legitimate defenses — are victimized by weak, groundless, or frivolous claims only because a defense is not economically justified? Who knows how many people suffer wrongs and injustices because of a rule that puts the economic burden of securing justice upon the wronged rather than upon the wrong-doer?

Where the cost of litigation is relatively large, then, the person with a strong case would likely be encouraged to assert his claim, and the one with a strong defense to a similarly uneconomic case would be encouraged to make his defense, by the prospect of being made entirely whole if successful. Thus, the virtue of a system allowing the winning party to recover his attorneys' fees from the unsuccessful party — and its potential contribution to the availability of legal services — is in its probable tendency to make the traditional legal process truly responsive and accessible to what must surely be a vast number of people who have not heretofore been able to afford representation.

Most of what has thus far been said presumes parties of roughly equal power or means and parties on whom considerations of cost can normally be expected to have considerable effect. The pernicious impact of the present system of allocating the expenses of litigation may be magnified, however, where significant disparities in power or means exist between the parties. Obviously, to the extent that one party is better able than the other to afford the expense, the effect of expense in determining the outcome of litigation is increased. In addition, where the disparity is great, the more powerful party may be able to afford to prolong litigation in order to increase the already high cost burden that must be borne by the other party, thus using expense tactically to defeat claims that might otherwise have prevailed on their merits or to crush defenses that might otherwise have been invulnerable.

Moreover, disparities in power also tend to increase the potential for arbitrary or irresponsible action. This may be especially true with respect to litigation by corporations and governmental agencies, where the decision that forces an individual to assume a heavy burden of expense in order to protect his rights is made by an essentially anonymous bureaucrat who has little or nothing to lose personally, regardless of the end result of the litigation. The individual citizen who, because of an arbitrary or irresponsible decision by a faceless bureaucrat, must defend his rights against the awesome power of government or big business is in an unenviable position. Surely, when he is able to fight his cause through to the end and win, he is entitled to be made completely whole.

The argument is sometimes made that relatively few cases can be described in terms of "strong" or "weak." Disputes often involve intermediate degrees of strength or weakness, and sometimes the parties' cases are evenly matched. But this observation merely points up the superiority of a system that would allow recovery of attorneys' fees by the successful party. Under such a system, effective access to the courts would depend upon the party's own evaluation of, and faith in, the merits of his case. The present American system says to the man with a small case, "Regardless of the merits of your cause, you cannot have justice because your case is not worth it." A system allowing recovery of attorneys' fees would say, "If you really believe in your cause — enough to assume the risk of paying your opponent's attorney's fees if you lose — then you can have justice regardless of how small your case is." The latter seems vastly superior.

2
*Legal Service
Financing Programs*[13]

An entirely different kind of reallocation of the burden of legal expenses is involved in the legal service financing programs

13. For a description of the pioneer program see Bar Ass'n of Erie County (**129**).

now engaging the attention of the bar. Many such programs are
springing up around the country. They vary in detail, but all
employ the familiar time payment principle.

Typically, an agreement is entered into between a local bar
association and a bank or other lending institution. Under it, the
lending agency agrees to grant installment loans at specified
rates to qualified clients for the payment of lawyers' fees. Thus,
instead of attempting to shift the burden of legal expenses to
someone other than the person using the legal services, such
financing programs seek to spread it over an extended segment
of the user's own earnings. Consequently, many people can, in
theory at least, afford legal services that they would not be able
to purchase if they had to pay the entire fee at the time the
service was received.

The questions of ethics and propriety that were at first raised
against these plans seem now to have been substantially laid to
rest (*ABA Eth. Ops.*, No. 320), and the bar seems to be accepting
them enthusiastically (see 8; see also **299**:468, n.125; **310**). There
remains, however, a question that is essential from the standpoint of availability of legal services: Will legal service financing
programs in fact cause significant numbers of people to use
lawyers' services who would not otherwise have done so?

While such programs may be of benefit to both lawyers and
clients in a number of ways, they come with serious limitations
built in. To begin with, legal expense financing is available only
to qualified clients—those with good credit ratings and good
prospects of repayment. Thus, they exclude at the outset many
of the clients and potential clients who most need help in meeting legal expenses. Moreover, because most programs contemplate only modest publicity, much of the financing will be
done, in the immediate future at least, for people who have
already sought out a lawyer. It may be that the availability of
financing will one day become a matter of such common knowledge that people will go to lawyers' offices with the expectation
that the fees will be financed much as they now go shopping for
television sets with a similar expectation. If so, such programs
may ultimately be a factor in stimulating the use of lawyers'
services by people who now do not use them. But for now, and
for a good while in the future, it is likely that legal service
financing will be used mainly by people who would have taken
their problems to lawyers anyway. Financing programs may thus

relieve lawyers of the burden of carrying many unpaid accounts, but they probably will not immediately bring in many new clients.

One further limitation is of some importance. Legal services must compete with a potential client's other needs and desires for a share of his limited financial resources. This is so with respect to his future earnings no less than with his current income. The extent to which a man may be willing to encumber future income in order to purchase legal services in preference to other services or goods is limited. Thus, even the person who does have a good credit rating and good prospects of repayment may opt for a television set instead of estate planning, even though the latter becomes as easily financed as the former. The main value of legal service financing, it would seem, is that it gives him at least the opportunity to choose the estate planning.

3
Legal Expense
Insurance Proposals[14]

The marked success of medical insurance has prompted many lawyers to speculate about the feasibility of some kind of insurance for legal services (e.g., **82**; **288**). Such speculation has been founded generally on the assumption that similarities between legal services and medical services make the medical insurance experience a suitable model for a legal expense insurance program. On the other hand, some critics, pointing out important differences between medical and legal services, have expressed serious doubt about the feasibility of insurance for legal expenses (e.g., **127**).

Most proposals for legal expense insurance contemplate spreading the burden of legal expenses in two ways, only one of which involves genuine insurance principles. Under orthodox theory, insurance spreads among all members of an insured group the burden of substantial losses incurred fortuitously by

14. The first definitive work on the subject is the preliminary feasibility study done by Professor Preble Stolz of the University of California School of Law (Boalt Hall) (299:417-76). It was conducted under the auspices of the American Bar Foundation as an adjunct to the Project on Availability of Legal Services and at the request of the American Bar Association Special Committee on Availability of Legal Services. This careful study, which made use of the best available actuarial advice, is the source of much of the following brief discussion.

only a few members of the group. Although the loss occurs randomly among group members, its incidence in the group as a whole is predictable. Thus, pure insurance for legal services would be limited to major legal expenses that might be expected to be incurred by only a relatively small number of insureds in any given period—such expenses, for example, as those arising from a serious criminal charge, negligence suit, divorce, or the like.

However, most legal expense insurance proposals include, as well, many lower cost services that are, or might be, used frequently by nearly everyone covered by the program. These services include such things as the preparing of simple legal instruments and the giving of routine legal advice. Indeed, one of the arguments most commonly made in support of legal expense insurance is that it may encourage people of moderate means to seek legal help and advice before their problems have become so serious as to require expensive remedial action. Coverage for such services is clearly not insurance in the true sense. Rather, it is in the nature of budgeting or prepayment of anticipated expenses. It spreads the burden over the insured's own earnings for a period of time before the services are used, much like loan or time payment plans spread it over the client's earnings for a period of time after the services have been used.

The combining of both insurance and budgeting elements in one so-called "insurance" program is not novel. Medical insurance, although perhaps predominantly insurance in character at its inception, has now come to include a substantial budgeting element, with some programs now covering even routine visits to a doctor's office. And even automobile insurance, viewed by many people as true insurance, seems to be more nearly budgeting than insurance in its comprehensive coverage, which includes such losses as glass breakage.

Although they do so differently, both insurance and budgeting elements contribute to what is probably the greatest problem associated with legal expense insurance—marketability. In the case of the insurance element, many of the major legal expenses that might be included in an insurance program are already being handled in other reasonably satisfactory ways. For example, the cost of defending negligence actions is included in conventional casualty insurance policies, and the cost of prosecuting negligence actions is dealt with by means of the contingent fee device. Other major legal expenses involve problems that most people would find so difficult to imagine happening to *them* that they would not see any need to use insurance to protect themselves against the risk. The expense of defending oneself against serious criminal charges—except, perhaps, for those that might result from the operation of automobiles—is probably of this type. Divorce, another common major legal expense, involves a remedy against which a substantial number of people have moral or religious scruples. The person whose beliefs preclude his own use of a particular legal service or make his use of the service unlikely is not apt to be enthusiastic about assuming part of the burden of another's use of it. As a result of such problems, it becomes difficult to find enough suitable major legal expenses to make a really attractive insurance package from the marketing standpoint.

The problem with the budgeting element is perhaps equally troublesome. Few people who now go to lawyers for routine legal services really have trouble paying for them as they use them. Thus, for these clients a prepayment scheme fills no urgent need. The budgeting element of legal expense insurance proposals is therefore actually directed at people who do not now consult lawyers for help and advice in small or routine matters. The theory seems to be that people will make greater use of legal services if those services are already paid for. This theory may be sound. But it comes up squarely against the marketing problem: How can people be induced to pay in advance for legal services that they cannot now even be induced to use?

Advertising may be part of the answer. Perhaps it would be possible to do more to "sell" legal services through the advertising of legal expense insurance than it has ever been possible to do in "selling" them directly. Still, legal expense insurance would not appear to be a highly attractive "package" for purposes of marketing.

If legal expense insurance is salable at all, it will probably be on a group basis. Although in this event, such insurance would have to compete with other group benefit programs, there may be reason to hope that it would be marketable to groups when it might not be marketable to individuals. Employers, because of their special interest in sustaining the productivity of employees, might well be receptive to an insurance program that would relieve employees of the burden of major legal expenses when such expenses do occur and encourage employees to have their minor legal problems taken care of before they become serious. With interests generally embracing the welfare of their members, unions also might be receptive to programs that offer genuine benefits, even though the members might not have purchased the same benefits individually.

Legal expense insurance would have to compete as well with other possible group methods of obtaining legal services. Group legal services,[15] for example, would seem to have an advantage over insurance in enabling the group to select lawyers who are experts in the fields of law of concern to group members, and to assist in bringing lawyers and group members together. Insurance, on the other hand, is an attractive alternative because it would preserve for the individual his free choice of attorneys and because it would relieve the group of the burden of administering a legal services program.

The marketing of legal expense insurance on a group basis may also be responsive to another of the problems of such insurance. In the absence of controls of some sort, any kind of insurance would be purchased most readily by those who were likely soon to be claimants. Obviously, a program that insures a disproportionately large number of people who already have or soon will have claims is in a doubtful economic position. Consequently, most insurance programs have adopted restrictions to control their exposure to risk. Life insurance companies, for instance, typically either reject applications from prospective insureds deemed unacceptably high risks or accept applications at higher premium rates than standard. Similar controls are used in medical and automobile insurance. In addition, another kind of restriction is also used in medical insurance to deal with adverse selection; insureds become eligible for certain benefits — obstetrical benefits are the most common example — only after a specified waiting period.

Knowledge of behavior and causation does not yet appear adequate to permit the identification of individual prospective insureds presenting high risks of legal expense insurance claims, however. And there are no neatly defined gestation periods for most legal problems. Thus, these controls are not at present

15. See chapter 7 *infra*.

feasible for legal expense insurance. Instead, adverse selection would probably best be handled, at least at the outset, by marketing such insurance on a group basis rather than individually, controlling the incidence of claims through selection of the group to be insured. While it may not be possible to predict whether individual applicants will be acceptable insurance risks, it should be possible to predict generally that the incidence of legal problems among the members of a given group with fairly stable characteristics will be within acceptable limits for insurance purposes.

Another problem is the possibility of abuse or over-use of insurance benefits. Under orthodox insurance doctrine, abuse occurs whenever an insurance benefit is utilized to secure or pay for a service that would not have been used by the insured except for the insurance benefit. Obviously, abuse tends to raise the amount that must be paid out in claims and, in turn, the price of the insurance.

Legal expense insurance would appear to be especially susceptible to this kind of abuse. There are two reasons. First, one objective of such insurance, at least with respect to small and routine legal problems, is to encourage the use of lawyers' services. But because the principles involved are budgeting principles and not insurance principles, the problem is not too serious. To the extent that an insured's contribution, whether made by himself or by someone else, is in fact simply prepayment of routine and more or less certain-to-be-incurred expenses, he and all other insureds can make full use of the insurance benefit without upsetting the economic balance of the program.

The second and more serious reason for the susceptibility of legal expense insurance to over-use is that many of the major problems that might be included in an insurance program are not really fortuitous in their occurrence. Indeed, their occurrence is to one degree or another within the control of the insureds. While it is unlikely that many people would commit crimes, obtain divorces, or adopt children merely because the legal fees were covered by insurance, the availability of an insurance benefit might induce a good many people to utilize a service like estate planning when they would not have done so in the absence of insurance. While it may be desirable to encourage people to make greater use of such "optional" legal services, their inclusion in an insurance scheme without adequate controls would probably necessitate raising the price of the insurance to an unmarketable level.

There is another problem. The amount of legal service to be devoted to a given legal problem is largely within the control of the client and the lawyer, both of whom, under an insurance plan, have an interest in the lawyer's devoting as much time and effort as possible to the problem. Moreover, the amount of service that might be devoted to a problem is highly elastic. Thus, if insurance were to provide what was in effect a blank check for legal services, the tendency in many cases might be to abuse the insurance benefit by the application of a greater amount of time and effort than the cases would otherwise justify.

There are a number of possible approaches to the problem of over-use of insurance benefits. One is to limit the benefits offered, excluding those that present the greatest danger of abuse, and restricting others. This approach may reduce over-use by eliminating the more tempting opportunities, but it also limits both the marketability of the insurance and its efficacy as an aid in meeting legal expenses.

Another possibility is to adopt a fixed schedule of fees for specific services, thus removing part of the lawyer's incentive to provide more service than the case requires. This approach would take some of the elasticity out of the cost of insurance benefits, but it would also leave insureds only partly protected in extraordinary cases where the legal services that were legitimately required exceeded what would be covered by the set fees. In addition of course, there is the difficulty of formulating fee schedules as well as the virtual certainty that any system of rigidly fixed fees would be unacceptable to the bar.

Still another approach is the device of coinsurance, under which the insured remains obligated to pay a significant portion of the expense—the first one hundred dollars, for example, or a percentage. Coinsurance does seem to be a workable control, although it is by no means a complete one. Indeed, effectiveness in limiting over-use of benefits seems to correspond roughly to the extent to which it leaves the burden of legal expenses on the insured. Still, a middle ground might be reached where insurance would provide adequate protection while permitting useful and significant coverage.

This sketch of the principles and problems of legal expense insurance should serve to suggest some of the difficulties to be expected in any attempt to develop a workable insurance system. But the problems do not appear insurmountable. A preliminary study has concluded that a system of legal expense insurance has reasonable prospects of proving feasible (299:476). In response, the American Bar Association, upon the recommendation of its Special Committee on Availability of Legal Services, has undertaken to sponsor experimental programs that should eventually provide a definitive answer to the question of feasibility (29:231). Legal expense insurance may never come to be a complete solution to the problem of the cost of legal services. If it does prove workable, however, it should be a significant help in making legal services available to people who need them.

4
Legal Service Subsidies

The proposal that public funds be used to assist people to meet legal expenses contemplates spreading the burden among the taxpaying public. This discussion will review two main proposals for doing so. The first is an indirect subsidy; taxpayers would be allowed to claim personal legal expenses as deductions in the computation of income taxes. The second is a direct subsidy of the type embodied in the English Legal Aid and Advice Schemes.

a
**Income tax deductions
for legal expenses**

It is sometimes suggested that people might be encouraged to use lawyers' services by a modification of the income tax laws to permit individuals to claim deductions for personal legal expenses, much as individuals now may with medical expenses (423:§ 213), and as businesses now do with legal expenses classifiable as business expenses (423:§ 162). This, of course, is simply a form of subsidy, seeking to spread among all taxpayers — in the form of higher taxes to compensate for the loss of revenue to the government — that portion of an individual's legal expenses represented by the actual tax saving from the deduction.

Such deductions may afford people some help in meeting legal expenses, but they involve three problems. First, there is the political problem of getting the necessary legislation enacted. Second, tax deductions for legal expenses would tend to give the greatest benefit to those who need it least, and the least benefit to those who need it most. And third, there may be some question about the real effectiveness of the device as an incentive to the use of lawyers' services.

The history of the medical expense deduction does not shed much light on the political problem. In 1942 the demands of a world war made necessary substantial increases in federal income taxes. The medical expense deduction appears to have been offered and adopted as a means of mitigating for individuals this increased tax burden (318:1612). The proposed medical expense provision allowed extraordinary expenses to be deducted from individual income subject to taxation — "extraordinary" expenses being those in excess of an amount (expressed as a percentage of income) regarded as normal and routine for medical expenses. Among witnesses appearing before congressional committees to support the medical expense deduction were the Tax Advisor to the Secretary of the Treasury and representatives of the Teachers' Union of the City of New York, the National Lawyers' Guild, the National Association of Retail Druggists, and the Congress of Industrial Organizations. The gist of their testimony was that a person who incurs an extraordinary burden of medical expenses during a given year should be relieved of a part of the burden of increased wartime taxes for that year (318:1611–23, 2042–43, 2115–20, 2200–2206, 2304–2308; 319:1676–78).

One might only guess about the reception Congress would give to a bill providing for a legal expense deduction, or about the sources of support for such legislation. As high wartime taxes have become more or less permanent, the same argument that supported the medical deduction would appear to be applicable to a legal expense deduction. Moreover, the legal expense deduction would surely present far less of a political problem than would a proposal for a comprehensive subsidy system. On the other hand, the use of tax laws to accomplish special ends not related to the collection of revenue — particularly through tax-avoidance measures that amount to subsidies for special interests — seems today to be meeting with increasing disfavor.

One characteristic of tax deductions is that their benefit to the taxpayer is proportional to the tax rate: $100 of deductible legal expense would save a taxpayer in the lowest tax bracket $15.40 in federal income taxes under present rates (423:§ 1). The same $100 of legal expense would save the taxpayer in the 55 percent bracket $60.50 (423:§ 1). It might be argued that $15.40 would be more significant to the man with a low income than $60.50 would be to the high-income person. Still, this kind of graduated subsidy would seem to be less than ideal as a method of assisting persons of moderate means to pay legal expenses because it would give comparatively little help to those who need it most.

The same reasoning suggests that, as a practical matter, a tax deduction would offer only slight incentive toward increased utilization of lawyers' services by people of moderate means. It seems unlikely that many people presently give a great deal of consideration to the prospect of tax deductibility in deciding whether or not to seek medical services. Little reason exists for believing that it would be otherwise with legal expenses. A man will not ordinarily spend $100 for services he doesn't think he needs in order just to get a $15 tax saving. Thus, although a legal expense tax deduction might be of some value in assisting people to pay for legal services, there are serious limitations on the effect it could be expected to have on the use of lawyers' services.

b
Direct
legal service subsidies

Perhaps the best example of a direct subsidy is the Legal Aid and Advice Schemes that have been in operation in England and Wales since 1949.[16] This program is funded by the British government but administered by the Law Society, the national organization of solicitors. The system presently consists of three

16. The Legal Aid and Advice Schemes (the term "scheme" carries no unsavory connotations in Great Britain) have been described by a number of commentators. E.g., 166:508-21; 247; 249; 328.

parts: the Statutory Advice Scheme, the Voluntary Advice Scheme, and the Statutory Assistance Scheme.

Under the Statutory Advice Scheme, an eligible applicant is entitled to obtain up to half an hour of consultation and advice from a participating solicitor of his own choice either without charge or for a minimal fee.[17] All fees paid are added to a governmentally subsidized Legal Aid Fund, from which the solicitor is compensated at the rate of £1 ($2.40) for a half-hour advice session (**424**:§ 7(8); **426**).

The Voluntary Advice Scheme is a supplementary program offered by the solicitors participating in the Statutory Schemes. Under it any person, regardless of his means, may obtain half an hour of consultation and advice for a fee of one pound (see **249**:23; see also **211**). The solicitor keeps this fee, which, of course, is the same as the compensation he would have received from the Legal Aid Fund for advice given to a client who qualified under the Statutory Advice Scheme.

Legal services beyond simple advice are covered by the Statutory Assistance Scheme. In matters related to litigation a person is eligible for legal aid under this program if his means are below specified levels.[18] In addition, he must satisfy a committee of local solicitors that he has reasonable grounds for asserting or disputing his claim or for defending or being a party to the proceedings to which his application relates (**424**:§ 7(8)). An applicant who is thus determined to be eligible for legal aid is then entitled to obtain the services of a solicitor of his own choosing and, where necessary for the trial of a case, a barrister. The statute provides specifically that the relationship between the solicitor or barrister and his legal aid client is to be precisely the same as with other clients (**424**:§ 1(7)).

A person receiving legal aid may be required to contribute to the Legal Aid Fund in accordance with his means.[19] In matters

17. An applicant who is receiving National Assistance (welfare) pays nothing; one whose disposable capital does not exceed £125 ($300) and whose disposable income is less than £7/10 ($18) per week pays only 2/6d (30 cents) for the half-hour of advice. Capital considered "disposable" for this purpose is for the most part property in excess of the applicant's dwelling, furniture, clothing, tools, and a limited amount of other property. Disposable income is income in excess of a specified sum, the amount depending upon the number of dependents the applicant must support and upon other relevant factors (**424**:§ 7(8); **426**).

18. To be eligible an applicant must not have disposable income exceeding £700 ($1,680) a year nor disposable capital exceeding £500 ($1,200) (**425**; see also **428**).

19. The recipient of legal aid may be required to contribute a sum not more than one-third of the amount by which his disposable income exceeds £250 ($600) a year and

not involving litigation, however, legal aid is available only to those applicants whose resources are below the levels at which contribution to the Legal Aid Fund would be required (**425**:§ 5 [1949 Act], § 1(2) [1960 Act]).[20] Again, the solicitors and barristers providing services under the Legal Aid Act are compensated from the Legal Aid Fund, generally for 90 percent of the fees allowed by court or, for some services, according to an established schedule (**425**:§ 6 (5), (6), Sched. 3 [1949 Act], § 2 [1960 Act]; see also **427**). Virtually the entire legal profession participates in the Legal Aid and Advice Schemes (**211**).[21] Furthermore, because the Schemes cover a large portion of the population,[22] a substantial amount of the work now being done by English lawyers is done under the Legal Aid and Advice Schemes.[23]

Variations of the English Legal Aid and Advice Schemes are now in operation in other countries.[24] In the United States the subsidy approach has been utilized primarily as one method of compensating assigned counsel in criminal cases under the Criminal Justice Act (**430**) and in a few limited "Judicare" experiments funded under the Legal Services program of the federal Office of Economic Opportunity (**255**; **274**; **264**). These Judicare programs operate primarily in rural areas where indigent persons may obtain the services of private lawyers of their own choice, with the fees being paid out of governmentally provided funds. Unlike the English Legal Aid and Advice

the amount by which his disposable capital exceeds £125 ($300) — not exceeding, of course, the amount that the Fund may have paid out on his account (**425**:§ 3 [1949 Act]).

20. Thus, it would appear that a person whose disposable income was below £250 a year or whose disposable capital was below £125 would be eligible for legal aid both in matters involving litigation and in those not involving litigation, while he would not be required to make any contribution to the Fund. A person whose resources were above those levels but below £700 a year of disposable income and £500 of disposable capital would be ineligible for legal aid in matters not involving litigation; in matters involving litigation, he would be eligible for legal aid but would also be liable for a contribution. A person whose disposable income exceeded £700 a year and whose disposable capital exceeded £500 would be ineligible for legal aid of any kind.

21. Cf. **249**:38 estimating the participation of the profession at approximately two-thirds.

22. It has been estimated that three-quarters of the English people come within present eligibility standards (**249**:31, n.82).

23. Some 119,815 applications for legal aid were granted, and advice was given to another 63,196 people, under the Statutory Schemes in 1966-67. See **184**:194-95. The Law Society estimates that about half of the serious cases brought are assisted under the Scheme (**186**:2).

24. These include schemes in Ontario, Canada (**208**; **246**; **281**), and in Hong Kong and Scotland (**249**:44).

Schemes, both the subsidies under the Criminal Justice Act and
the experimental Judicare programs are limited solely to the
indigent. Neither do they provide for any contribution by the
recipient of the services. And, of course, under the Criminal
Justice Act, counsel are assigned and not chosen by defendants.

Much of the comment on the English Legal Aid and Advice
Schemes has been favorable (**211**; **247**:1029 et seq.; **184**:31–33),
and some observers appear to favor adoption of the system on a
comprehensive basis in the United States (e.g., **249**:42–44;
281:89–90). Moreover, where the only alternative appears to be
an institutionalized salaried lawyer system, even otherwise
skeptical bar groups seem to favor the Judicare-type of subsidy,
at least when it is limited solely to services for the indigent (e.g.,
255:91–97; see also **134**). On the other hand, there has been
some criticism of the English system (see **185**; **264**:142–45), and
there appears to be a good deal of opposition to its importation
into this country, even in its attenuated Judicare form (e.g.,
264:127–52; **69**:291; **163**:428; **207**; **224**:113; see also **210**).

A number of criticisms are made of the English system. Those
who look at it primarily from the point of view of legal aid for
the poor complain that it makes no provision for law reform
activities and that it is ineffective in reaching the poor and
overcoming the barriers that keep them from seeking legal help.
The system is also regarded as being unduly restrictive in the
kinds of cases in which it offers help and as being too expensive.
Viewed as a comprehensive system to serve people of moderate
means as well as the poor, the English subsidy program is seen
as inappropriate to the American situation for two other reasons:
There is the question of its ideological acceptability to the
American public and the question of its acceptability to the
American legal profession.

The first two objections seem of comparatively little weight.
While the Legal Aid and Advice Schemes have not been completely effective in reaching the target population, and while law
reform has not thus far been a notable product of the Schemes,
there appears little reason for concluding that methods of
achieving both objectives *could* not be developed within the
context of a subsidy system. The other problems are more
difficult, however. While a subsidy is clearly responsive to the
problem of the cost of legal services, and thus might do much to

increase the public's utilization of such services,[25] would the bar and the public be willing to accept it and pay for it?

The problem of political ideology is especially difficult because the American electorate is far more sharply divided than the English on the question of the proper role of government in the affairs of citizens. Sentiment favoring an essentially passive role is still very strong in this country, and such sentiment may be expected to constitute a major obstacle to the adoption of any comprehensive subsidy system. It is true that political sentiments change, and that many governmental activities now almost universally accepted were at one time vigorously opposed as outside the government's proper sphere.[26] Where this has happened, the benefits to the public from such activities have come to be seen as justifying the resultant enlargement of the role of government. A comprehensive legal service subsidy may one day become similarly acceptable. But for now, political ideology will surely be a major deterrent to acceptance of any "American Legal Aid and Advice Scheme."

The bar's fear of "socialization of the legal profession" is likewise a serious consideration. It is interesting, however, that the English legal profession views the Legal Aid and Advice Schemes as means of *avoiding* "socialization" (see **247**:1030, 1033). The Law Society, seeing the nationalization of medical care and anticipating a similar development with respect to legal services, took the initiative by formulating its own plan for comprehensive legal services (**247**:1030, 1033). In so doing, the English legal profession was able to secure the adoption of a program that leaves direction and control substantially in the hands of the profession itself (**424**:§§ 8–14). To be sure, the subsidy comes from the government, and substantive changes in the program require legislative ratification. And, of course, The Law Society must report periodically to Parliament on its administration of the program. Still, both the effective direction of the program and its actual administration remain with the legal profession. It may be doubtful whether the American legal pro-

25. It is estimated, for example, that litigation has increased by seventy-five percent since the Legal Aid and Advice Schemes were inaugurated, although it is impossible to tell how much of that increase is attributable to the Schemes (**249**:39). In sixteen years some 1,125,010 applications for legal aid were received, of which 831,664 were granted (**187**:27).

26. Social security, for example.

fession could secure adoption of a government subsidy program leaving such a high degree of control with the profession, even by means of such timely action as that taken by The Law Society. And without the retention of control by the profession, there is perhaps reason to fear that a subsidy system would cause a large part of the bar to become mere employees of a government bureaucracy.

To give perspective to the problem of the expense of a subsidy system, perhaps it would be helpful to view it as a problem of equal justice. The ideal of the American legal system is equal justice under law. The principal mechanism provided for achieving it is the adversary litigative process, which in practice has come to require the representation of adversaries by competent counsel. Thus, assuming that the litigative system is in fact an appropriate dispute-resolving mechanism — and this must be the assumption, for no other mechanism is presently available for the resolution of most kinds of disputes — the validity of the concept of equal justice under law rests upon the actuality of representation by competent counsel. Perhaps this is just another way of stating the old truism that lawyers, as officers of the court, play an indispensable role in the administration of justice. But however it is stated, the fact is that as the litigative system now functions, equal justice can be had only if both sides to the dispute are fully represented by competent counsel.

On the other side of the issue is the widely held notion that the economic burden of litigation should rightly fall on those who use the litigative process. This notion has been accompanied by a fear that the courts would be swamped in frivolous cases if the poor man were given the same options as the rich man with respect to litigation. These two ideas have also been responsible for much of the resistance over the years to the concept of free legal aid for the poor, as well as for the resistance to measures for relieving poor litigants of the burden of ordinary court costs. They have given way only grudgingly to the idea that equal justice requires that some help be given to poor litigants.

But individualistic notions about the burden of the cost of litigation require a closer look. Lawyers' fees and so-called court costs are but part of the real cost of litigation — only the tip of the iceberg. Underneath lie other costs that should also be considered as costs of litigation: the expense of building and maintaining courthouses, of paying the salaries of judges, sheriffs, bailiffs, clerks, and reporters, of keeping records of various kinds, and even of maintaining police forces. These and many other expenses are quite properly viewed as part of the over-all cost of administering justice. And in paying them out of public funds *society does in fact subsidize litigation.*

Why does society subsidize the litigative process? The reason, manifestly, is that the resolution of disputes through some peaceful process is essential to public order and safety. Thus it is entirely appropriate that public funds be used to provide such a process. Moreover, because any such system must rest ultimately upon the confidence of the people in its fairness, the equality of the justice dispensed is of vital importance.

Taken to its logical conclusion, the individualistic notion that it is somehow wrong to have the costs of litigation paid by anyone but the litigants would mean that all the costs of administering justice would have to be paid by the individual parties, with the administration of justice becoming a self-supporting enterprise. As a result, the courts would be effectively closed to all but the very wealthy, and even they would be able to use litigation for only the most weighty and economically important matters. A situation in which the courts—the only alternatives to violence—were closed to the vast bulk of society's problems and to all but a tiny minority of society's members would be completely intolerable. Perhaps equally important, a society which has developed even the most rudimentary notions of fair play and justice must recognize a moral obligation to see that disputes are resolved on the basis of their merits rather than on the basis of the relative power of the contestants.

So, then, the matter comes back to the idea of "equal justice," which must mean that disputes are resolved according to the merits of the respective cases and not according to the power of the respective parties. Moreover, except in Orwellian-style "double-think," the concept of equal justice permits of no qualifying adjectives. If all litigants are to be equal—i.e., if merits, not power, are to govern—then no litigants can be "more equal" than others.

This may be the best light in which to view the question of the expense of litigation. What justification can there be for permitting the rich man to indulge his whims by using the publicly subsidized court system to bring frivolous or uneconomic cases, while denying the same option to the poor man? Is it only because the one can afford the additional expense of lawyers' fees, while the other cannot? If so, then such discrimination is completely unjustifiable under any acceptable concept of equal justice. If merits rather than power are to govern, then either the poor man must have the same options as the rich, or the rich as well as the poor should be foreclosed from frivolous or uneconomic use of the publicly subsidized litigative process. Interestingly, the small claims court is in some ways a limited—albeit not entirely successful (see, e.g., 298)—attempt to do the latter, denying both rich and poor the assistance of counsel in the small cases submitted to it.

The partial subsidizing of litigation through the maintenance of courts and the litigative machinery, as well as the halting steps that have been taken to provide legal services to the poor, are in large part a striving by society toward the as yet unattained ideal of equal justice under law. Viewed from this perspective—and questions of political ideology aside—the essential issue with respect to legal service subsidies becomes a question of allocation of resources. How much is society willing to spend to ensure that disputes will be determined on their merits and not according to the power of the parties? How much is America willing to pay for equal justice?

Even the English commitment is not a total one. The legal aid recipient must still satisfy a local committee of lawyers that he has reasonable grounds for bringing or defending his cause, and considerable criticism has been directed at the system for being excessively restrictive in granting legal aid. Presumably, the rich Englishman may still get his frivolous cause into court. Nevertheless, the subsidy concept provides a viable theoretical base for achieving equal justice under law.

C
Conclusions

This brief survey describes, at least in a general way, some of the measures that might be taken to reduce the price of lawyers' services and to assist people of moderate means in paying for them. While each of the measures discussed might have some beneficial effect, none promises an immediate and conclusive solution to the whole problem of legal expense. Discussion of them tends to lead however toward other, perhaps more basic, questions.

This is especially so with respect to the proposal for comprehensive legal service subsidies. Even if it were to be accepted that the concept of equal justice under law required a comprehensive subsidy system or some comparable method of achieving genuine equality for all people in the adjudication of disputes, and even if such a system were ideologically acceptable, important questions would remain: Are the legal processes that are to be subsidized adequate and responsive to society's problems? Particularly with respect to small claims and minor disputes, is it justifiable for society to spend more to subsidize litigation than the matters being litigated are worth? Does this make any more sense for society as a whole than it does for individual litigants? Does every dispute or every claim really require full-scale formal litigation? Or might some of them be resolved satisfactorily through less involved and less costly procedures?

There are no easy answers. But it seems noteworthy that a number of dispute-resolving and claim-deciding mechanisms are developing as alternatives to formal litigation. Some of them, indeed, are of long standing. Administrative procedures, mediation arrangements, small claims tribunals, ombudsmen, advice bureaus — all have arisen or are arising at least partly in response to the same economic pressures that are producing legal service loan plans, legal expense insurance, and legal service subsidies.

It is unlikely that any new legal process or institution will completely eliminate the problem of expense as a barrier to equal justice — at least not in the immediate future. Thus, efforts to reduce the price of lawyers' services by increasing the efficiency of law practice will probably continue to be appropriate. So, too, will efforts to assist people of moderate means to pay the price. The organized bar's prompt and concentrated attention to these problems is therefore in order.

Specialization

Specialization in law practice has long been a controversial subject. Some see it not only as an inevitable development in a complex age, but also as a definitive answer to many of the bar's problems (**312; 168; 167**).* Others view it as a divisive force that threatens to destroy the legal profession (**54; 343; 278**). Much has been said on both sides, and the dialogue continues to be spirited (**99**:87, **144; 90; 98; 89**:707; **121; 123; 148; 162; 229; 313; 350**). American Bar Association consideration of the subject has now spanned some fifteen years (**52; 30; 49; 33; 50**:261; **50**:607; **51**), and a committee of the State Bar of California has recently made specific recommendations for a statewide system of certification of legal specialists (**87**).

Attention will be given here to only two aspects of the subject. First, consideration will be given to the probable effects of specialization on the availability of lawyers' services to people of moderate means. And second, an analysis will be made of some of the attitudes and assumptions that appear to underlie much of the opposition to specialization in the practice of law.

A
Specialization and Availability of Lawyers' Services

As discussed earlier, the demand for lawyers' services is largely determined by the terms and conditions under which the

---

*Citations in boldface type refer the reader to the numbered "Works Cited" at 297–313; where numbers immediately follow the boldface reference, the reader is referred to specific pages in that work.

services are offered to the public. Among the factors identified as likely to have some bearing upon a potential client's decision about the use of a lawyer's services are: (1) the quality of the service offered; (2) its price; (3) its accessibility; and (4) the potential client's knowledge and attitudes about law, lawyers, and legal services. These factors are in turn affected by the kind and nature of the nonlegal and nonlawyer-supplied alternatives. What relationship does specialization have to these factors and thus to the use, or potential use, of lawyers by people of moderate means?

1
The Quality of the Service

There is little room for doubt that specialists can provide legal services superior in quality to those performed by generalists. Other things being equal, any given service, legal or otherwise, can be better performed by one who devotes his entire time and attention to that kind of service than by one who spreads his talents and attentions over a broad field. This is obviously true of the manual skills: an experienced cabinetmaker can be expected to do better cabinet work than a general carpenter. The principle is certainly no less true in the field of law, which requires great knowledge as well as skill. If proof were required, we would need only to look to the extent to which large corporations are beginning to staff their legal departments with specialists,[1] to the growth of large departmentalized law firms[2] in response to

1. Letter to author from Mrs. Frances Utley, Manager of A.B.A. Lawyer Placement Information Service, Oct. 31, 1956; see also Bracken (76).
2. On the trend toward partnership practice, see Smith & Clifton (286), and *Lawyer Statistical Report* (57:18). Current data are not available to show trends in the size of law partnerships, although a trend toward larger partnerships is suggested by older statistics reported in *Survey of Current Business* (301). It should be noted that the trend toward larger partnerships, though easily seen in contemporary big city law practice, is quite likely to be understated in statistical comparisons, at least when expressed in percentage terms. This is because most of the many solo practitioners now entering partnership practice probably do so as members of two- or three-member firms. Thus, the statistical comparisons may not quite show so dramatically the additional fact that, at the same time, the previously existing firms are now also becoming larger. Data to show the extent to which law firms are becoming departmentalized, or to show the nature of such departmentalization, do not exist, although the phenomenon is easily observed in most large law firms. Perhaps the subject deserves more detailed empirical study than it has thus far been given.

the demand from business clients, and to the public's increasing use of nonlawyer specialists for tasks that have heretofore been regarded as lawyers' work (**154**:70; **271**; **262**; **332**:209; **243**; **272**). In addition, one major reason for the rise of Group Legal Services is the ability of at least some group service programs to offer specialized service of higher quality than would otherwise be available to group members. The only really remarkable thing about this aspect of the subject is the continued refusal of some lawyers to acknowledge that better quality legal services can be made available to the public through specialized practice than can be provided by general practice.[3] Fortunately, recent evidence indicates that most lawyers probably do recognize the benefits to the public from specialization (**88**:147–48, 183–84).

2
Price

Price may well be the weightiest factor affecting the prospective client's decision whether to use a lawyer's services or to solve his problem in some other way. It is also an element almost surely affected by specialization, although there is some disagreement as to the nature of the effect. Proponents of specialization argue that it will lower the price of legal services, while those who oppose it contend that the effect will be just the opposite (**144**). The price of a specialist's services will be higher, they say, because he must recoup from clients the cost of the extra training he has taken and because he may have fewer clients and would therefore have to charge them higher fees.

This paradoxical aspect of the dispute stems from a tendency on the part of both sides to view price as an isolated phenomenon, whereas in fact it has meaning only in relation to the service rendered. The real issue is whether the price of a service is low or high in relation to the service's value to the potential purchaser. A specialist's fees may be higher in some instances than those of a generalist when computed in terms of hourly rate

---

3. E.g., Teschner (**305**), who takes the rather extreme position that experience in practice is irrelevant to legal problem solving—even incompatible with legal reasoning (see also **304**).

or annual income, but are they higher in relation to the value of the services performed? Or, to pose the same question another way, could a generalist match the quality or value of the specialist's services at the same or a lower fee? Speaking generally, the answer must be negative;[4] so long as the matters in issue are those for which lawyers' skills are genuinely required and economically justified, the inexorable economics of production favor the specialist. Matters that the specialist can handle on a completely routine basis at modest fees require custom-made solutions when handled by a generalist, resulting in either an economic loss to the lawyer or a relatively high price to the client—a situation that, in fact, prevails with respect to many of the services lawyers now perform for the public. Legal jobs that the specialist can do on a custom basis, with relatively small expenditures of time and effort, will require larger amounts of time in study and research from the generalist, with correspondingly larger fees as a result. And jobs that require the specialist to exert the utmost in time, effort, and professional skill are likely to be beyond the ability of the generalist to perform within reasonable limits of time and price.

3
Accessibility

Specialization, by itself, is only indirectly related to the element of accessibility of legal services: If the bar should adopt a specialization system permitting specialists to make their expertise known to the public, for instance, the accessibility of legal services would be considerably enhanced.[5] Certain other applications of the specialization principle—for example, specialization in the context of Group Legal Service plans—may also help to make legal services more readily accessible to the public. But the mere fact of specialization would seem to have little direct effect upon the accessibility of lawyers' services.

---

4. According to one commentator, statistics for a recent 15-year period—a period characterized by tremendous growth in specialized medical practice—reveal that while doctors' real incomes increased substantially, the prices of doctors' services actually *fell* relative to the general price level (121).
5. See chapter 4 *infra*.

4
*Public Knowledge
and Attitudes*

The bar has long worried about its "image." This is an en-
demic concern that probably arises at least partly from public
antagonisms and antipathies rooted in the very nature of law and
law practice. Law involves disputes, and lawsuits have losers as
well as winners. Attitudes growing out of both distaste for controversy and disappointment in litigation are all too readily
transferred to the lawyers who play such a highly visible role in
the legal process. Today, however, an additional threat to the
lawyer's image exists in what seems to be the public's decreas-
ing faith in the lawyer as a satisfactory source of solutions to the
problems of the individual. Such a decrease is illustrated statis-
tically in the various opinion polls[6] and practically in the rise of
unauthorized practice of law (see **154**:74; **271**; **262**; **332**:209; **243**;
272).

Loss of faith in the lawyer's omnicompetence may well have

6. In a public opinion survey conducted in Texas several years ago, for example, less
than half of the respondents indicated that they would go to a lawyer if they needed help
in drawing up a real estate lease or deed; the majority replied that they would seek this
kind of help from a title company, a real estate man, a notary public, a banker, or some
other source (**307**). Much the same thing was found by the pioneering Koos study, which
is especially significant in its undertaking to develop information about the attitudes that
keep people from seeking help from lawyers (**177**). A pilot study in Michigan in 1949
revealed that 23 percent of the respondents acknowledged having sought non-lawyer
help with problems which they, themselves, identified as "legal," and that most of those
who did so were completely satisfied with the results (**216**). A 1949 Iowa study suggested
that, although lawyers may be regarded as the primary source of help with regard to law
suits and wills, as high as 40 percent of the public would not go to a lawyer for help in
drawing up a real estate lease or deed, and 66 percent would go to a tax collector, banker,
CPA, or other source in preference to a lawyer for help in filling out an income tax return.
Furthermore, the Iowa study showed that the use of lawyers was highest among manage-
rial and professional people, and lowest among skilled, semi-skilled, and unskilled, and
farm laborers (**161**:22-23). A similar poll in Minnesota indicated that less than 17 percent
of the public would go to a lawyer for help in making out an income tax return (**344**).
More recently, the Missouri Bar—Prentice–Hall Survey has made essentially the same
kind of findings. Of those respondents who had at some time in the past had a will
drafted, 76 percent had gone to a lawyer to have it done. Of those who had written leases
or contracts drafted, only 34 percent had the service performed by lawyers. Of those who
had bought *or* sold real estate, only 15 percent had used a lawyer's services in connection
with the transaction. And only 7 percent of those who had prepared income tax returns
had sought a lawyer's help, while a total of 42 percent had gone to accountants, "tax
specialists," or notaries public (**220**:19-20). These figures do not represent the public's
"need" for legal services, of course, nor even the "demand." Rather, in a very general
way, they suggest something of the extent to which people appear to regard lawyers as
desirable or undesirable sources of help with problems that might possibly be appropriate for the application of lawyers' skills. Of course, studies of social status have some
limited relevance to the question of the public's faith in the lawyer as a source of help
with problems, at least to the extent that such faith may be one element of status (see
261:54-57).

something to do with the growing tendency of people of moderate means to look elsewhere for help that they might otherwise have obtained from lawyers. Today's "man-in-the-street" is probably much less inclined to place his trust in all-knowing shamans than in astrophysicists, nuclear physicists, biochemists, and their like, whose compound titles suggest complete competence in narrow but vital fields of human knowledge. Is it any wonder, in an age in which even divine omniscience is commonly denied or questioned, that people are skeptical of the tradition-bound lawyer who proclaims himself competent to solve any and every problem brought to him?

Specialization thus may have a vital contribution to make to the public's attitudes about lawyers. People may never really love lawyers; unfortunately, Sandburg's hearse horse will probably continue to snicker down through the ages (270).[7] But if lawyers are equipped and organized to offer the public truly competent, expert service in tasks that really need doing, then it will not be unreasonable to expect people to continue to respect lawyers and to trust them with many of their most difficult problems.

B
Attitudes and Assumptions
Underlying Opposition
to Specialization

The foregoing discussion suggests something of the social utility of specialization in law practice by indicating its potential effects upon the elements that determine whether a prospective client will take his problem to a lawyer or seek other means of solution. In the discussion that follows, the intent is to probe some of the attitudes and assumptions that appear to underlie much of the opposition to specialization in law practice.

The recent survey conducted by the State Bar of California indicates that lawyers—at least California lawyers—generally acknowledge the benefits to the public from specialization in the

---

7. "Why is there always a secret singing
   When a lawyer cashes in?
   Why does the hearse horse snicker
   Hauling a lawyer away?"

practice of law and favor specialization (88:147-48, 183-84). At the same time, there still seems to be a substantial amount of opposition, not only to certification or other means of regulating specialization, but also to the concept itself.[8] And much of this opposition seems to be rooted in fear of specialization as a rather threat to the legal profession or a segment of it.

There appear to be two kinds of fear. One is largely economic; specialization is seen as a threat to the economic interests of a great many lawyers. The other is ideological; specialization is perceived—although sometimes only vaguely—as a challenge to some of the basic attitudes and assumptions of traditional law practice, cherished attitudes and assumptions that many lawyers are not yet ready to question.

1
Specialization
as a Threat to
Economic Interests

Though there seems to be a rapidly growing trend toward the employment of legal specialists in corporation legal departments,[9] our main concern here is with private practice. And specialization does involve the economic interests not only of specialists in private practice but of general practitioners as well.

Legal specialists in private practice today are mostly concentrated in the large law firms.[10] This is because, under the profession's present ethical restrictions, relatively few solo practitioners or members of small firms are able to attract enough business in any single field of practice to make possible specialization in the fullest sense of the word. Solo practitioners and small firms often do eventually concentrate to some extent in certain fields of practice, and in even the smallest of partnerships a pragmatically developed division of labor is a rather

8. See note 3 *supra;* ABA Committee on Unauthorized Practice of Law (54); Wham (343); and Siddal (278).

9. See note 1 *supra.*

10. There is little statistical information to substantiate this statement, but perhaps its truth is so self-evident as not to require proof. It may be illustrated, however, in a number of ways, including information obtained from observations of the ABA Lawyer Placement Information Service with respect to the amount and sources of demand for the employment of legal specialists. See note 1 *supra.*

generally accepted practice. But comparatively few solo practitioners or members of small firms ever reach the point where it
is economically feasible for them to give up general practice,
even though they might prefer to do so or might feel truly
competent in but a single field.

Large firms, on the other hand, are able — through firm reputation, through the eminence of senior partners, through established relationships with the business community and with
other firms, and through similar factors — to obtain lucrative legal
business in the volume necessary to support themselves either
as specialized law offices or as general law offices offering specialized services in a number of fields through internal departmentalization. These large firms have developed programs for
recruiting, training, and supervising the lawyers they employ,
thus creating a built-in de facto specialization system. Some
lawyers may as a consequence be apprehensive that a recognition and certification plan administered by the bar could ultimately result in loss of control by the large firms over the
recruitment, training, and discipline of specialists. Furthermore,
any program that contemplates allowing the public to learn
which lawyers are recognized as specialists also appears to pose
at least some threat to established channels of obtaining business. Some present de facto specialists may therefore fear that
the solo practitioner who attains recognition as a specialist
would, if he were permitted to inform the public of his qualifications, draw away clients who would otherwise have gone
through the established channels to their own large firms.

We may only speculate about the extent to which these fears
actually exist and, if they do, the extent to which they may be
justified. It seems unlikely that many large businesses with their
continuing needs for a broad range of specialized legal services
would turn to using solo specialists instead of the com-
plete-service large law firms. The fact that most lawyers practicing in large firms appear to accept the need for specialization
and its regulation seems to confirm this. Indeed, recognition of
specialization should, in the long run, prove an economic boon
to large law firms and the lawyers who choose to practice as
specialists.

The economic threat that specialization presents to the solo
general practitioner and the member of the small general practice firm is clear and immediate, however. If the legal

specialist is permitted to make his expertise known to the public, he will inevitably attract some of the general practitioner's potential clientele, a great many of whom are "one-shot" clients or infrequent users of lawyers' services.[11] Given the choice and an awareness of their need for specialized service, many of them might be expected to take their legal problems to specialists rather than to generalists, particularly if specialists' fees were not too high. The same threat would probably also exist with respect to the general practitioner's more-or-less regular clients, although possibly to a lesser extent; the regular client is more apt to appreciate the value of a continuing relationship with a lawyer who is thoroughly familiar with his particular affairs.

Even if specialists were prohibited from making their special qualifications known directly to the public, specialization would nevertheless appear to constitute an economic threat to the generalist. As de facto specialization continues to grow and as the law becomes more technical and difficult, pressure will increase on the general practitioner to refer to specialists those clients whose problems are beyond his competence. But there is now no safe way for him to do so. Because today's specialist is usually a member of a large firm offering a complete line of services, the generalist who finds it necessary to refer a client to a specialist runs a substantial risk of losing the client.

There is another dimension to the economic threat that specialization presents to the solo practitioner and the small general practice firm. Many a medium-sized or large firm owes its growth to a single business client acquired when both the firm and the business were small. Because at the beginning no one else would serve the client at the small fees it was able to pay, the small firm did so, partly as a speculative investment. As the client grew and its problems proliferated, the law firm developed special skills, risking its time and energy in acquiring requisite skills as the client's need arose. The payoff was realized in the form of large and profitable fees when the client had grown to the point where it could afford them. Then, having developed these special capabilities, the firm was able to attract other clients having similar needs.

Most if not all small firms work in the hope that such a client will one day walk in the door. The chances of this happening

11. The surveys mentioned in note 6 *supra* tend also to show the infrequency of use of lawyers even by those individuals who do use them (327).

today are probably much less than they were a generation ago. Changes in the structure of business and in the complexity of law make it less likely that the generalist will be able adequately to serve the walk-in business client and therefore less likely that he can keep such a client. Nevertheless, the hope that one's professional ship will come in is strong. The fear that recognition of specialization will reduce or destroy chances of obtaining such a client — not a groundless fear, by any means — is clearly one of the sustaining forces in the resistance to recognition of specialization.

Of course, counterpoised against these economic threats is the possibility that recognition of specialties might offer the general practitioner an opportunity to achieve recognition as a specialist himself and to develop a specialized practice. The kind of specialization system adopted will, of course, have much to do with the extent of this opportunity.

Specialization may threaten the presently existing economic interests and expectations of some lawyers. At the same time, it offers opportunity for economic benefit to others. Furthermore, by equipping the bar to serve the public more effectively, specialization promises to contribute to the future economic well-being of the entire profession and thus to the economic interests of future generations of lawyers. And, most importantly, it offers significant benefits to the public. To what extent, then, is economic self-interest acceptable as a justification for lawyers to continue to practice in ways that do not best serve the public interest and for the bar to protect them in such practice? Does the bar have the right to deny to the public — or to itself — the benefits of specialization simply to protect the economic interests of lawyers who cannot or will not adapt their practices to the needs of the times?

If the legal profession is to be described honestly in terms of Roscoe Pound's oft-quoted definition, "a group of men pursuing a learned art as a common calling in the spirit of a public service" (253:5), then the answer must be that economic self-interest can never be more than an incidental factor in the bar's decisions about specialization. Opposition to specialization in law practice is conscionable only if some paramount *public* interest requires that the public be denied its benefits; limitations on specialized practice are tolerable only to the extent that they are required to further other more important public interests. The following discussion of specialization as a challenge to attitudes and assumptions rests largely upon this fundamental premise.

2

Specialization as a
Challenge to
Attitudes and Assumptions

The lawyer's view of himself and his profession is based upon a number of attitudes and assumptions, some of which are directly challenged by the concept of specialization in law practice. Thus specialization comes to be seen as a threat to the institutional identity of the profession and to the lawyer's own personal identity as a professional. It may be well, then, to spend some time examining these challenged attitudes and assumptions. Four of them are of special concern: (a) the assumption of omnicompetence; (b) the egalitarian ethic; (c) the myth of noncompetitive practice; and (d) the ideal of the independent client's lawyer.

a
The assumption of
omnicompetence[12]

It is sometimes assumed by lawyers, as a basic premise underlying traditional law practice, that the "compleat" lawyer should be able to solve any and every legal problem presented to him. In the abstract this premise might appear to be at least partly valid. Given an unlimited amount of time for preparation, a good lawyer probably *can* handle any legal problem. But the premise becomes subject to serious question when applied to the conditions of modern law practice, in which time is the dearest of commodities. When a difficult question arises in a field with which he is unfamiliar, today's lawyer is rarely granted enough time to make himself an ad hoc expert. Many lawyers recognize this and readily acknowledge their limitations, but some cling persistently to a pose of omnicompetence. In addition, although many lawyers may individually acknowledge their limitations,

12. See generally 99:87–103.

the organized bar, when dealing with the problems of the profession, frequently indulges an assumption that lawyers are omnicompetent.

Perhaps a reference to the historical development of the American lawyer will provide some helpful insight.[13] The English legal profession, though well along in its development at the time of the colonization of America, was not one of the institutions immediately transported intact to the new colonies (253:130–35). By the time of the Revolutionary War, however, a well-educated and highly trained bar had developed (253:135–74).

Then came what Pound calls the American bar's "era of decadence," the period from 1836 to 1870 (253:223–42). This was the era of Jacksonian democracy, that great frontier-dominated age of the common man, which saw the legislative decimation of requirements for admission to law practice. By 1860 thirty of the thirty-nine states had eliminated all requirements for a definite period of preparation for law practice, and requirements had been substantially relaxed in the other nine.

The most important reason for this lowering of standards is what Pound called "faith in a natural right of every man to pursue any calling of his choice," and a complementary "faith in the ability of any man to do anything" (253:233, 236). In the field of law, this faith in the ability of the common man was subject to but a single condition: the practical requirement that to study or practice law, a man had to know how to read and write. Thus, though the lawyer of that era was a "common-man lawyer," even he was uncommon to the extent that he was more or less literate in a society in which literacy was far from universal. And there were some, of course, like Lincoln, who were decidedly uncommon in every respect.

The assumption of the lawyer's omnicompetence began, therefore, as an assumption of the omnicompetence of the common man. It was the product of a relatively simple and democratically romantic age, with simple laws and institutions and

13. The following historical discussion is taken largely from Pound (253:77-163, 223-42). See also Chroust (105); Haar (145). Note, however, that Pound's thesis that colonial law was substantially unrelated to the law developed by the newly independent country in the post-Revolutionary era has been subjected to criticism (174:873). It is submitted, however, that this criticism does not impair the validity of Pound's analysis of the development of the legal profession in the post-Revolutionary period.

with correspondingly simple demands upon legal practitioners.
The subject matter of law practice was made up predominantly
of problems relating to land and a still-simple commerce
(**160**:295–96). Furthermore, the functions that lawyers were expected to perform with respect to these problems were narrow
in scope (**160**:301–302). The lawyer of the Lincoln era was first
and foremost an advocate. He represented clients in the courts;
the counseling and drafting tasks he performed were either
incidental to litigation or done with law suits in mind. Consequently, a lawyer's success in practice depended far less upon
his knowledge of a still small body of substantive law than upon
his mastery of the idiosyncracies of local procedure, his forensic
ability, and his quickness of wit (e.g., **68**:37–39). The common
man of the mid-1800's, armed with a degree of literacy but with
comparatively little legal training, was able to function adequately in the role required of him as a lawyer.

The renascence of the legal profession as a learned calling
appears to have begun about 1870 (**253**:253–69). Pound attributes
this largely to the development of strong and active bar associations, beginning with the Bar Association of the City of New
York in 1870 (**253**:254). It might be suggested, however, that
though the raising of professional standards has been accomplished principally through the efforts of bar associations, both
the rise of the modern bar association and the restoration of the
profession as a learned calling have really resulted from the
demands of social change. As society developed beyond frontier
simplicity, it came to require more from its legal practitioners
than the relatively unlearned common-man lawyer was capable
of giving, and as this fact became more and more apparent, so
also did the need for higher professional standards.

Restoration of the legal profession as a learned calling required, of course, denial of the proposition that any man is able
to do anything—and more specifically, denial of the idea that the
minimally trained common man is competent to practice law.
But conceptually, the step taken was not so great as it might at
first seem, moving only from the assumed omnicompetence of
the common man to the assumed omnicompetence of the
learned man. Consequently, the assumption of the lawyer's omnicompetence is, even today, really just a reaffirmation of that
earlier faith in the ability of the common man—but, of course, he
is now a common-man-gone-learned.

An essentially simplistic view of law and legal problems and a narrow view of the scope of the lawyer's functions were implicit in the Lincoln era's faith in the ability of the minimally trained common man to know and practice law. The survival of these views appears largely responsible for the continued vitality of the assumption of the omnicompetence of the modern lawyer. Are the law and legal problems of modern America sufficiently simple to be mastered by any one man, however learned? Are the functions required of the modern American lawyer sufficiently narrow in scope and homogeneous in character to be effectively performed by any one man, however talented? And should conclusions about the structure of the legal profession rest upon the assumption that they are?

Just as social change once caused the role required of the lawyer to expand beyond the capacity of the untrained or minimally trained common man, thus stimulating the development of the legal profession as a learned calling, so today an almost explosive expansion in the complexity of society has caused the law and legal problems, as well as the number and variety of lawyers' functions, to swell far beyond the capacity of any one man. This expansion is well illustrated by the expansion of law school curricula.[14] Another example is the rapidly expanding demand for lawyers with specialized or highly concentrated legal experience, as reported by the ABA's Lawyer Placement Information Service.[15] And, of course, all lawyers are aware of the overwhelming proliferation of legal materials — decisions, statutes, regulations — with which the modern lawyer must cope. Simply keeping up with the change in the law has become a more-than-full-time task.

If the assumption of omnicompetence is no longer valid — and there can no longer be any real doubt that it is not — why do lawyers continue to cling to it so tenaciously? The question would probably best be answered by a psychologist, but the

14. For example, in 1860 the course of study at the Columbia University Law School consisted of: Personal Rights, Contracts, Real Estate, Equity Jurisprudence, Evidence, Mercantile Law, Torts, Admiralty, Pleading and Practice, Medical Jurisprudence, and Political Science (139:408, n.111). By contrast, the 1959-1960 *Announcement* of the same law school listed some eighty courses and seminars, including: Regulated Industries, Trade Regulation, Taxation of Distributions of Wealth, Business Planning, Collective Bargaining, International Financial Counseling, Legislative Development of Law, Oil and Gas Law, Problems of the Labor-Management Relations Act, Problems of Atomic Energy, Effects of Taxation on Business Policies and Practices, Urban Redevelopment, and Water Resources and Uses (111).

15. See note 1 *supra*.

common-man origin of the assumption and the still strong egalitarian ideal in American life would seem to have something to do with the phenomenon. Too, it may be a kind of defensive mechanism, generated by insecurity. Recognizing that the times require more than an individual general practitioner is able to provide, some lawyers may be afraid to acknowledge that they cannot do everything for fear the public will think that they cannot do anything. And so they cling to a pose of omnicompetence in the hope that no one will discover their fallibility.

It may also be that lawyers are apprehensive about the relationship to law practice—and particularly to specialized practice—of new and different fields of learning. To an ever-increasing extent, the modern lawyer—and again, particularly the specialist—finds himself involved with other disciplines often thought by lawyers to be either unduly mundane or forbiddingly esoteric. Furthermore, many of these disciplines may be viewed as competing with the legal system as problem-solving processes. Professor Gerhard O. W. Mueller has put it this way:

> Who is talking your language, my friend from the tax department? It's not the guy who teaches forms of actions. No. It's an accountant, a business manager, a welfare worker, a G-man, an actuary, a social engineer, a banker. And who is talking your language, my friend in international law? It's a geo-physicist, a geo-politician, a diplomat, a trader, an economist. And yours, my friend in Municipal Corporations I or II? An urban planner, a public health planner, an architect, an engineer, a sonar physicist. And yours, brother in criminal law? A sociologist, a psychiatrist, a psychologist, an economist, a statistician (**223**:411–13).

In the face of such strange new worlds, with atmospheres of unknown—and possibly even hostile—nature, the lawyer may well find the cocoon of traditional law practice, with its familiar air of torts, contracts, and civil procedure, all too comfortable and safe. Thus, he may be tempted to try to preserve traditional practice against the encroachment of nonlegal disciplines by claiming for the legal system—and for himself—an exclusive omnicompetence that doesn't exist.

Finally, and perhaps most importantly, lawyers may be loath to abandon the pose of omnicompetence in favor of specialization because of what specialization suggests about the law itself. First, and most obviously, it suggests that the "seamless web" analogy might have to be abandoned, or at least modified. If specialization is possible and desirable, then clearly the law *has* some seams.

Specialization suggests something else about the law as well. The bar has traditionally been committed to the legal process, administering the formal norms of the law, as the best device for resolving conflict and maintaining order in society. But as legal specialists become familiar with other fields of knowledge and other disciplines related to their specialties, they cannot help but become aware that the traditional legal processes are not society's only means of social control; they may even be prompted to question whether, or how effectively, legal processes accomplish their objectives and whether, in a given field, they are actually the best, or even the most acceptable, available conflict-resolving devices. Of course, one need not practice law in a specialized field to ask questions like these. The legal realists — Holmes, Frank, Llewellyn — began asking them years ago (e.g., **156**:443–63; **133**; **196**; **195**). The point here is that once the pose of omnicompetence is abandoned, such questions become far less avoidable than heretofore, and it may be that some lawyers cling to the fiction of omnicompetence simply to avoid having to face such thorny problems.

It should be clear, at any rate, that the assumption that an individual lawyer is capable of solving all legal problems and performing all legal services does not square with the facts of modern life and is invalid as a foundation for the bar's rejection of specialization in law practice. Neither that assumption nor the implications that flow from assertion of its invalidity requires that the public be denied the benefits of specialization by lawyers.

b
The egalitarian ethic

The foregoing discussion leads to consideration of the legal profession's egalitarian ethic — the assumption that all lawyers are equal in ability. Few lawyers really believe this to be so, of course, as witness the care used by all law firms in selecting out-of-town counsel to handle even minor matters. Nor does the public believe it. But in regulating the practice of law and in dealing with the problems of the profession itself, lawyers act as if they believe all lawyers to be equal, and apparently they want the public to believe likewise. Thus, the egalitarian ethic operates as a notable force in much of legal profession thought and activity—a sort of extra-legal fiction.

The egalitarian ethic may be seen in the bar's all-too-often indulgent approach to professional discipline; for example, disbarment or suspension for incompetence is rare, except perhaps for outright mental incapacity. It may also be seen in the operation of Lawyer Referral Services, many of which admit any licensed lawyer to the referral panel and insist that clients be referred to them in strict rotation. It is likewise evident in the unauthorized practice principle that holds all lawyers to be competent and all laymen incompetent to perform legal services. One of the best examples of the bar's egalitarianism appears in the controversy over specialization. The theme appears again and again throughout the literature on the subject; specialization cannot be recognized or condoned because it simply is not fair or right when all lawyers are equal to allow some to set themselves up above others by claiming special competence in particular fields of practice. Whether the argument be specialization's supposed threat to the unity of the bar or its claimed tendency to impair professional discipline, underneath runs the same thread: faith in the equality of all lawyers and a concomitant antagonism toward anything that would tend to suggest inequality, much less recognize or formalize it.

The assumption that all lawyers are equal is unsound and unacceptable as a reason for rejecting or opposing specialization in law practice. It is unsupportable, either empirically or by reason. The only real issue is the extent of variation among lawyers, and here we are handicapped by lack of reliable data. Of the many books that have been written about the legal profession and lawyers, most are quite subjective and tend to idealize the lawyer.[16] Only recently have there been even the begin-

---

16. This is especially so of the many biographical and autobiographical works (e.g., 155; 120; see also 191; 199; 179). The Survey of the Legal Profession, under Arthur T. Vanderbilt and Reginald Heber Smith, undertook as early as 1947 to collect statistical data about lawyers, but the scope of that study precluded probing the issues raised in any significant depth (73). Too, the triennial *Lawyer Statistical Report*, compiled by the American Bar Foundation from statistics furnished by the publishers of the *Martindale-Hubbell Law Directory*, makes available current general statistical information, the value of which will tend to grow as it accumulates over periods of time sufficiently long to show trends. And, of course, there continue to be numerous economic surveys of the bar,

nings of serious attempts to conduct sound sociological studies of the legal profession. Information now becoming available, however, particularly the Carlin, Handler, Johnstone-Hopson, Ladinsky, Smigel, and Warkov-Zelan studies, reveals a far wider variation among lawyers, both in ability and in ethical attitudes and behavior, than anyone in the profession had previously dared acknowledge (92; 91; 147; 166; 180; 181; 284; 152; 338).

History and tradition have a great deal to do with the bar's reluctance to acknowledge differences in the ability of lawyers, of course. Another reason appears to exist, a reason with interesting implications. The lawyer plays a fundamental role in the adversary system. Under it, disputes are resolved through a kind of formalized forensic battle, from which the tribunal is supposed to be able to discover the truth of the matter being fought out. But the validity of this system of forensic contest rests upon a presupposition that the advocates are equal; the system would be intolerable if the results were to depend not upon the merits but upon the abilities of the advocates. Abandonment of the egalitarian ethic would appear as a denial of this presupposition and thus of the validity of both the adversary system and the lawyer's role as an advocate. Lawyers simply could not accept their function in the system without some assurance that they are, in fact, instruments of justice rather than injustice.

Thus, a dilemma arises because the adversary system presupposes the equality of lawyers who are far from equal. The bar has attempted to accommodate itself to this dilemma in a most interesting way.

An informal and largely unrecognized stratification has grown up within the bar, together with the de facto specialization already mentioned. It is easily seen in the large law firms which recruit primarily from among the better graduates of the more prestigious law schools. Some of the large firms concentrate in particular fields of practice while others conduct more generalized practices—though with a fairly limited range of kinds of clients—offering a variety of specialized services through internal departmentalization.

---

studies that concentrate primarily on lawyers' fees and incomes (e.g., 67; 173; 248). A few books, such as MacKinnon's (200), do focus with significant effect upon specific aspects of law practice. And finally, the Missouri Survey combined a public survey and a survey of the bar, though it did not delve significantly into the characteristics of lawyers and law practice (220).

Even the individual general practitioner has a place in this stratification; his clients are different from those of the large firm, and the problems they present are also different. In addition, although he still claims omnicompetence and seeks to retain his privileged position as a practitioner of the whole law, his practice is actually being increasingly restricted in scope by the encroachments of lay specialists and of Group Legal Services, and by the competition of the larger firms. It may not be accurate to say that he is already a specialist, but the trend is unmistakable, and some elements of the general-practice bar are indeed becoming specialists of sorts. Unhappily, the tasks being left to the general practitioner are more and more coming to be jobs that no one else wants to do. The most striking example is given by the Carlin study of urban solo practitioners; with a limited clientele, the lawyer described by Carlin is reduced to the role of specialist in uneconomic and unattractive legal jobs (see 92:206). This study may well prove prophetic for general practice as a whole, as the gap grows ever wider between what the individual general practitioner claims to be and what he actually is.

A peculiar but significant result of this informal and largely unrecognized stratification-specialization is that the lawyers who face each other in the legal arena tend to be, in most instances, roughly equal in ability. The Harvard-trained corporation lawyer rarely appears in court against Carlin's big-city solo practitioner, primarily because differences in their respective clienteles produce differences in the kinds of problems to be solved as well as in the courts and agencies in which the problems are contested. Litigation, whether in a federal district court or in a local justice-of-the-peace court, and administrative proceedings, whether before the SEC or before a local board of health, typically involve adversaries who in each instance are of roughly comparable ability and also have at their command roughly comparable facilities and resources.[17] And, significantly, this gener-

17. One notable exception to this generalization is, of course, defense of indigent persons accused of crime in states where variations of the assigned counsel system are still retained. Here, all too often the lawyer assigned to defend an indigent, particularly one accused of a noncapital offense, is inexperienced—at least in the criminal law—and has neither the funds nor resources even to begin to develop an adequate defense, while the prosecutor has not only ample experience and skill in the prosecution of criminal cases but also has the resources of the state at his disposal (see 279). Of course, lawyers' usual attitudes about the criminal law and criminal practice lend themselves readily to rationalization of the inequalities encountered in this field.

ally unacknowledged stratification-specialization, by creating in fact a kind of rough equality in the forum, permits the entire bar to continue to indulge its egalitarian predisposition and to ignore the reality of inequality—simply because the lawyer is not frequently confronted by the fact of inequality in the form of a lawyer of disproportionate ability on the other side. Acceptance of specialization is an overt and formal recognition of inequality, a step that is much too extreme for many lawyers as long as inequality can be ignored.

The adversary system may become a mechanism of injustice, and the lawyers who participate in it may become instruments of injustice, however, when this kind of rough equality between immediate adversaries is not achieved. This happens most often when the person of moderate means is drawn into a legal conflict with a large institution, governmental or private. In those instances, the contest all too often finds the individual general practitioner without adequate knowledge and experience in the field of practice involved and without sufficient resources, facing a battery of experienced, well-financed specialists. The results are all too frequently unjust. And here, of course, the myth of equality is a means of reassuring lawyers of the moral validity of their roles as advocates in the adversary system.[18]

This analysis not only reaches the conclusion that the egalitarian ethic is false and that its implications do not require that the public be denied the benefits of specialization, but it also suggests what may be the most valuable contribution specialization can make to the administration of justice and to the future of the legal profession. Though this incipient and rudimentary stratification-specialization fails to produce true equality between adversaries with sufficient consistency either completely to satisfy the requirements of equal justice or to afford lawyers full assurance of the moral validity of their roles as advocates in an adversary system, it does, generally, result in a *rough* equality where an absolutely intolerable inequality would otherwise prevail. The ultimate development of a national and well-controlled system of specialization, in which all clients would have ready access to lawyers who are genuinely expert in the kinds of

---

18. This is one area in which group legal services may offer the public a significant advantage. The group-secured, group-retained, or group-employed lawyer is likely to have both the necessary expertise and the resources at his command to meet the large institution's counsel on a more-or-less equal footing.

problems for which those clients need help, may achieve a more consistent and more perfect equality between adversaries than is now the case. If so, the contribution of specialization may be to make the adversary system work even better and more justly and to make the lawyer's position in society vastly more useful and substantially more secure.

c
**The myth of
noncompetitive
law practice**

The idea that the legal profession is above competition is old and strong. It also inhibits the bar's acceptance of specialization in law practice, for the quite obvious reason that recognition of specialists would enhance the competitive position of those lawyers who are or who become specialists.

The idea that lawyers are above competition is a myth, of course. The practice of law in modern America is highly competitive, both among lawyers and between lawyers and nonlawyers. This is so by virtue of the kind of society in which lawyers must practice. In order to be successful, they must find ways of making their services competitively attractive as compared with the alternatives available to the public. Those who are successful have done so, and, as the "how-to-build-a-practice" books attest, so, too, must those who wish to be successful (e.g., 309:3–13; **268; 260; 267; 256**).

Most lawyers are well aware of the competitive nature of law practice, but collectively, through the organized bar, they persist in basing their decisions about the regulation of the profession on the premise that law practice can and should be noncompetitive. This myth is a historical remnant of the early English bar, a small and intimate group of barristers with independent means, "who did not have to worry about earning their keep, and who traditionally looked down on all forms of trade and the competitive spirit characteristic thereof" (**122:**210). The premise is clearly inapplicable to the large, heterogeneous, and geographically scattered American bar, whose members must earn their keep. But the force of tradition has preserved it as the underlying basis of many professional restrictions — those on advertising and solicitation in particular. It is also one factor inhibiting specialization in law practice.

The myth of noncompetitive law practice also owes much to the two assumptions already discussed—the assumptions that lawyers are equal and that they are omnicompetent. As long as lawyers see themselves in this light, there is little room or reason for competition among them; and unseemly competition with nonlawyers appears unnecessary because the bar deems itself justified in using other measures to stifle outside competition.

In a society founded upon the competitive doctrine of free enterprise, however, restrictions upon competition, even when based upon sound and legitimate reasons, are acceptable only when absolutely necessary to effectuate other overriding public policies. Because the assumption that law practice is or can be noncompetitive, like the assumptions that lawyers are omnicompetent and equal, is clearly unsound, it provides insufficient support for denying to the public the benefits of specialization in law practice.

d
**The ideal
of the client's
lawyer**

One ground of opposition to specialization is a belief that the rise of specialists threatens to eliminate general practitioners and to deprive the public of the valuable functions that generalists perform. Because of the fairly common notion that the ideals of the profession are exclusively characteristics of traditional general practice, specialization appears as a challenge to the legal profession's cherished assumption that the public's legal needs can best be served by lawyers who deal directly with individual clients in a relationship embodying the elements of confidentiality, trust, professional independence, and individual responsibility—in short, the ideal of the client's lawyer functioning in the context of the traditional lawyer-client relationship. This ideal, almost universally accepted by lawyers, runs throughout the arguments on specialization (see especially 144:140-42).

Experience supports the bar's belief that law practice is of greatest value to the public when it consists of direct service to clients through relationships based upon confidentiality, trust, professional independence, and individual responsibility. Much of what is good about the legal profession may be reasonably and honestly attributed to this ideal. But there is a fundamental fallacy in the conclusion that this ideal is necessarily incompatible with, and therefore threatened by, specialization in law practice. The fallacy is, of course, in the further assumption that the ideal of the client's lawyer can be realized only by the traditional general practitioner practicing in the time-honored ways. In fact, the present impasse in the bar's intramural fight over specialization has probably resulted at least partly from the profession's failure to recognize that the two stark and over-drawn alternatives customarily discussed do not exhaust the possibilities for solution to the problem.

To a remarkable extent, labels have made the argument. The choice has been seen as an election between "the general practitioner"—an idealized character sliced out of his place in history, his development forever arrested and his characteristics forever fixed—and "the specialist"—more a technician than a learned artist, knowing all there is to know about an insignificantly small legal subject but almost nothing about people or about law as a whole. With the alternatives for choice so posed, it is little wonder that the legal profession has been divided, or, perhaps that it has thus far preferred to retain its commitment to "the general practitioner." But may it not be possible that the ideal of the client's lawyer is separable from the institution of "the general practitioner?" If so, other alternatives may be possible.

A great deal of the sentiment that causes the old-fashioned general practitioner to be regarded as the only possible manifestation of the ideal of the client's lawyer stems from the fact that in the past he has been its principal manifestation. Furthermore, because specialization does seem to threaten the general practitioner, it may be only natural that fraternal sympathy should cause the bar to offer the generalist's main virtue as a justification for his preservation as an institution. Too few lawyers realize, however, that the threat to the general practitioner is not really from specialization, but from his own inability to meet the demands of modern society, and that law practice might possibly be made to serve society's needs without sacrificing the ideal of the client's lawyer. Although old-fashioned general practice may become extinct, the valuable functions now being performed by the general practitioner as a client's lawyer need not become so.

The assumption that only the old-fashioned variety of general practitioner can be an ideal client's lawyer probably also results at least in part from an uncritical acceptance of a mistaken notion about the English legal profession, where the generalist solicitors are said to act as client's lawyers and the specialist barristers as lawyers' lawyers. Barristers are specialists—in advocacy, of course, but also in other fields of practice—and are isolated from the public by the rule that they may obtain cases only by referral from solicitors. But solicitors who function as client's lawyers are not necessarily generalists. *Many solicitors do, in fact, specialize,* and they are coming more and more to associate themselves together in firms of sufficient size to permit individual members to concentrate in limited fields of law or practice (see **229:85–86**; see also **166:359–85**).

Perhaps the bar's insistence that the client's lawyer must be a traditional general practitioner also arises partly from a failure to distinguish form from function. Because the general practitioner has been the traditional client's lawyer, it is assumed that the role is a product of the institution of general practice, whereas, instead, it is probably produced by the complex of circumstances that both create and act upon the practitioner (**91:165–82**). Indeed, it may be entirely accurate to say that most general practitioners embody the ideal of the client's lawyer because they are lawyers and not because they are general practitioners.

This might be illustrated by one element of the ideal of the client's lawyer—professional independence. A lawyer's independence in the exercise of his professional judgment is far less likely to be the result of the specialized or general nature of the service he offers than of his attributes as a lawyer and of the pressures generated by the social, institutional, and work settings in which he functions (**91:170–76**). Indeed, in many instances a senior partner in a large law firm may exercise his professional judgment with infinitely more independence in advising the president of a large corporate client on a highly specialized problem than a financially pressed solo practitioner might do in advising an affluent and locally influential individual client on a rather routine general problem. The point is, of course, that traditional general practice has no monopoly upon professional independence, nor upon the other elements of the ideal of the client's lawyer, and consequently, preservation of the traditional lawyer-client relationship for the benefit of the public does not require the rejection of specialization.

This point is confirmed by the facts of current American law practice, as Harrison Tweed, describing the modern large law firm, has so perceptively observed:

> The law firm makes available to its clients a number of lawyers, each of whom possesses at least one of the special skills needed by clients. Thus it comes about that, generally speaking, a firm must include a partner who spends most of his time in court and another who is thoroughly grounded and absolutely up-to-date in tax matters. A third must be expert in labor negotiations and be able to give sound advice in that area. There is a demand for one partner with the ability to advise business clients on broad and crucial questions of policy although he may be less expert in any one area of the law than his partners. Generally speaking, *each client of the firm looks to one particular partner as his lawyer*—the lawyer to whom he brings his legal problem for initial discussion unless it happens to be of such a peculiarly specialized nature that this preliminary step would involve a waste of time. Thus, from the large firm there may be obtained by a client precisely the close and confidential counseling which is in the best tradition of the Bar. (312).[19] (Emphasis added.)

19. Tweed then went on to say:

When corporations began to take the place of individuals as a lawyer's clients, it was feared that there would be impairment of the traditional relationship. To anyone who looks closely today it is clear that there was no basis for this fear. It arose from the erroneous conception that the relationship between the lawyer and his corporate client is not a human one but is an artificial one between a corporate entity on the one hand and a large partnership on the other. In fact, the advisory process between counsel and corporation is this: Most of the matters requiring legal advice are comparatively minor and somewhat technical. They are considered and discussed and decided by a junior partner and a subordinate corporate officer. *The relationship between them is almost precisely the same as that between the old-fashioned general practitioner and his client-friend of long standing.* It is true that the corporate officer is not receiving advice on a personal matter but on a corporate question. But the interest of the corporation in the solution is much more indirect and remote than is the interest of the officer. His job depends upon his ability to get the right answer. And it is here that the lawyer, able to view the matter with detachment and impartiality but with understanding and sympathy, becomes indispensable to his opposite number. And as a result of the decision of many questions over a considerable period of time, the relationship becomes as intimate a one and contains as much reliance and confidence as any attorney and client relationship can yield.

This is the way that corporate advising operates all the way up and down the line. Each member of the firm is in constant contact with the corporate officers on his level—there are usually several of them to one lawyer. It generally happens that as the corporate officer goes up in the hierarchy so

Tweed's point needs little elaboration: even the de facto specialist in the large firm serving corporate clients is a client's lawyer in the highest sense of the term. If this is true, can it reasonably be contended that the lawyer who serves moderate-income individuals must be an old-fashioned general practitioner in order to retain the worthwhile elements of the traditional lawyer-client relationship? Is there anything about moderate-income clients that would render the relationship any less confidential when they consult specialists than when corporate clients do so? Would the trust relationship be in any way impaired? Would the lawyer be any less independent in the exercise of his professional judgment? Would not his responsibilities be precisely the same? And would not the force operating to motivate him to fulfill his obligations and to discharge his responsibilities to his clients — especially the force of professional pride — remain the same?

The profession will make a grave mistake if it commits itself to the position that traditional general practice is the only acceptable expression of the ideal of the client's lawyer. The position is not only unsound, but it also results in the erection of protective walls — including rules inhibiting specialization in law practice — around the general practice of law, both impairing the bar's ability to serve the public and arresting the natural evolutionary development that will keep the profession responsive to the demands of a changing world.

C
Specialization
in Medical Practice

Those who advocate the extension of specialization in law practice often draw liberally from the experience of the medical

---

does the lawyer. Frequently the close business and legal association and the personal intimacy exist for twenty-five years or more. And it remains very intimate and thoroughly typical of the traditional ideal even when it exists between the highest officer of the corporation and the senior partner. The corporate interest in the matters considered by them may be greater, but it is nonetheless a fact that the personal element is generally predominant. After all, the force which drives the lawyer to the hard work he must do is not the pay for the particular job or the continuation of his employment but the pride which he can take in the soundness of the advice given. Thus, although money may come from the corporation, the lawyer's satisfaction comes from having dealt successfully with the problem presented and that was the problem of the individual who headed the corporation (312). (Emphasis added.)

profession (144:11–47; 167:539; 121:442). There are significant differences between the two professions, of course, and consequently care must be exercised in looking to doctors for solution to lawyers' problems. There are also important similarities, however, and the bar would appear to have something to gain by giving careful consideration to the experience of the medical profession.

Most importantly, the experience of the medical profession provides a striking demonstration of the utility of specialization, especially in enhancing the quality of medical treatment. The subject of quality has already been discussed, however, and will not be treated further here.

A recent report on "The Graduate Education of Physicians," prepared for the American Medical Association by a distinguished Citizens Commission, is of particular interest, as it presents another aspect of the subject deserving of close consideration (106). The report describes the growth of specialization in the medical profession and the corresponding decline of general practice, leaving what the Commission regards as a serious gap in the medical services available to the public. Although high quality specialized treatment for specific acute conditions is readily available to the public, present sources of the kind of continuing and comprehensive care that used to be furnished by general practitioners are unsatisfactory, and people are thus increasingly forced to become their own diagnosticians in deciding which kinds of specialists to consult, to resort to self-treatment for many minor and routine ailments, and to turn to hospital emergency rooms for help not only in emergencies but also in situations involving many other kinds of medical problems (106:34).

Thus, according to the report, one of the public's most pressing needs is for a reliable source of continuing and comprehensive medical care of high quality (106:35–36). To fill this need, the report proposes that the old-fashioned general practitioner be replaced by a specialist in continuing and comprehensive care—a "primary physician" as he is called (106:37). At first this might appear to be merely a semantic change—what lawyers would call a distinction without a difference. But the proposal does contemplate important differences. First, the primary physician's training would be as long and as thorough as for any other specialty. Second, he would be accorded full status as a specialist. Third, he would function not as a mere referral service or clearing agency for specialists, but rather would, as the "epitome of over-all competence" (106:39), offer comprehensive and continuing treatment that would make use of all the available medical resources—including the skills of specialists and the facilities of hospitals—that might help to solve a patient's total problem or contribute to his total, long-range health care. The report compares this "primary physician" to a football quarterback, "utilizing effectively the talents of different members of the team" (106:39). And fourth, the report stresses the interesting idea that the most effective utilization of such "primary physicians" would be in group practice with other "primary physicians," each concentrating in some degree in a different field of medicine (106:55–56).

This is an intriguing concept, but it is not entirely without problems, even in its proposed application to the medical profession. Will it be possible, for example, to convince significant numbers of prospective doctors that the rewards to be anticipated from this type of practice—status, income, professional satisfaction—are sufficiently high, in comparison with those to be obtained from the established specialties, to justify a full eight years of intensive medical training? And what of the plan's impact upon existing specialties and subspecialties, especially those—pediatrics, for example—that do offer continuing and comprehensive care to patients? Moreover, although the public might be expected to welcome this new kind of doctor, will not public acceptance depend to some extent upon the medical profession's ability to convince the public that the "primary physician" is in fact something more than the general practitioner he replaces? And finally, what of the plan's impact upon present general practitioners?

This report on graduate medical education raises some interesting questions about specialization in the law. Is the public need for continuing and comprehensive legal care in any way comparable to the need for such medical care? If it is, does the experience of the medical profession mean that greater specialization in law practice will inevitably lower the level of continuing and comprehensive legal care available to the public? Might means exist for providing such care to the public while also providing the benefits of specialization? And, more point-edly, might the "primary physician" concept have some appli-cation to law practice?

At first glance, continuing and comprehensive care would appear to be equally important to the legal well-being of the lawyer's client as it is to the health of the doctor's patient. Indeed, the retainer fee and the corporate law department would both appear to be manifestations of client need for contin-uing and comprehensive care. However, while the incidence of injury and disease, and therefore the need for continuing and comprehensive care, is probably at least as great among people of moderate means as among the well-to-do, the incidence of legal problems among persons of moderate means may not be entirely the same as among the wealthy and among business organizations. Granted that any person would benefit from hav-ing his affairs subject to the constant attention of a lawyer, however infrequent his actual need for some specific legal ser-vice, as a practical matter the person of moderate means prob-ably has greater need for a ready source of diagnosis of his occasional legal problems and referral to appropriate legal spe-cialists than for continuing and comprehensive care.

Even though there may be some public need for continuing and comprehensive care, it does not appear that greater special-ization in law practice will necessarily impair the ability of the bar to fill that need. It is true that the number of physicians in general practice has decreased markedly in recent years (106:34), and there can be little doubt that this decrease is largely attributable to an equally marked growth in medical specialization. Nor can it be doubted that this decrease has in fact caused adequate continuing and comprehensive medical care to become less readily available to the public than before. Extension of specialization in law practice might similarly be expected ultimately to reduce the number of lawyers engaged in traditional general practice. But it is by no means clear that the result would also be to make continuing and comprehensive legal care less available to the public. Indeed, large law firms and corporate law departments, which already involve a fairly high degree of de facto specialization, presently appear to be providing such care to their clients on a completely adequate basis. It would therefore seem likely that if people of moderate means do in fact have significant need for such service, those needs could be filled in similar manner—through law firms of legal specialists—in all areas, except rural areas incapable of supporting such firms.[20]

It would thus appear that the "primary physician" concept has, at best, only limited application to the practice of law. In addition, any attempt to translate the idea into a "primary lawyer" concept would encounter the problems already mentioned with respect to its application to the medical profession and some special difficulties as well. It is significant, for example, that while only about one-third of the country's practicing physicians are now in general practice (106)—and their numbers are diminishing—more than half of all practicing lawyers are solo practitioners (57:18), most of whom are general practitioners, and surveys have indicated that in some states as many as 90 percent of the lawyers still consider themselves to be general practitioners (144:58–59). The absence of well-developed and well-defined specialties in the bar also creates problems with any kind of "primary lawyer" concept, as the number and variety of legal specialists upon whom a primary lawyer might call are limited, and the institutional arrangement for their utilization is completely inadequate.

Differences between legal education and medical education might also be a factor. Although, as the AMA report points out, present graduate medical training is in need of revision and improvement, still the medical profession does have an existing educational structure that is reasonably effective in training specialists, and the basic medical schools themselves have long since been raised to a fairly high and more-or-less uniform level of quality (106:9–17). Thus, to initiate a training program at the graduate level for a new "primary physician" specialty would require relatively moderate changes and additions. Legal education is quite another matter, however. Even basic legal education varies widely in quality, with substandard law schools still flourishing, while facilities for specialty training at the graduate level are few and limited in capacity and range. Consequently, the training of "primary lawyers" would present considerable difficulties.

It is quite clear then, that the experience of the medical

20. Note that modern rapid communication and transportation may now make some kind of dispersed partnership arrangement entirely feasible for practice in sparsely populated areas.

profession with respect to continuing and comprehensive care is not likely to be duplicated by the legal profession. Because of the essential differences between the practice of medicine and the practice of law, the needs of the public for continuing and comprehensive legal care are quite different from their needs for such medical care. And because of the patterns of specialized practice already developing in the legal profession, increased specialization in law practice probably will not leave a gap that would deprive the public of needed continuing and comprehensive legal care. Should such a gap develop, however, the "primary lawyer" idea might eventually be an appropriate adjunct to specialized law practice.

D
Specialization in the English Legal Profession[21]

The English legal profession is also sometimes mentioned as a possible pattern for the development of specialization in American law practice (229). This is to be expected, of course, both because of the English profession's historical relation to its American offspring (144:7–9) and because some of its elements do appear relevant to the issues American lawyers are now seeking to resolve.

The aspect of the English legal profession that appears most closely related to specialization in American law practice is its division into two branches and the specialization scheme this division has produced. Barristers, of whom there are now approximately 2000 in practice (166:360), have the exclusive right of audience in the higher courts. They are thus specialists in advocacy, although, as will be discussed shortly, they also offer special expertise in other fields as well. But while they have exclusive access to the higher courts, barristers are denied direct access to clients—a barrister may do legal work for a client only upon instructions from a solicitor.

Solicitors, who now number approximately 20,000 in practice (166:359) are therefore the clients' lawyers of the English legal

---

21. This discussion of specialization in the English legal profession is derived largely from Johnstone and Hopson (166:366–531; see also 214:11–35).

profession, dealing directly with clients in the performance of counseling, drafting, and other legal functions. A client who requires representation in litigation in one of the higher courts, or who needs legal services requiring special expertise not possessed by the solicitor, may be referred to an appropriate barrister, or the solicitor may obtain the advice or assistance of a barrister. But a client referred to a barrister remains the client of the solicitor who referred him, even to the extent that the barrister's fee is paid by the solicitor and not directly by the client. The services a barrister may perform for a client are limited to those called for by the solicitor's instructions, and a barrister may not accept employment from a client to handle matters beyond those for which the client was referred to him.

It will be readily seen that this arrangement provides the solicitor with assurance that referral of a client to a specialist will not result in loss of the client. The result of this assurance has been to encourage the free use of specialists by solicitors.

The English system thus does appear to embody principles that may have application in American practice. Unfortunately, however, many of the generalizations made about the English experience, and many of the conclusions drawn from it, appear to rest, at least in part, upon a few fairly serious misconceptions. Indeed, the English legal profession is actually somewhat different from the institution American lawyers generally believe it to be.

One common misconception is the notion that the division between barristers and solicitors is a purely functional one, with the solicitors acting exclusively as counselors and the barristers solely as advocates. But, as Johnstone and Hopson have pointed out, the division is not nearly so simple and sharp (166:359; cf. 214:11-12). Although barristers do have the exclusive right to appear in the higher courts, solicitors do a substantial amount of trial work in the lower courts and in administrative tribunals. Similarly, barristers, who are often expert in specialized fields of substantive law, frequently function as counselors in matters unconnected with litigation. Indeed the observation has been made that the two branches are in many ways competing professions (166:359).

Another mistaken belief is that the solicitor's supposed lower status reflects inferior professional competence. To be sure, the barrister still enjoys some advantage in status, but that advantage is based more upon tradition and on his continued monopoly in the matter of important government appointments – including appointments to higher judgeships (**166**:382–84) – than upon any superior professional competence (**166**:394). In fact, the solicitor's legal training is generally more comprehensive and thorough than that of the barrister, and the requirements for admission to practice as a solicitor are substantially more demanding than those for admission to the bar (**166**:378–81).

Still another frequently entertained misconception is the idea that the solicitor is necessarily a general practitioner and that he typically practices alone or in a small firm. Although most solicitors, like most American lawyers, still regard themselves as general practitioners, and although many still do practice alone or in small firms, more and more they are coming to concentrate in limited fields of practice and to associate themselves together in the larger firms that make such concentration most productive (**166**:365, 372; see also **214**:12–13).

Another mistaken idea about the English legal profession is that matters requiring outside help are referred only to barristers and never to other solicitors. Although this is generally so, there are exceptions. Most American lawyers are aware, of course, that solicitors in the outlying areas frequently have "London agents" to whom they refer matters requiring on-the-spot attention in London. It is not commonly known, however, that many London solicitors are coming increasingly to make use of other solicitors who specialize in trials before particular London minor courts, mainly because such cases are uneconomic unless handled on a volume basis (**166**:371; **229**).

And finally, there is a possibility that the English legal profession may eventually abandon its division between barristers and solicitors. Fusion continues to be the subject of spirited debate with a variety of arguments – both cogent and specious – on both sides (**166**:385–95). Of the arguments favoring fusion, Johnstone and Hopson are most sympathetic to contentions that the divided profession: (1) is wasteful of legal manpower;[22] (2) is unnecessarily expensive, mainly because of the duplication of effort involved in briefing counsel (**166**:391–92); (3) perpetuates an unfair status system (**166**:394); and (4) lacks solidarity and

---

22. It is said that in recent years the bar has been substantially underemployed, while solicitors have had more work than they can handle (**166**:381–82, 389–90).

unity of purpose (**166**:394–95). Of the arguments opposing fusion, they regard as most persuasive the system's influence in creating effective specialization by "granting to a subgroup monopoly rights over certain work tasks; encouraging others in the profession to refer matters to the subgroup by removing the danger that it will steal clients away from the referrers; and fostering appropriate specialist selection by placing on knowledgeable professionals — here solicitors — principal responsibility for choosing specialists when needed" (**166**:396). Although Johnstone and Hopson decline to predict the outcome of the debate, they point out that considerable support now exists for various specific measures — e.g., common entrance and training requirements for the two branches and easier transfer from one branch to the other — that can be expected to result ultimately in a gradual blurring of the distinction between barristers and solicitors (**166**:396–98).

Perhaps the most obvious conclusion to be drawn from this — and maybe the most significant as well — is that the English and American legal professions face many of the same problems and are now in the midst of much the same kind of transition. Furthermore, the growing tendency of English solicitors to become specialists themselves and to join together in firms of sufficient size to make specialized practice productive would seem to indicate that the parallel development in American law practice is sound. Beyond these two conclusions, the English experience provides two other relevant ideas: (1) if specialists are isolated from the public, generalists may be encouraged to refer difficult matters to specialists; and (2) the job of selecting a specialist may be done effectively by informed generalists. It remains to be seen whether these ideas can be applied to American law practice.

E
Practical
Problems

Any attempt to establish a formal system of specialization raises a number of issues. Who is to operate the system? On what basis are qualifications for recognition as a specialist to be determined? In what fields of practice is special proficiency to be recognized? And how are such recognized specialties to be utilized?

1
The Regulating Agency

The regulation of law practice is and will no doubt continue to be a prerogative of state government. Consequently the appropriate regulatory authority in each state will have the ultimate power to decide whether and in what manner lawyers are to be permitted to hold themselves out as specialists, what qualifications they must possess to be entitled to do so, and in what fields such recognition may be accorded. For this reason and because of variations in law from state to state, it is sometimes suggested that national regulation of specialization is impossible and that all regulation should therefore be left to the states. Indeed, some state bar organizations are now beginning to consider the establishment of their own regulatory systems in order to fill the obvious vacuum left by inaction at the national level (e.g., **87**; see also **244:6**; **245:4**).

Although the power to regulate law practice does rest with the states, it does not follow that each state must—or should—operate its own separate specialty recognition apparatus, with fifty different sets of standards administered in fifty different ways. Undue provincialism in the admission of lawyers to practice in the several states unnecessarily hampers the mobility of competent lawyers and thus impedes desirable movement of the supply of legal services to meet the demands of a highly mobile society. This result is inimical both to the interests of the public and to the vitality of the profession. Much the same thing might be said of the recognition of special proficiency—a plurality of provincial specialization systems oriented toward local idiosyncrasies and dedicated primarily to the protection of local lawyers will never fully meet the needs of the public or the profession.

Furthermore, differences in state laws are exaggerated. Their similarities are much greater and more significant than their differences; were this not so, the national law school would be an impossibility. The new graduate of a national law school in

Massachusetts, Michigan, New York, or California is quite able to adapt quickly to the demands of law practice in Florida, Missouri, Texas, or Oregon, despite differences in state laws. Any difficulty he may have comes not from the need to learn new law but from the need to learn the *techniques* of law practice, which are not presently taught in any law school. Can it seriously be asserted that a lawyer who has acquired expertise in a special field of law could not adapt as well, or better, to specialized practice in different states?

Not only are present differences exaggerated, but those differences are diminishing rapidly. Increasing activity in the development and promotion of model legislation and uniform laws—to say nothing of the swift expansion of federal law into fields heretofore covered by state laws—promises in the future to create an ever greater degree of similarity in the laws with which lawyers in all parts of the country will be working. A state-by-state approach to recognition of special proficiency is thus by no means imperative.

One suggested alternative would be a system based upon state-by-state recognition of proficiency in fields where the statutes and decisions of the respective states are said to be unique and controlling—e.g., land law, corporation law, and trial practice; regional recognition in fields that are regional in character—e.g., oil and gas, mining, and water law; and national recognition in fields truly national in scope. This approach does appear to have some merit, at least as a possible intermediate step, in the event that national recognition should prove to be not immediately attainable. Still another alternative would be to leave the recognition of special proficiency entirely to the states, providing at the national level a set of recommended or "model" standards, much as the American Bar Association has traditionally done with respect to ethical standards through its Canons of Professional and Judicial Ethics.

While it now seems likely that regulation of specialization will develop on a state-by-state basis, nationwide uniformity of standards would nevertheless appear to be desirable. It is to be hoped, then, that the movement presently working toward uniformity in bar admissions standards will also ultimately produce uniformity in the regulation and recognition of specialists in law practice.

2
Qualifications for
Recognition as a
Specialist

This is perhaps the most difficult problem involved in the subject of specialization. Not only does it involve difficult policy questions and practical problems, but to some extent it also raises the question of what specialization really means. It has been suggested that a distinction should be drawn between the terms "specialist" and "expert," with the former being used to indicate only limitation of practice to a single field or concentration primarily in one field, but with no implication of any expertise. Such a line is impossible to draw, of course, because the public will inevitably infer a claim of expertise from the title "specialist," regardless of its definition by the bar. And clearly, expertise is the essential element of the whole concept of specialization. Its objectives are to enable the public to identify lawyers who have some claim to special expertise and to provide some assurance that the claimed expertise in fact exists.

Because the term "specialist" does imply expertise, two serious questions must be answered. First, what level of proficiency does use of the term "specialist" require? Second, how may the existence of special proficiency be determined?

The level of proficiency required by the term "specialist" is, of course, that level necessary to protect the public who rely on it. This, in turn, can probably be defined only in terms of the level of proficiency thought to be reasonable by lawyers presently practicing in the various specialized fields. Thus it becomes apparent that qualifications for specialized practice will have to be formulated, at least at the outset, with reference to presently existing standards of practice.

Determining the existence of special proficiency is a practical problem. Possibilities include examination, formal training, experience, rating by colleagues, and various combinations of these. Self-evaluation is also a possibility.

a
Examination

Determination of special proficiency through examination has at least the appearance of simplicity, directness, and objectivity. As an immediate answer to the problem, however, it presents a serious difficulty. This difficulty is, of course, that of deciding just what is to be measured and finding reliable means of measurement.

The ultimate objective is to determine proficiency in a limited field of practice, but proficiency involves knowledge, skills, temperament, professional commitment, and any number of other elements. Measurement, if possible at all, will be extremely difficult, and there is considerable reason to doubt that the capability presently exists to measure proficiency in law practice — specialized or general — with any degree of accuracy. Certainly the bar's experience thus far in the administration of examinations for admission to law practice provides little encouragement for the success of specialty examinations; it still remains to be demonstrated conclusively that bar examinations have significant effect in determining the professional competence of applicants for admission to practice.

Even if effective specialty examinations were presently possible, those lawyers now practicing as specialists would not be likely to accept examination as a method for their qualifying as certified specialists. Thus, at best, examination could be utilized only for the qualification of future specialists.

b
Formal training

Formal academic training also presents some problems as a method of creating and identifying special expertise. First, although formal training may contribute to expertise, it does not guarantee proficiency as a practitioner, at least as legal education is now conceived. Completion of a specialized course of graduate study at a recognized law school may signify possession of a fairly high degree of special knowledge and perhaps even some special skills, depending upon the field of study and the nature of the course. But it probably would not signify proficiency as a specialized practitioner any more than completion of basic law school today signifies proficiency in general practice. Second, a system of specialization based on formal academic training would require a major expansion of presently existing graduate legal education facilities, an expansion that can be expected to take place only with the passage of time and the manifestation of genuine demand. And third, de facto specialists now in practice could not be expected to accept a system that would require them to go back to school in order to gain official recognition as specialists.

c
Experience

Experience in practice may produce expertise, and experience would be acceptable as a test to present specialists. But it, too, raises some problems, not the least of which is the matter of evaluating experience.

Practice of long duration, although it may lead to proficiency and thus may be relevant to the issue, is no sure sign of proficiency. A lawyer may be incompetent even though he has somehow managed to survive as a practitioner for many years. Similarly, the fact that a lawyer has handled a substantial number of cases of a particular kind may indicate that he possesses special proficiency, at least to the extent that a successful practice is in fact the result of satisfactory performance. But again, this fact alone is not conclusive without reference to the specific nature of the cases handled and the actual quality of performance. And when the inquiry goes beyond these readily discerned criteria — number of years in practice and number and type of cases handled — it becomes essentially subjective and extremely difficult to evaluate.

Another problem with the use of experience as a measure of special proficiency is the danger that it may foster development of legal specialties as closed crafts, unfairly discriminating against young lawyers and those who do not happen to belong to the established group and who thus may not have ready access to the opportunity of obtaining suitable experience in a chosen specialized field.

d
**Rating
by colleagues**

Perhaps the best known and most ambitious attempt to determine professional proficiency through rating by professional colleagues is the rating system employed in the *Martindale-Hubbell Law Directory* (209). Through discreet inquiries to judges, bar leaders, and prominent lawyers, the *Martindale-Hubbell* publishers attempt to obtain an evaluation of the professional competence of the lawyers listed in a given community.

This same approach is sometimes suggested as a method of determining special proficiency for the purpose of certification. The idea has some appeal as a matter of theory, since a lawyer's colleagues at the bar and the judges before whom he argues are no doubt better qualified than almost anyone else to evaluate his professional proficiency. But as a practical matter, this approach is subject to some reservations. The *Martindale-Hubbell* system is based essentially upon hearsay, and while anonymity may encourage informants to be frank, it may also invite evaluation on bases other than proficiency. It is said that in some communities an "a" rating in *Martindale-Hubbell* is more a sign of social acceptance than of superior proficiency, and indeed it is fairly common to find "c" or "b" rated lawyers who are actually more proficient than certain "a" rated lawyers in the same community. On the other hand, a system that did not leave informants anonymous would probably lose much in terms of frankness, as the temptation would be great to report favorably on almost everyone.

e
Self-evaluation

Of the various possibilities for determining the existence of special proficiency, self-evaluation by the individual lawyer provides the least assurance of actual proficiency. It nevertheless deserves consideration.

Whatever validity self-evaluation may have rests, of course, upon the basic integrity of the bar. Most lawyers are honest and will not deliberately claim for themselves special proficiency that does not exist. But at the same time there may be lawyers who honestly overestimate their own ability, and those few members of the profession who are lacking in integrity can be counted on to exploit any opportunity to claim special expertise, regardless of actual ability. Thus, while self-evaluation may involve few of the difficult implementation problems of other methods of determining the existence of special proficiency, it provides substantially less protection to the public.

It is sometimes suggested that protection to the public might be increased by the addition of certain safeguards. For example, it has been proposed that a lawyer be permitted to hold himself out to the public as limiting his practice to a special field. This, of course, is a form of self-evaluation of proficiency, and it does carry an implication of expertise. As a general matter, it also provides some assurance that the expertise actually exists. The fact that a lawyer is willing to limit his practice to a single special field and to risk his professional fortunes on one kind of practice, forgoing the right to supplement his income by dabbling in other fields, may be taken at least as evidence that he is in earnest with respect to the field of practice to which he has limited himself. And, if he does not already possess special expertise, concentration in one field of practice can normally be expected eventually to produce it. Thus, generally speaking, the lawyer who limits his practice to a single field is probably somewhat more likely to possess special proficiency than the lawyer who simply proclaims himself to be a specialist.

It is also possible that self-evaluation of special proficiency might be coupled with certain easily applied objective tests — i.e., a specified number of years of practice in the field or a specified number of cases handled — in order to provide increased protection to the public. Obviously, the lawyer who claims himself a specialist but who can also show at least a few readily ascertainable indicia of real expertise is more likely to be proficient than one who cannot.

f
A beginning
step

An earlier draft of this chapter speculated that the legal profession was not yet ready for a certification system that would embody effective measures for determining lawyers' qualifications. That speculation seems to have been wrong, for a recent survey of California lawyers suggests that the bar generally favors specialization and is ready to accept a suitable certification system (88). Moreover, a committee of the California State

Bar has recommended a system for adoption on an experimental basis (87).

Limited initially to three fields of specialized practice, this system would be tried statewide for a specified time, with periodic reevaluation to determine whether it justified continuation or expansion. The proposed plan provides for the certification of lawyers as specialists on a voluntary basis, but it does not require a certified specialist to limit his practice to the specialty. Indeed, a lawyer may be permitted to obtain certification in more than one specialty.

The proposed system makes uses of three of the foregoing five methods of determining qualifications. In addition to a "grandfather clause," which provides for certification solely on the basis of experience, it contains provisions for certification as a specialist upon a showing of experience and formal training, together with the passing of appropriate examinations. Moreover, the plan calls for re-certification every five years, although not necessarily by examination.

Adoption of this proposed certification system would constitute a bold step forward by the California Bar. It is to be hoped that the step is taken.

3
*Fields of
Special Practice*

A good deal of apprehension appears to exist about the supposed danger of "overspecialization" in law practice. In part, this is a concern that excessive specialization may impair a lawyer's professional ability; by focusing in too narrow a field, he may lose the breadth of understanding needed to deal adequately with a client's problem. And, in part, it is a fear of undue factionalization of the profession. The second of these two concerns may be quite justifiable, although there is some question about its relevance to the public interest. The first, however, seems somewhat specious.

Presumably, pressure for recognition and regulation of specialization in a given field of practice arises as a result of de facto specialization in that field, and de facto specialization is a product of client demand. It is difficult to imagine the existence—at least for very long—of any significant client demand for a degree of specialization that impairs the ability of lawyers to handle client problems. Thus, client demand itself may be expected to have a good deal to do with determining how much specialization is enough.

A decision to recognize a particular field of practice as a specialty is not a decision to extend specialization into an area where it did not previously exist, but rather it is a decision to undertake to protect the public by regulating a field in which lawyers are already practicing as specialists as a result of client demand.

Specialization's possible divisive effect upon the legal profession has already been mentioned. Although only indirectly related to the public interest, this aspect of the problem is of legitimate concern to the profession, and perhaps deserves to be considered in relation to the recognition of particular fields of specialized practice. But here the analogy to the medical profession may be somewhat misleading. It may very well be that a substantial part of the problem of factionalization in the medical profession lies in the independent character of medical specialty boards. Indeed, the best argument for prompt action by the organized bar to regulate specialization may be that it will forestall action by independent specialty organizations and thus actually inhibit excessive factionalization.

It would appear, then, that specialization should ultimately be recognized and regulated in every field in which a substantial number of lawyers practice as specialists. For the present, however, practical problems of feasibility indicate that regulation would best be undertaken in only a limited number of the major fields of practice.[23] A modest but sound beginning should provide experience that will permit eventual extension of the system into every field in which it is needed.

4
Use of
Specialties

The point has already been made that specialized legal ser-

[23]. The proposed California system would begin with the fields of workmen's compensation, criminal law, and taxation (87:511–12).

vices can probably be provided to the public most effectively through law firms made up of legal specialists and offering a wide range of expertise. Two other aspects of the use of specialties require mention, however. The first involves the extent to which lawyers certified as specialists may be permitted to hold themselves out to the public as specialists. The second involves the referral of cases to specialists by generalists.

The question of lawyers holding themselves out to the public as specialists, but one facet of the general topic of advertising and solicitation by lawyers, will be treated at some length in the following chapter. For now, it would appear sufficient to observe that making special expertise more readily available to the public is one of the main objectives of the recognition of specialized practice. Within reasonable limitations applicable to all lawyers, the certified legal specialist should therefore be permitted to make his special expertise known to the public.[24]

The traditional English legal specialist, the barrister, is isolated from the public by rules of practice. He may have no clients of his own but may serve only those referred to him by a solicitor. Furthermore, he may do no work even for a referred client beyond that requested in the solicitor's instructions. It follows that he is not permitted to advertise or otherwise make his expertise known to the general public. As a result, the services of barristers are not readily available to the public—except through the agency of solicitors. But at the same time, solicitors are encouraged to use specialists because there is no danger that barristers will keep referred clients as their own.

The informal system of specialization now existing in American law practice retains one of these aspects of the English profession but not the other. The American public may have direct access to those de facto specialists presently practicing, although the bar provides nothing at all to help them find and select the right one; but the American lawyer is deterred from making free use of specialists by the fact that he has no assurance that clients sent to them will ever return to him. Indeed, the risk of losing such clients is substantially increased by the fact that most de facto specialists practice in large com-

---

24. The California plan would modify traditional restrictions on advertising and solicitation to permit a lawyer certified as a specialist to make the fact of such certification known in conventional legal directories or law lists, in classified sections of telephone directories, and in dignified notices circulated to other lawyers (87:514).

plete-service firms that are well qualified to handle any kind of problem the referred client may ever have.

No one would seriously urge, at this point, that the American bar be divided into two branches, with specialists denied all access to clients except by referral from other lawyers. Indeed, the public interest would seem to be best served by preservation and improvement of direct public access to specialists. At the same time, it also appears that full acceptance and effective use of specialization by the American bar will not be possible unless some way is found to asure lawyers that clients they refer to specialists will not be lost as clients.

It is doubtful that any way will be found, however, unless specialists are prohibited from accepting other employment from referred clients. Such a restriction limits the client's freedom of choice, of course, and thus is tolerable only if it furthers some public interest of compelling importance. It may nevertheless be that the benefit to the public from the encouragement of the referral of cases to specialists is sufficient to justify the limitation.[25]

F
Conclusions

There can be little real question about the social utility of specialization in law practice. It holds great promise for improving the quality and lowering the cost of the legal services available to the public. At the same time, it should contribute substantially to the improvement of the administration of justice by enhancing the effectiveness of the adversary system. In so doing, it cannot help but make the lawyer more useful to society and hence more secure.

The attitudes and assumptions that prompt much of the resistance to the extension and improvement of specialization in law practice are not acceptable. Lawyers are not and cannot be omnicompetent in the complex world of today. Lawyers are not uniform in ability and therefore fungible. The public is entitled

25. The proposed California system would prohibit a certified specialist to whom a client had been referred by another lawyer from enlarging the scope of his representation or retaining the client upon completion of the referred matter. Indeed, under the provisions of that plan, the specialist should not thereafter again represent such a referred client without first notifying the lawyer who made the referral (87:511).

not only to acknowledgment of this fact by the legal profession, but also to some effective system that will enable people to locate a lawyer specially qualified to do a given legal task. Lawyers compete with each other and with nonlawyers for the privilege of furnishing law-related services to the public; the mistaken notion that they do not or should not compete is not sufficient justification for restrictions on law practice that unnecessarily inhibit the extension and improvement of the legal services available to the public. The ideal of the client's lawyer is the very essence of the legal profession. But the ideal is not an exclusive property of old-fashioned general practice; legal specialists can be — and are — lawyers, in the highest sense of the word.

Has the time not come for the legal profession to establish a rational and equitable regulatory system for specialized law practice? By providing the public with an effective and convenient means of locating legal specialists through a system offering some assurance of the actual competence of lawyers who claim to be specialists, the profession would be acting in the highest tradition of public service.

Bringing Lawyers and Clients Together

Making legal services more readily available to the public necessarily involves the question of how lawyers and clients are brought together. A person with a problem will not obtain the services of a lawyer unless he recognizes that his problem is one to which a lawyer's services may be appropriate, unless he is convinced that employment of a lawyer is worth the cost and is a more desirable method of solving the problem than other possible alternatives, and unless he is able to find a capable lawyer willing to handle the matter on agreeable terms. To the extent that lawyers' services are in fact appropriate, effective, and priced at acceptable levels, then the public's utilization of them will be determined in large part by what is done by the lawyer or by others to inform the public about law and lawyers and to facilitate contact between lawyers and the people who need their help.

A
The Nature and
Scope of the
Problem

The traditional model for bringing lawyers and clients together is expressed in the introductory sentence of Canon 27, as originally adopted by the American Bar Association in 1908: "The most worthy and effective advertisement possible, even for a young lawyer, and especially with his brother lawyers, is the establishment of a well-merited reputation for professional capacity and fidelity to trust" (13:75).* Although this statement does not appear in subsequent versions of the Canon, the model it describes is implicit in present restrictions on the activities of lawyers in obtaining legal employment: A lawyer should obtain his clients through a deserved reputation for competence and integrity (6, Nos. 27, 28, 35, 40, 43, 45, 46).

This traditional model presumes the existence of conditions that will make its operation possible. It presumes that prospective clients will be able to recognize that the services offered by the lawyer are appropriate and desirable solutions to their specific problems—an ability which is a function of the knowledge and sophistication of the prospective clients, the complexity of their problems, and the nature and variety of the lawyer's services. It presumes that the community is small enough to make the lawyer reasonably visible and accessible to all who might have cause to use his services. And it presumes that communication among members of the community is sufficiently free and effective to permit the lawyer's qualifications to become known by prospective clients without any special effort by the lawyer or by anyone acting for him.

The most obvious situation embodying these conditions is small-town law practice as it once existed.[1] In years past, the typical lawyer practiced in a little, homogeneous, closely knit community, where everyone was known to everyone else. With the small town's highly efficient system of informal internal communications, a reputation—professional or otherwise—could be quickly made or lost. Although the average person in that setting was probably not very knowledgeable or sophisticated, his problems were correspondingly limited in variety and simple in nature. The lawyer's practice was thus apt to involve a fairly narrow range of services relating to common and comparatively uncomplicated matters. Consequently, even the least sophisticated member of the community was able to recognize his legal problems and knew the kinds of services a lawyer

*Citations in boldface type refer the reader to the numbered "Works Cited" at 297–313; where numbers immediately follow the boldface reference, the reader is referred to specific pages in that work.

1. This idea is not new. The late Karl N. Llewellyn made the same point thirty years ago: "The canons of ethics on business-getting are still built in terms of a town of twenty-five thousand (or, much more dubiously, even fifty thousand)—a town where reputation speaks itself from mouth to mouth, even on the other side of the railroad track" (194:114; see also 253:223–42; 160:295–302).

offered for their solution. He was also likely to know what those services would cost and to know, or be able to find out easily, a good deal about the qualifications of available lawyers.

Remarkably, the conditions that made the traditional model work in the small town seem to be paralleled by those in the setting in which today's large firms practice — the community of property and commercial clients in the large city. This community is relatively small, homogeneous, and closeknit, and its communications are good. Although its members often have highly complex problems, their knowledgeability and sophistication more than compensate, so that they are able to recognize legal problems and see the appropriateness and desirability of the varied and highly specialized legal services available to them. Furthermore, when they do decide to get legal advice or services, they are likely to obtain them from large firms with which they already have established relationships. And even where they do not already have lawyers of their own, their business, professional, and social contacts provide them with a ready source of reliable information about the capabilities and cost of available lawyers and firms, so that selection of counsel is relatively easy and safe. The existence of these "small-town" conditions in the community of property and commercial clients no doubt has much to do with the fact that the large firms serving the business community are generally able to follow the traditional model of building a clientele almost wholly through reputation, while at the same time the members of that community make near-optimum use of lawyers' services. Moreover, it seems highly improbable that any measures taken to increase the utilization of lawyers by the general public would have any significant effect on the use of lawyers by property and commercial clients or alter the channels through which they presently obtain legal service.

The community of the urban poor, to take the other extreme, does not duplicate the conditions of the nineteenth-century small town. Its members are not sufficiently knowledgeable and sophisticated to make effective use of lawyers for the solution of their problems. Information about law, legal rights, remedies, and the qualifications of lawyers is not readily available, nor is such information easily communicated to and within the community. And, of course, the poor are generally unable to pay the fees of private lawyers. As a result, the traditional model has never worked to supply the poor with adequate legal services, as the long history of organized legal aid clearly demonstrates (see generally 84).

This fact no doubt accounts in large measure for the development of organized legal aid outside the pattern of private law practice. If the present trend continues, it may well be that the great bulk of legal services for the poor will eventually come to be provided by salaried lawyers working through institutionalized legal service programs. Furthermore, although advertising and solicitation activities by organized legal aid agencies are still occasionally challenged on the ground that they violate the ethical restrictions applicable to private lawyers, such activities are coming more and more to be regarded as unique and outside the scope of traditional ethical inhibitions (*ABA Inf. Eth. Ops.*, No. 992; see also *ABA Eth. Ops.*, No. 148; *ABA Inf. Eth. Ops.*, Nos. 786, 888; **72; 265; 381; 370**). Whatever might be said about the desirability of these developments (**77**), their continuance may mean ultimately that the private bar will come to be involved only incidentally in serving poor clients. By the same token, measures taken to bring together private lawyers and clients of moderate means can probably be expected to have but slight effect upon the poor and upon that segment of the bar engaged in serving them.

But what about people of moderate means? Is the traditional model still valid with respect to them? In modern urban America, is informally acquired public knowledge about lawyers' reputations adequate to bring together lawyers and the people of moderate means who would benefit from the services lawyers offer? Or is something more needed to cause this large segment of the public to make optimum use of lawyers' services?

There is reason to doubt that the traditional model is still adequate. The problem may be summed up in the word "urbanization." Megalopolis, not the small town of bygone days, is coming to be the setting for both modern life and modern law practice.[2] This fact has important implications with respect to the availability of legal services to persons of moderate means.

2. The fact of an existing concentration of population in urban settings is indisputable, and the trend toward even greater concentration in the future is unmistakable. In 1940 standard metropolitan statistical areas contained nearly 70 million people—52.6 percent of the total population of more than 130 million (**316**:5,16-17). In 1950 they contained nearly 85 million—56.1 percent of the total population (**316**:5, 16-17). By 1960 they had grown to over 112 million—62.9 percent of the population (**316A**:19). And by 1965 it was estimated that metropolitan areas had a combined population of nearly 124 million—64.4

To begin with, the conditions of increasingly complex urban life cause the individual to encounter more and more situations calling for the kind of help lawyers are equipped to give. With ever-larger numbers of people living close to one another, the fundamental business of getting along together becomes more difficult; as a result, interpersonal problems and disputes tend to increase in frequency and consequence. In addition, the growing involvement of the individual with large nongovernmental institutions—employers, labor unions, insurance companies, credit agencies, and the like—further expands the potential for conflict and increases the need for professional guidance in the systematic adjustment of differences. A third factor is the continuing expansion of governmental regulation of individual activities.

The number and complexity of these varied contacts and relationships, besides increasing the incidence and seriousness of problems, also tends to make recognition of their legal implications more difficult. Perhaps this is best exemplified by the field of consumer credit, where a remarkable expansion in the availability and use of credit has been accompanied by the proliferation of ingenious new credit devices. As a result, the average person has at best only a vague appreciation of the legal implications of his everyday credit transactions. For instance, while most borrowers in 1918 probably had a fair understanding of the nature of the responsibilities they undertook when they signed promissory notes and real estate or chattel mortgages, today's borrower is unlikely to have even the slightest inkling of the legal obligations he assumes simply by accepting a credit card, to say nothing of the obligations created when he uses it. And much the same observation could be made with respect to revolving charge accounts, check-credit schemes, and other similar arrangements.

It would also appear to be significant that the individual is usually at a substantial disadvantage in terms of power whenever he comes in conflict with government or with large private

percent (316A:19). Moreover, these great concentrations of people are now beginning to merge into complex "strip cities," of which the gigantic tangle sprawling from Boston to Washington, D.C., and including New York, Philadelphia, and Baltimore, is the best example. Several of these "strip cities" are even now readily identifiable, already embracing over half the country's metropolitan areas and containing half the entire population of the United States (339:2). There is no reason to believe that this trend will be reversed (see also 140).

institutions. He is at a disadvantage not only in his lack of knowledge about his obligations, about his rights, and about possible remedies, but also in having grossly inadequate resources to protect his interests against powerful institutions.

Urbanization also affects the individual's ability to find the help he needs to solve his problems and pursue his remedies. In the first place, the lawyers who practice in the cities are not usually where the people are. Much of the urban population growth in recent years has taken place in the areas contiguous to the central cities. Thus, many people of moderate means live in neighborhoods and communities that, although integral parts of the urban complex, are somewhat dispersed geographically. The lawyers, on the other hand, tend to be concentrated in the city centers.[3]

This concentration may have utility for the providing of legal services to a property and commercial clientele, both because of visibility to prospective clients and because of the economies of proximity to the courts and to business and financial institutions, but it poses a considerable obstacle to the use of lawyers by persons of moderate means. For one thing, lawyers located in the business section of the city are not constantly visible to most of the public. As a consequence, people with problems calling for legal services may simply fail to think of lawyers as possible sources of help. For another, the inconvenience of the lawyer's location almost surely discourages many people of moderate means from utilizing lawyers when they might otherwise have done so, if only because of the difficulties of travel within the metropolitan area. If the reluctance of shoppers to go into the city centers forces department stores and other retail businesses to build neighborhood and suburban branches, similar reluctance no doubt affects the use of downtown lawyers by persons of moderate means.

Lack of communication among people in the cities also affects their use of lawyers. The city dweller may not even know the name of his next-door neighbor, and even in the suburbs the patterns of communication are quite different from those typical

3. For example, the Chicago metropolitan area has over 6 million inhabitants. Of these, nearly half live outside the City of Chicago (316A:18, 20). Yet, of the approximately 11,000 lawyers in private practice in the Chicago metropolitan area (209:vol. 2, 1–260), nearly 9500 have their offices in the city proper (57:86). Furthermore, most of these are located in the downtown area (letter from Jacques G. Fuller, Executive Director of the Chicago Bar Association).

of the small town. In this setting it is virtually impossible for information about the services lawyers offer, or about the qualifications of particular lawyers, to be disseminated to any significant extent solely by word of mouth. Thus, whatever the downtown lawyer's reputation may be among his business clients, he is usually no more to the person of moderate means than a name on a building directory or one among several thousand in the classified telephone directory.

Another factor affecting the use of lawyers by people of moderate means is the pervasive effect of modern advertising and marketing techniques. Today's consumer has become conditioned to techniques that offer him goods and services in the most accessible, convenient, and attractive manner. They come to him pre-mixed, pre-cooked, pre-packaged, and easy to acquire. To expect people to pursue a completely self-reliant course in seeking out and securing the services of lawyers regardless of the obstacles is surely to expect too much. This is especially true of the so-called preventive legal services.

It should be apparent that the traditional model for building a law practice, based as it is on the public's informally acquired knowledge of law and lawyers, is inadequate in the metropolitan setting as a means of bringing together lawyers and moderate-income clients. Therefore, if such people are to make optimum use of lawyers' services, some effective supplement or replacement for the traditional model must be found. There are a number of possible solutions.

One is for lawyers to locate their offices in the neighborhoods of the cities and in the contiguous communities, with the primary objective of serving moderate-income clients. This possibility is being discussed in chapter 6 and will not be treated further here. Another is to provide lawyers' services to persons of moderate means through the groups and organizations of which the individuals are members. This is the so-called group legal service, in which the group or organization undertakes to perform some of the functions once accomplished informally in the small town setting. The group informs individual members about legal rights and the value of lawyers' services, assists in the selection of lawyers, and helps to bring lawyers and clients together on acceptable terms. This subject too is discussed in chapter 7. Still another possibility is the lawyer referral service, which is discussed in chapter 5. A fourth possibility, and the one with which this chapter is chiefly concerned, is to improve communication between the profession and the public in order to supply information no longer supplied adequately through the traditional model.

One way to improve communication between the profession and the public is to increase the effectiveness of the bar's collective efforts in the field of public information and education. Theoretically, it should be possible to devise a "public education" program that would in large measure compensate for the absence of small town conditions in the modern metropolitan setting. This would require effective mass public education programs, of course, coupled with equally effective lawyer referral programs. Unfortunately, prospects do not appear to be good for the development of such programs, at least in the near future. The tremendous cost of extensive use of the mass communications media would require large capital formation, and the diffusely organized bar has almost insuperable difficulties in raising large amounts of capital. While it is within the capacity of the profession to do much more than is presently being done, funds will probably never be adequate to sustain fully effective mass media communications efforts.

Another possible means of increasing the use of lawyers' services by persons of moderate means is the improvement of communications between individual lawyers and the public, perhaps by permitting lawyers greater freedom in offering their services to the public.

B
Conflicting Values

Significant values are brought into conflict by the suggestion that, in order to increase utilization of lawyers' services by people of moderate means, lawyers should be allowed more freedom in offering their services to the public. On the one side are those public and professional interests that might be served by permitting greater freedom. They include: the public interest in the ready availability of legal services; the interest of the profession in the improvement of the economic condition of the bar; and the interests of both the profession and society in the values of the free enterprise system as it relates to the purveying of legal services. On the other side are: the public interest in protection against misrepresentation and overreaching by lawyers; an interest of society in inhibiting the stirring up of litigation; an interest of at least some lawyers in the preservation of present patterns of economic advantage within the profession; and an interest of both the public and the profession in avoiding "the commercialization of the practice of law." Reasonable decisions about what lawyers should be permitted to do in order to increase the utilization of their services by people of moderate means require evaluation of these conflicting interests and of the values they embody.[4]

Three general observations might be made by way of preface to such an evaluation. First, the impact of present restrictions on the business-getting activities of lawyers seems to fall mainly upon the lawyers practicing alone and in small firms who now serve or attempt to serve people of moderate means. Lawyers presently serving the poor through organized legal aid programs and those presently serving property and commercial clients are substantially unaffected in any concrete way by existing restrictions. They would probably also be largely unaffected by modification of the present rules, except perhaps as changes might affect the professional "image." This possibility will be discussed later.

Second, advertising and solicitation are very different from most of the activities covered by the profession's ethical rules. While there are those who regard advertising and solicitation as inherently evil—even in their customary commercial and business applications—most people would reject the idea that such activities by themselves involve moral turpitude or venality. Indeed, even when engaged in by lawyers and against the profession's ethical rules, advertising and solicitation activities are quite different from disloyalty to clients, misappropriations of clients' funds, violation of client confidences, or perpetration of fraud upon clients or the courts. Henry S. Drinker made this point in his esteemed work on legal ethics, characterizing the profession's restrictions on advertising and solicitation as rules of professional "etiquette" rather than professional "ethics" (122:211; see also 368).[5]

4. For incisive critiques of the rules and the theories underlying them, see "A Critical Analysis of Rules Against Solicitation by Lawyers" (113), and Crabites (119).

5. Drinker went even further, characterizing the lawyer's duty not to advertise as "a duty to the traditions and amenities of an honorable profession," quite apart from his

And third, the question of whether lawyers are to be given greater freedom to make their availability and their qualifications known to persons of moderate means is not a choice between their being absolutely "noncommercial" (engaging in no business-getting activities whatever) and their being completely "commercial" (engaging in any and all such activities). Present restrictions already permit many advertising and solicitation activities, some of which are most effective in making lawyers' services available to some kinds of clients.[6] Rather, the question is whether lawyers should be permitted to engage in certain other similar activities designed to make legal services more readily available to persons of moderate means. And this question can be answered only through an evaluation of the conflicting values involved.

1
Values That May Be Served by Allowing Lawyers Greater Freedom in Obtaining Legal Employment

a
Greater availability of legal services

Whatever else may be the result, there can be little doubt that less stringent limitations on the obtaining of legal employment would enable persons of moderate means to acquire much more

---

duties to the public, the courts, his clients, or his colleagues (**122**:xii). It may be submitted, however, that the ultimate duty must always be to the public. While the lawyer's obligations to the courts, to clients, to colleagues, and to the profession may have some value in themselves, their final justification should be in the extent to which they benefit the public as a whole and can thus be said to be in the *public* interest. For example, the lawyer's duty to respect his client's confidence is of inestimable benefit to the client; but such communications are privileged because their protection is in the *public* interest—mainly to encourage clients to be open and candid with their lawyers. So the "duty to the traditions and amenities of an honorable profession" is really meaningful only if the next step is taken and the preservation of the traditions and amenities of the legal profession is shown to be in the public interest. Perhaps there is too great a tendency to presume that this is always so.

6. For example, lawyers are permitted to use such devices as shingles, letterheads, professional cards, undifferentiated listings in classified directories, and advertisements in law lists. The rules also at least tolerate the kind of civic and social activity and the sort of "soft-sell solicitation" usually recommended by the "how-to-build-a-law-practice" books (**296**:403-11). While most effective in bringing lawyers and clients together in many contexts—including the community of property and commercial clients—such activities do not appear well suited to the task of reaching people of moderate means in the urban setting.

information about law, legal rights, lawyers, and legal services than they now have. Such an increase in information would almost surely help people to recognize their legal problems, to see their need for lawyers' help, and to get in touch with the right lawyers more easily than at present. This would be so especially if that information were to include facts about the fields of law practiced by particular lawyers or about the special capabilities they possess. The end result should be increased public utilization of lawyers, with people of moderate means obtaining much legal help they would not otherwise get. This is clearly the most important value that may be served by allowing lawyers greater freedom to advertise and solicit legal business. It is a value of great significance to the public.

b
Economic benefit
to the bar

Increased utilization of lawyer's services by people of moderate means would, of course, benefit the bar as well as the public. More legal business obviously is of economic benefit to lawyers. There may also be some cause for hope that it would have the particular effect of improving the economic position of that segment of the bar presently underemployed. For while part of the profession is already fully engaged in well-paid service to property and commercial clients (and for that reason perhaps would not even be interested in an increased clientele among the moderate-income group), many lawyers are still underemployed and need more clients.[7] Relaxation of the restrictions on the obtaining of legal employment might well supply them.

c
Fostering
free enterprise

The free enterprise system is premised on the notion that the public is best served when goods and services are free to compete on an open market, on the theory that competition itself

7. Among these are many described by Jerome Carlin in his study of the solo practitioner in the large city (92; see also 130:16).

will be the most effective regulator of cost and quality. It is no accident, then, that in a society based on the free enterprise system, regulations designed to preserve competition are among the most significant of the restrictions imposed by government upon business activity. On the other hand, restrictions limiting competition can be justified only by the most cogent of public interest considerations.

Lawyers tend by nature and training to be independent of mind, and they have therefore usually been among the most ardent supporters of free enterprise. It seems strange, then, that they should themselves practice under a system of restrictions that substantially limits competition — and sometimes even forget that they do so. This system of restrictions, by preventing the operation of normal competitive forces, deprives the public of the benefits those forces would otherwise produce. Indeed, a respectable case could be made for the proposition that restriction of competition in the rendition of legal services is a major reason that many legal services have been priced out of the reach of moderate-income people. Of course, when such restrictions were adopted, they were aimed at preserving other values which the bar deemed to be sufficiently in the public interest to justify the limitation of competition. But limitation of free enterprise should never be permitted to continue beyond what may be clearly necessary to preserve values of direct and vital concern to the public.

The profession's own interest in avoiding unnecessary restrictions on competition also deserves mention. The lawyer's existense as a professional depends upon his ability to serve the public on terms that the public will accept. And this means simply that *he must compete effectively.* Competition from outside the bar is therefore a legitimate and serious concern of the legal profession, and one not entirely met by efforts to prevent the unauthorized practice of law by laymen.[8]

This is not to say that the bar's need to compete effectively necessarily justifies abandonment of controls over advertising and solicitation, or even that the need to compete should be the predominant factor in decisions about controls. But the need to compete is a factor, and it may be well to keep in mind that restrictions on advertising and solicitation are largely respon-

8. The observations made on this point thirty years ago by Karl N. Llewellyn are still timely and most trenchant (194:104–109).

sible for the lawyer's vulnerability to outside competition. The limitations on free enterprise that produce such vulnerability should not go beyond what the public interest clearly requires.

2
Values That May Be Disserved
by Allowing Lawyers Greater Freedom
in Obtaining Legal Employment

a
Protection of the public against
misrepresentation and overreaching

One reason often given for restricting the business-getting activities of lawyers is that the public needs such protection in order to avoid injury that might otherwise be caused by reliance upon exaggerated or misleading claims of ability by self-serving lawyers.

On its face this appears sound. Because legal services usually deal with important rights and interests, the quality of such services is especially important. Yet lawyers' abilities vary greatly, both in kind and in quality, and, unfortunately, a license to practice is not always a sure sign of competence. Furthermore, evaluating a lawyer's competence is a difficult task, even for other lawyers. It is perhaps understandable, then, that many members of the profession feel that the public needs the protection of restrictions intended to prevent lawyers from claiming special ability or from communicating anything to the public that might be taken as implying such a claim.

This reasoning might be persuasive if reasonable alternatives were available to the public to enable rational selection of counsel. But no such alternatives now exist. The inexperienced person has no reliable source of guidance in his choice of a lawyer, and it is he who is denied even the slightest bit of information about lawyers' abilities from lawyers themselves. Instead, he is forced to rely on the fiction that all lawyers are equally competent to handle all problems. How much, then, do such restrictions really benefit the public? Having to take "pot luck" from the classified directory may be preferable to an otherwise uninformed selection from among the competing claims of soliciting lawyers, but the difference does not seem great.

Moreover, are misrepresentation and overreaching by lawyers really such serious threats to the public, and are ethical proscriptions really necessary for the public's protection? There is reason for doubt. The laws of fraud, together with civil liability for any failure by a lawyer to perform as promised, would appear to offer substantial protection to the public against serious misstatements or exaggerations. A lawyer who would disregard the law with respect to fraud may be expected to demonstrate equal disregard for the ethical proscriptions.

There remains what might be called "minor puffing" as a possible sphere for the practical operation of the ethical rules in protecting the public. Here, the rules against advertising and solicitation seem to rest on the questionable premise that many lawyers who do not now engage in "minor puffing" would begin to do so if they were allowed greater freedom in obtaining clients. Is this so?

First, is there any real prospect of increased "puffing" by lawyers who already do advertise and solicit in violation of present rules? Probably not; they already seem to go about as far in exaggerating their abilities as they would go if the rules were modified to permit greater freedom. More importantly, is there really any danger that lawyers who now observe the rules against advertising and solicitation would begin to engage in minor "puffing" if they were permitted greater freedom in obtaining clients? Again, it is doubtful. Although advertising and solicitation activities may be more easily seen and thus more easily policed than exaggeration of ability, how many lawyers who now refrain from either advertising and solicitation or exaggeration of ability do so out of fear of disciplinary action?[9]

Moreover, advertising and solicitation activities do not, in themselves, involve the same basic moral standard as that brought into question by deliberate misrepresentation of ability. An honest lawyer might violate the restrictions against advertising and solicitation inadvertently, or even out of conviction that they are irrelevant and that such activities are necessary to make legal services adequately available to the public. But an honest lawyer could never deliberately misrepresent his own ability. It seems unlikely, then, that any great number of lawyers who now observe the rules against advertising and solicitation — regarding

9. Recent studies indicate that disciplinary action by the profession plays a relatively minor part in the control of the ethical behavior of lawyers (see 91:159-61; 147:77-86).

themselves, and being regarded by others, as honorable and ethical men — would violate the more fundamental standards of honesty and candor by engaging in "minor puffing" just because they were permitted to advertise and solicit. Even to suggest that this is so impugns the basic integrity of the entire profession.

It would seem, then, that present rules against advertising and solicitation by lawyers have, at most, only minor influence in protecting the public against misrepresentation and overreaching by lawyers. The rules may be justified solely for the function they perform in articulating an ideal of conduct, of course; but if this is the justification, it is not clear why that ideal should not be expressed in terms of integrity and candor rather than in terms of particular business-getting activities.

b
Inhibiting
the stirring up of
litigation

Present rules condemn the stirring up of strife and litigation as not only unprofessional but also criminal (**6**, No. 28; see also **122**: 63–66). The ethical interdictions thus appear to be a reflection of the policies underlying the common law doctrines of maintenance, champerty, and barratry. Over the years, these ancient doctrines have been substantially limited and modified, however, so that they have now lost their original rigor (**412**; see also **419**). Rather pointed criticism has also been directed at the premises upon which they were based (**259**:48–78; **232**:533–41). There is consequently some reason to question the "stirring-up-litigation" rationale as a ground for the rules against solicitation of legal business.

Prohibitions against the "stirring up of litigation" rest on two rather dubious premises. The first is the proposition that litigation is an evil in itself, and that nothing should be done to encourage it. The second is that, as a practical matter, the assertion of even legitimate claims must be discouraged in order to impede the bringing of fraudulent or frivolous actions. Neither proposition is persuasive.

The medieval idea that litigation is an evil in itself (**259**:68, 72) causes the legal system to be regarded as a wholly passive mechanism for the resolution of only those disputes that chance to come to it through the initiative of the parties. This view has important ramifications that are often overlooked.

To begin with, any legal system necessarily results in a rationing or allocation of justice somewhat different from that which would prevail in its absence, the nature of the allocation being determined by the nature of the system and the setting in which it operates (**151**:1–10). Next, even a passive mechanism encourages litigation; many issues that are eventually litigated would remain unasserted if resort to force were the only alternative. And finally, a purely passive system tends naturally to serve the interests of those prospective litigants who have sufficient knowledge and power to make effective use of it.[10]

Thus, the practical effect of the old belief about the evil nature of all litigation was to limit the use of the litigative mechanism to the strong, the wealthy, and the knowledgeable. It purported to say that all litigation was evil. In effect, however, it said that litigation had social value only when used by the strong to control the weak; it was an evil, and therefore to be discouraged, when used by the poor, the weak, and the ignorant to assert their rights against the strong. Such an allocation of justice might have been acceptable in a feudal society; but it seems wholly inconsistent with contemporary concepts of equal justice.

Equal justice under law, always an ideal of the American legal system, is not achieved simply by throwing open the courtroom doors. Not only must the substantive laws and the adjudicative processes be truly relevant to the needs of all citizens, but they must be truly accessible to all. And accessibility is not merely a matter of standing to sue; it is also a matter of money and knowledge. Indeed, it is the purest kind of sophistry to argue that the person of moderate means who has a legitimate claim but is not aware that the legal process may offer him a remedy, or who cannot afford or cannot locate the kind of help he needs to pursue the remedy, is nevertheless afforded equal justice merely because he may have a cause of action and standing to sue. Furthermore, the notion that the adjudicative mechanism should concern itself with only those claims that the prospective

10. This is perhaps best illustrated by experience with small claims courts, which were originally conceived as convenient and inexpensive forums for the adjudication of minor disputes. In many instances, however, they have come to be mere collection devices for the use of sophisticated creditors against naive and uninformed debtors (see **241**).

claimants deem of sufficient importance to assert on their own initiative overlooks the fact that people may fail to assert legitimate claims for many reasons — fear, ignorance, or lack of funds, for example — that have nothing at all to do with the importance of the claims to the prospective claimants but everything to do with the good to be derived by society from enabling such claims to be asserted.

The very fact that society even provides a litigative mechanism is in itself an acknowledgment of social value in at least some kinds of litigation. Furthermore, the idea that the assertion of legitimate claims may have social value and should be encouraged has long been recognized in particular situations. For example, under certain circumstances a corporation stockholder may be given standing in court to enforce rights of the corporation, or to prevent or remedy wrongs to the corporation, even though the stockholder has no individual claim and may have no interest in it other than his interest as a stockholder in the general well-being of the corporation.[11] Of course, the shareholder's interest in the well-being of the body corporate and in seeing to it that the corporation's rights are enforced is somewhat different from the lawyer's interest in the well-being of the body social and in seeing to it that the rights of individuals are enforced — but perhaps not so very different. At the least, the equitable doctrine of derivative suits is an acknowledgment that the social value of asserting some kinds of corporate rights is sufficient to justify encouraging litigation by permitting actions to be brought by parties who would not otherwise have standing to sue.

Perhaps the social value that may exist in at least some kinds of "stirring up" of litigation is most dramatically illustrated in the field of civil rights. Stirring up litigation among disadvantaged minorities whose basic constitutional rights are being violated and denied, thus encouraging them to assert their rights through orderly processes, may be one of the few real alternatives to disorder and violence.[12]

11. It should be noted that, although derivative suits involve the rights of the corporation and not those of the individual shareholder, there seems to be some authority to the effect that the shareholder bringing a derivative action must be able to show some ultimate loss or injury if the corporation's rights are not asserted (see 413).

12. Perhaps the most dramatic statement of this truism is the Final Report of the March 1968 American Assembly on Law and the Changing Society (5). This report charged the law, the legal process, and the legal profession with central roles in meeting the growing challenge to public order (see 308; 193; 222).

Even the business-getting activity that seems to be most deprecated by the profession—overt and aggressive solicitation of personal injury cases, usually called "ambulance chasing"—is not completely devoid of social value. The person who suffers an injury for which someone else is or may be liable needs the timely services of a competent lawyer. So far the profession has not provided any really effective method of supplying him with such services on an adequate and sufficiently prompt basis within the bounds of the ethical rules (see **64**). Whatever else it may do, "ambulance chasing" does address itself to that need, and although it may be deemed contrary to the public interest, the reason surely cannot be that it "stirs up" *legitimate* personal injury claims. Nor is it relevant that such "stirring up" may result in court congestion. If the litigative process has not the capacity to adjudicate all of society's serious legitimate claims, however brought to light, then perhaps the process needs changing.

If there is social value in the litigation of some kinds of claims, then the profession's objective should not be to discourage all litigation, or—worse yet—to discriminate among claims on the basis of the means, power, or sophistication of the prospective claimants. The objective should be to find some rational ground on which to determine which litigation is to be encouraged and which discouraged.

The social value of any litigation would seem to be most closely related to the legitimacy of the claims involved, and this would appear to be the right ground for determination. While the stirring up of frivolous or fraudulent claims is undoubtedly evil, the stirring up of legitimate claims that would otherwise go unasserted because of the prospective claimants' poverty, weakness, ignorance, or naiveté may in fact be a positive good. It would seem to follow that restrictions on lawyers' business-getting activities, at least when they are premised on a supposed public interest in preventing the stirring up of litigation, should focus on frivolous and fraudulent claims. A blanket rule against all stirring up of litigation seems clearly unjustified.

This leads to the second premise of the "stirring-up-litigation" concept—that, as a practical matter, the bringing of legitimate actions must be discouraged in order to discourage the bringing of fraudulent or frivolous ones. This premise is equally unsound. It carries with it quite unacceptable implications, not only about the venality of the bar but also about the inability of the courts to discover or to deal with fraudulent or frivolous claims. Furthermore, it assumes that those few lawyers who might be tempted to involve themselves in the bringing of such actions will somehow be more effectively deterred by rules against "stirring up litigation" than they are by existing laws and rules relating specifically to fraudulent and frivolous actions. This assumption is of doubtful validity. Those lawyers who might participate in the bringing of fraudulent or frivolous actions in the absence of rules against "stirring up litigation" are probably the same ones who now ignore existing rules and laws. There is no reason to anticipate that repeal or relaxation of the rules against "stirring up litigation" would prompt any significantly greater portion of the bar to begin instigating fraudulent or frivolous actions, or to doubt the ability of the courts to deal with such actions as might be brought. The remedy, if one is needed, should be directed to the fraudulent and frivolous claims themselves and not to legitimate ones.[13]

The foregoing discussion does not mean, of course, that the solicitation of business by individual lawyers is necessarily the right way to accomplish the positive good of bringing to light legitimate claims that would not otherwise be asserted. Other factors may still cause this kind of solicitation to be regarded as undesirable or may favor some different approach to the achievement of equal justice. The point is only that the ancient "stirring-up-litigation" rationale is no longer valid as a justification for blanket rules that unduly impair the lawyer's ability to reach and serve the public.

c
Preserving existing patterns
of competitive advantage
within the bar

Although lawyers generally are reluctant to admit that their private economic interests enter into the profession's decisions about permissible conduct, preservation of existing patterns of

---

13. The furnishing of security for expenses by plaintiffs in derivative actions demonstrates that the problem of frivolous actions can be handled by measures directed specifically at frivolous suits, without prohibiting or unduly impeding the bringing of legitimate suits.

competitive advantage within the bar is a factor to be considered
in evaluating controls over lawyers' business-getting activities
There can be little doubt that restrictions on advertising and
solicitation do have some effect upon patterns of economic advantage, or that at least part of the opposition to changes in the
restrictions is founded on fear that modification will upset existing patterns. Indeed, while discussions of the subject usually
begin in terms of "the public interest" or "the high ideals of the
profession," they can usually be expected to turn, at some point,
to terms like "competition" and "unfair advantage."

Lawyers must be concerned about their own economic interests, of course, even though they embrace a professionalism
that requires primary commitment to the public interest. This is
the real dilemma facing the modern legal profession, a dilemma
which may provide at least a partial explanation of the bar's
difficulty in applying the norms of the eighteenth-century English bar to the realities of modern law practice. The eighteenth-century English barrister, for whom the restrictions were
originally fashioned, did not have to make a living practicing law
and thus did not have to face the hard task of somehow accommodating a completely noncommercial norm to the demands of
economic necessity. The American lawyer has always faced this
task, however, and the problems arising from it are difficult and
persistent.[14]

Perhaps the most that can reasonably be asked of the modern
lawyer is an honest objectivity that will enable him to recognize
and acknowledge the extent to which economic considerations
do in fact enter into his personal decisions about professional
conduct. By openly and squarely facing the problem of either
accommodating personal economic interests to the public interest or choosing between them, the lawyer may be both encouraged and helped to make the "professional" choice—putting
the public interest first and letting the economic chips fall where
they may.

Such honest objectivity is the only conscionable course for the
legal profession in making its collective decisions about permissible conduct. Restrictions on the activities of lawyers in
obtaining clients must serve the public interest, regardless of

14. For a sharp exposition of the differences between the English and American legal
professions, see Crabites (119).

patterns of economic advantage within the bar. Perhaps the
converse is also true. Restrictions giving one lawyer competitive
advantage over another cannot be justified unless such restrictions are in fact necessary to the public interest.

How would existing patterns of economic advantage be
affected by changes in present restrictions on advertising and
solicitation? Any attempt to estimate the effect is necessarily
somewhat speculative, of course, but there may be some value
in such speculation.

One factor to be considered is the prospect that large law
firms may in the future undertake to serve clients of moderate
means. Should this happen, many solo practitioners and small
firms would find it difficult to compete, and most legal business
would probably gravitate to the large firms. It appears improbable, however, that the large firms will undertake to expand
their practices to include large numbers of clients of moderate
means — at least not in the immediate future. Most of them seem
already to have more lucrative business than they can conveniently handle; the main problem of the large firm today is
often that of finding enough capable new lawyers to sustain the
quality of service while expanding to meet the demand. Service
to clients of moderate means is not likely to appear economically
attractive by comparison. In addition, the style of the law practice that might be required in order to provide legal service to
such clients on an economically sound basis is apt to be quite
different from the style of the law practice in which the large
firms are now engaged, and they may be somewhat reluctant to
make the necessary transformation. The large firms may thus be
expected to continue to concentrate on property and commercial
clients, regardless of changes in the rules on advertising and
solicitation, leaving to others the job of providing legal services
to people of moderate means. The competitive position of the
large firms would probably therefore remain undisturbed; they
would neither gain new clients nor lose old ones.

Any increase in clientele resulting from relaxation of the rules
against advertising and solicitation would therefore seem likely
to accrue to small firms and solo practitioners. But how would
these new clients be distributed among this segment of the bar?
Would present patterns of competitive advantage be preserved
or disrupted? Here there appears cause to anticipate changes in

competitive advantage. While the large firms are not likely to undertake extensively to serve clients of moderate means, it would appear probable that the more solidly established and better organized small firms would do so if allowed to engage in activities reasonably calculated to reach such clients. It might well be that these stronger small firms would expand to become large firms especially designed to serve clients of moderate means. As a consequence, other small firms and solo practitioners not absorbed in such expansion might either be forced to combine themselves into larger and more efficient units or be squeezed out of the practice of law.

But here some hard questions must be asked. How would the *public* be hurt? If, in fact, large firms or expanded small firms were able to gear up to serve persons of moderate means with more, better, and less costly legal services, would not the public be benefited, even though some other small firms and solo practitioners might be injured economically or squeezed out? And if so, could the profession justify rules denying such benefits to the public in order to preserve present patterns of competitive advantage? Of course, no one knows at this stage whether either large firms or small firms would undertake to serve people of moderate means on any great scale, even if greater freedom in advertising and solicitation were permitted — or, indeed, whether they could, in fact, gear up to provide such clients better service at lower cost. But asking questions serves to illustrate the basic principle: In the profession's decisions about restrictions on intra-bar competition, the public interest, not private economic advantage, must govern.

The relationship of group legal services to patterns of economic advantage should be mentioned in passing. Group legal services are arrangements in which legal services are rendered to individual members of organized groups by lawyers who have been provided, recommended, or secured by the organizations or groups. Recent decisions of the Supreme Court of the United States have held such group activities to be constitutionally protected (392; 364; 409), and it has been proposed that lawyers should be permitted to participate in group programs that pose no undue threat to their independence of professional judgment and action (31; see also chapter 7 *infra*).

Group legal services obviously involve a substantial competition problem. To the extent that group programs and private lawyers are in fact vying for the same clientele,[15] the group's ability to advertise and solicit, free of the profession's ethical restrictions, places the private lawyer at a competitive disadvantage. A certain amount of such competitive disadvantage may be unavoidable.[16] This disadvantage might well be reduced substantially, however, if private lawyers serving people of moderate means were given greater freedom in obtaining clients. This might be especially so if the private lawyers were allowed to make known to the public at least some information about special proficiency. To the extent that this might be so, the bar's interest in preserving present patterns of competitive advantage may actually be served rather than disserved by the modification of present restrictions to give lawyers greater freedom in obtaining clients. However this may be, the ultimate answer to the problem of competitive advantage must remain the same: The public interest must always be paramount to the lawyer's interest in private economic advantage.

d

**Preventing "the commercialization
of the practice of law"**

The reason most often given for the rules restricting advertising and solicitation by lawyers is that such rules are necessary to prevent "the commercialization of the practice of law" (**230:678**). This hazy generalization, while it often invites emotional rather than rational responses, does embrace concepts deserving careful analysis.

15. Group programs may, in fact, reach a substantially new group of clients who would not otherwise make use of lawyers' services. This was not the case in either *BRT* or *UMW*, of course, but it was surely the case in *Button*. There is some reason to believe that the growth of group programs in the future will tend toward serving clients who were not previously, and would not have become, clients of private lawyers.

16. Many of the activities that serve to attract clients to group legal service programs are tied in closely with other legitimate group activities. It would therefore be extremely difficult to impose the legal profession's restrictions upon such activities. Moreover, one of the chief utilities of the group arrangement is its function in reaching people who need help and inducing them to use the service. At least some advertising and solicitation in connection with group legal service programs would therefore appear to be both necessary and in the public interest. A court or legislature would probably find it difficult to justify restrictions not clearly required to protect some important public interest. Unless there is some change in the restrictions imposed on private lawyers, then, group programs will probably always enjoy some competitive advantage.

(1)
Commercialism,
the professional image,
and public confidence

It has long been fashionable for lawyers to be concerned about the image of the profession. At least part of this concern flows from a belief that the bar's image as a noncommercial enterprise is essential to public confidence in the profession, in the law, and in the legal process.[17]

In considering image, it might be well to keep in mind the possibility that the lawyer's view of himself is not necessarily the public's view. While the public's view of lawyers may be influenced to some extent by professional traditions, it seems likely that more immediate and visible characteristics have much more to do with it—such characteristics as the lawyer's independence, his power in the community, his relative affluence, his verbal skill, and the somewhat mysterious nature of his functions and of the settings in which they are performed. Thus, it is just possible that the profession's noncommercial tradition looms somewhat less large in the public mind than in the lawyer's.

This observation leads to some obvious questions. What is the real source of public confidence in the legal profession, and how do the rules against advertising and solicitation relate to it? Does public confidence really rest on the existence of such rules?

More basically, does advertising necessarily impair public confidence? Apparently not, at least in other fields of endeavor. Banks, for instance, once sought public confidence through neo-classic building facades, names smacking of antiquity and imputing dependability—e.g., "SECVRITY FIDVCIARY GVARANTY BANK AND TRVST"—and appropriately conservative appearance and behavior on the part of officers and employees. Today, however, they suffer no apparent lack of customer confidence, even though they have turned to modernistic buildings adorned with abstract art and have accepted the use of extensive and aggressive advertising to cultivate a "friendly banker" image. Too, the engineering profession seems to enjoy a high degree of

---

17. This is at least suggested in Drinker's statement: "Also in so much as lawyers are officers of the court, advertising and solicitation by them would lower the whole tone of the administration of justice" (**122**; see also **238**:186).

public confidence, even though it permits its members to advertise—provided they do not do so "in a self-laudatory manner" or in a manner "likely to discredit or unfavorably reflect upon the dignity or honor of the profession."[18]

The point, of course, is not necessarily that the legal profession should emulate either bankers or engineers. Rather, the point is that the basic source of public confidence is not in the trappings of the profession, but in the genuine competence and integrity of its members. Without genuine competence and integrity, together with genuine commitment to the public interest, no amount of image-building can long preserve public confidence: with them, other factors become relatively less important.

As a result of better training and of more careful screening of prospective lawyers before they are admitted to practice, the general quality of the American bar is generally thought to be higher now than it has been in over a hundred years—possibly higher than it has ever been. Yet a close and honest look at the bar cannot help but lead to the distressing conclusion that there are still some lawyers who do not deserve public confidence. Effort spent in further upgrading the quality of the bar would therefore appear to be one of the best ways to increase public confidence in the profession.

But assuming competence and integrity to back up the image, what effect might advertising and solicitation by lawyers be expected to have on public confidence in the legal profession? Only conjecture is possible, of course. It has been suggested that "many of the most desirable clients, imbued with high respect both for their lawyer and his calling, would have no use for a lawyer who did not maintain the dignity and standards of his profession and would instinctively resent any attempt by another lawyer to encroach on their relation" (122:212).[19] It may be seriously doubted, however, that many people of modest means really see the practice of law as a "noncommercial" enterprise, or that they would be especially shocked or alienated by adver-

18. National Society of Professional Engineers, *Code of Ethics* (225); see also their *Opinions of the Board of Ethical Review* (226), Nos. 59-1, 60-1, 61-1, 61-3, 61-7, 62-2, 62-4, 62-8, 62-15, 63-3, 63-7, 63-8, 63-9, 64-1, 64-8, 64-12, 65-7, 65-10, 65-13, 65-17, 66-3, 66-4, 66-7, 66-9. Note, however, that most other professions appear to have restrictions on advertising and solicitation similar to those of the legal profession (see 61; 60; 59; 62).

19. Perhaps it should be pointed out that advertising and solicitation do not necessarily involve encroachment on the relationships between fellow lawyers and their clients; instead, such activities may operate merely to reach new clients.

tising and solicitation by lawyers. Of course, the nature of the business-getting methods employed might well have a good deal to do with the public's reaction. While misleading or offensive advertising and solicitation could very well impair public confidence, there seems to be little real danger that honest and dignified efforts to attract clients would have any significant effect.

A similar conclusion suggests itself with respect to the effect of advertising and solicitation upon public confidence in the law and the legal process. Furthermore, although the lawyer is in some ways a symbol of the law and the legal process, he is not their only symbol and maybe not even their most important one. Many people no doubt identify the judge and the policeman with the law and the legal process at least as closely as they do the lawyer. Moreover, it seems clear that respect for law and legal processes is determined chiefly by how well these processes operate to resolve the individual's problems. Delay, undue bother, excessive cost, and outright injustice are almost surely the principal reasons for public disrespect for the law and the legal process. The lawyer's noncommercial image, if indeed he really has such an image, would seem to have relatively little to do with it.

(2)
Commercialism,
professionalism,
and the lawyer

Behind the generalization that advertising and solicitation threaten to "commercialize the practice of law" lies another concept that requires examination. Its essence is the notion that the bar's noncommercial tradition may be an important factor in inducing the lawyer to conform to those other professional norms so vital to the proper performance of his extremely difficult role. Of course, this idea raises questions about what a profession really is and about what membership in a profession means. This is probably not the place to go deeply into those most difficult questions, but a few observations about some aspects of professionalism seem called for and may be helpful.

A simple and direct relationship between professional restrictions on business-getting activities and lawyers' compliance with other ethical norms is hard to see and even harder to demonstrate. For example, it would be difficult to show that the publication of information about the specialized nature of a lawyer's practice has a direct bearing upon his loyalty to his clients. Indeed, patent and admiralty lawyers, who are now permitted to make such information known (6, No. 27), would no doubt deny that any such relationship exists.

If there is a connection between restrictions on the obtaining of clients' and lawyers' conformance to other professional norms, it is probably to be found in whatever contributions such restrictions may make to what has been called the "style" of the legal profession. According to this thesis, the lawyer's function as an adviser and representative of contending parties in an adversary context requires his adherence to the highest standards of honesty and fidelity. At the same time, because of the peculiar nature of the adversary system and of his function in it, the lawyer is confronted with almost unlimited opportunity, and is subjected to extraordinary pressure, to deviate from such high standards. As a result, he would find it virtually impossible to perform his demanding role without the help and protection of the traditions and amenities making up the professional "style" or milieu.

This traditional professional milieu is seen as serving three important functions. It may insulate the lawyer against the additional pressures that would flow from unrestricted competition for clients. It may foster his conception of the practice of law as a high and noble calling. And it may give him the rewards of status and prestige needed to sustain him in his difficult role. The supposed end result is a higher level of adherence to the fundamental norms of honesty and fidelity.

This seems to be what Henry Drinker had in mind when he explained the continued existence of the traditional rules against advertising and solicitation in the following terms:

> Several considerations have led to the persistence of these rules of professional conduct and their inclusion in the Canons of Ethics.
>
> In the first place, while American lawyers are by no means as intimate a fraternity as the English barristers with whom these rules originated, still they differ radically from the milkman, the liquor dealer, or the manufacturer of cigarettes in being yesterday an antagonist and today a colleague on the

same side of the counsel table. They also differ in being
members of a profession. This is not a fancied conceit, but a
cherished tradition, the preservation of which is essential to
the lawyer's reverence for his calling—as well as to his regard and esteem for his fellows at the bar (122:211).

Is this theory sound? Do the profession's restrictions on advertising and solicitation actually provide the lawyer with appre-
ciable insulation against the pressure of competition? Are they
truly necessary to the lawyer's high conception of his calling or
to his prestige and status? Are they so essential to the professional milieu that their absence would seriously impair the lawyer's capacity to perform his professional functions in a genuinely professional way?

There is some reason for skepticism about the supposed effect
of present advertising and solicitation rules as "insulation"
against the pressures of competition within the profession. The
point was made earlier that, while such restrictions may have
something to do with patterns of economic advantage within the
bar, they do not significantly hamper the large firms in obtaining
property and commercial clients. Instead, the impact of present
rules is chiefly upon lawyers practicing alone and in small firms.

At the same time, it is the solo or small firm lawyer who is
under the greatest competitive pressure, despite the supposed
insulation of the rules. Indeed, the pressures of competition
could hardly be more severe than they presently are among
those lawyers whose practices are made up primarily of clients
of moderate means (92:142–49; 147:31). The reasons are obvious.
These solo and small firm lawyers are unable to compete with
the large law firms for the more lucrative legal business, both
because they lack access to the channels through which such
business is obtained and because they lack the capacity to offer
the kind of service the large firms can offer. They are also
subject to fairly intense competition for the remaining business,
not only from other lawyers, but also from laymen and lay
agencies. In addition, the traditional model is no longer effective
in bringing lawyers and moderate-income clients together in the
urban setting. Yet lawyers practicing alone and in small firms are
further handicapped by rules forbidding the use of the only
business-getting methods that might be at all effective in attracting the one large but relatively untapped source of business
open to them.

It is perhaps understandable, then, that compliance with rules against advertising and solicitation is not universally high. While the rules are generally accepted by large firm lawyers, upon whom they have little economic impact, they gain far less acceptance among at least some urban solo and small firm practitioners (91:49–52; cf. 147:103-15). Disparity in compliance with the rules only adds to the competitive pressure upon the lawyer who seeks to serve moderate-income clients within the bounds of the rules. As a practical matter, therefore, present restrictions on advertising and solicitation would seem rather limited in their effect as "insulation" for lawyers against the pressures of competition. For many lawyers, they may in fact only intensify the pressure.

If present rules against advertising and solicitation fall somewhat short of affording protection against competitive pressures, might they nevertheless contribute to the lawyer's conception of his calling and thus tend to support him in his adherence to high professional standards? Here, although assessment tends to be largely conjectural, the conclusion may be somewhat more affirmative.

Far too little is yet known, of course, about why lawyers comply or fail to comply with ethical standards. This is no doubt the main reason that the profession's ethical code continues to rest largely upon assumptions that are substantially untested, except as their past validity may be borne out by historical experience. However, recent sociologial studies have begun to identify important situational factors that affect ethical conduct. They suggest as well that basic ethical attitudes may also be significant determinants of lawyers' behavior with respect to ethical standards (91:133-49; 147:125-34). So far this element of ethical behavior has not been extensively explored, however, except for Carlin's tentative suggestion that the big-city lawyer's social background may have a good deal to do with his basic ethical attitudes (91:147), and for Handler's thought that the socializing effect of the lawyer's years in practice might be important for lawyers practicing in smaller communities (147:127).

Here, perhaps, is where the primary relevance of the professional milieu may be found. While basic ethical attitudes may be essentially the products of social background, they would seem at the same time to be affected by a number of motivating factors to which the traditions and amenities making up the professional "style" may be especially pertinent. Simple idealism, for example, is a strong element in the character of the truly professional lawyer. So, too, is pride—particularly pride in accomplishment and in excellence for its own sake. The need to feel that one occupies an important place in the scheme of things and that the functions one performs are significant and worthwhile would seem to be of especially great force with respect to the professionalism of lawyers. Too, there is desire for prestige and status in society and desire for the esteem of colleagues.[20]

The relevance of the professional milieu is clearly in the effect it may have upon these basic motivating factors. Surely the idealism, the pride, and the sense of relevance and significance that seem to help motivate the lawyer to conform to basic ethical standards are buttressed by the knowledge that he is a member of a body with roots going deep into antiquity, a body traditionally recognized as one of the learned professions, and a body historically as well as contemporarily involved deeply in the ordering of society. So, too, the lawyer's desire to share in the status and prestige that society has traditionally accorded the legal profession and, by earning collegial esteem, to share in the bar's traditionally close spirit of fraternalism must surely help to encourage honorable behavior.

It may be, then, that this is where the noncommercial tradition and the rules regulating the business-getting activities of lawyers have functions to perform. By fostering the lawyer's conception of his calling as a high and noble one, "above the level of a trade or business," and by regulating business-getting activities that might otherwise interfere with such a conception, the tradition and the rules may contribute significantly to the professional milieu and, through it, to higher professional conduct. Moreover, while Carlin attributed the variance between the ethical behavior of "elite" lawyers and that of their "non-elite" fellows primarily to situational factors, might it also be at least partly attributable to a variance in the extent to which different segments of the bar actually share in the professional milieu? The tendency of the small-firm lawyer toward a lower level of compliance with professional norms than that main-

---

20. Indeed, social control among scientists is said to be largely based upon the desire for collegial esteem, although, presumably, they are also motivated by some of the desires described above (see **146**:52-56).

tained by the "elite" lawyer may indeed be caused mainly by
his greater exposure to opportunities and pressures to deviate
and by his lesser exposure to the influence of highly ethical
colleagues. But it may also stem partly from the fact that he does
not share fully in the amenities of professionalism—the fraternalism, the status, the prestige. If this is so, then perhaps one
way to raise the level of ethical conduct would be to find some
means of bringing the "little" lawyer into full fellowship in the
profession.

Although it is difficult to evaluate this function of the noncommercial tradition and the rules against advertising and solicitation, it does appear to be a significant one. Perhaps, as Drinker
suggested, it is the only satisfactory explanation for the continued existence of such rules in the modern American legal profession.[21]

Where does the balance lie between the values that may be
served and those that might be disserved by present restrictions
or by modifications that would give lawyers greater freedom in
obtaining clients? This question requires difficult value judg-
ments, of course, but possibly the above discussion has served to
narrow the issue somewhat.

One value appears to predominate among those favoring the
liberalization of present restrictions: It is the benefit to the
public from vastly greater access to lawyers and their services.
Similarly, one value stands out as most important among those
favoring the preservation of the restrictions in their present
form: This is the value most commonly spoken of as "preventing
the commercialization of the practice of law"—preventing impairment of the professional milieu and thus of the lawyer's
ability to perform his difficult functions in conformance with
basic professional norms.

The dichotomy is, then, a simple one: The prospect of making
lawyers' services more readily available to people of moderate
means through relaxation of the rules against advertising and
solicitation must be weighed against the threat such modification might pose to the professional milieu and thus to the
lawyer's ability to conform to high standards of conduct in the
performance of his professional functions. The weighing may be
less simple than the dichotomy, however. It is difficult to es-

21. See pp. 154–55 *supra*.

timate what effects a particular rule or change may have upon these two conflicting values. Judging where the greatest good lies once the effects have been assessed may be even more difficult. Still the judgment must be made, and it cannot help but be a better one if it is made with an understanding — or at least an awareness — of the values involved. The primary objective of this book has been, of course, to facilitate such understanding and to encourage the making of such decisions on the basis of those values.

Whatever one may think about the relative weights of the two main values in conflict, there should be no disputing the fact that the balance is now far overweighted in favor of the professional "style." Indeed, the bar has rarely even recognized that availability of legal services to persons of moderate means is at all involved in the restrictions on advertising and solicitation. As a result, decisions about the rules have often been made as if their effect upon the traditions and amenities of the profession were the only consideration.[22] Clearly, the availability of lawyers' services to people of moderate means is a factor, and a crucial one. It deserves great weight in any decision about the conduct of lawyers.

Perhaps repetition of a point made earlier is in order: The choice is not between complete "commercialization" and absolute "noncommercialism." Fairly intense competition already does in fact exist within the profession, and present rules are directed only at certain manifestations of it. Thus, due consideration to availability of legal services requires only readjustment of an extant line between prohibited and permitted competitive activities. The objective is to give the public greater access to lawyers. It may be possible to readjust the line in such a way as to produce optimum utilization of lawyers' services by people of moderate means, with little or no adverse effect upon the professional milieu. But even if this were possible, it would nevertheless be appropriate to ask of the restrictions that now impair the public's access to lawyers: What price professional style?

---

22. One example is Canon 46, which imposes tight restrictions on the notices a lawyer may send to other lawyers to announce his availability to act as an associate in a particular branch of the law or legal service. See especially *ABA Eth. Ops.*, Nos. 145, 183, 184, 194, 228, 251, 263, and 264, which hold, in effect, that such notices may not contain any information bearing upon the lawyer's qualifications. But see *ABA Eth. Ops.*, No. 301.

C
Some Possibilities for Change

1
Dignified Efforts To Reach
and Serve the Public

Some thoughtful critics have proposed that lawyers be permitted to use whatever means they deem suitable to reach and serve moderate-income clients, subject only to the limitation that such efforts must be in keeping with the "dignity and honor of the profession." ("Dignity and honor" are no doubt meant here to embrace not merely decorum or good taste but also conformance to the basic professional ideal that service is paramount to personal gain. If so, it would surely include the prohibition of such specific excesses as misrepresentation, promises of results in litigation, and disparagement of fellow lawyers, the courts, or the law itself.) This proposal would mean, of course, that lawyers would be free to engage in many of the activities now prohibited as "advertising and solicitation," provided they did so in a "dignified" manner. Where does the balance lie between the conflicting values in this proposal?

There can be little doubt that such a change in the restrictions would produce an incalculable improvement in public access to lawyers, with resulting benefit to both the public and the profession. More legal services would be rendered to people of moderate means; lawyers would obtain more clients.

Who, or what, would be harmed by it? Is there a significant risk of injury to the professional milieu and thus to the lawyer's capacity to conform to basic standards of conduct in the performance of his difficult professional functions?

As noted earlier, the impact of present restrictions is primarily on small firm and solo practitioners. The rules leave large firms substantially unhampered in reaching the property and commercial clients they serve. It is unlikely, then, that such a change would in any way tarnish the large firm lawyer's conception of his calling or lower the level of his conduct. He might not like being identified with lawyers who would engage in business-getting activities that are now prohibited, but it is doubtful that this would cause him to be any less honorable in his own practice.

Nor should such activities by solo and small firm lawyers diminish the professional milieu significantly in their own eyes or reduce their capacity to conform to basic standards of professional conduct. Indeed, giving solo and small firm lawyers a realistic set of limitations, limitations that may even reduce competitive pressures by giving large numbers of new clients reasonable access to them and their services, might actually enhance their conception of their calling and help them to conform to the basic norms. The lawyer who is given the means of competing effectively and who sees that the rules are not really stacked against him may well be induced to make a greater effort toward genuine professionalism.

But is it possible to enforce rules requiring only that lawyers be "dignified" and conform to the professional ideal that service is paramount to personal gain? Are those concepts too vague and subjective to serve as standards of conduct? If they are, then what of "honesty" and "fidelity," the ideals that must ultimately govern all the lawyer's professional conduct? And is there really any good reason why the ideal of service above personal gain, however vague or subjective it may be, should be thought to be adequate as a guide in the setting of fees but not in the obtaining of clients?

Much is made of the improvement in the legal profession over the past seventy-five years or so; and there is reason to believe that the quality of the bar has indeed risen substantially since the period Roscoe Pound called the bar's "era of decadence," between about 1836 and 1870 (**253**:223). Moreover, the rules against advertising may have had something to do with bringing about that improvement (although better education and higher admission requirements are the more likely reasons). But is the profession not now at the stage where lawyers' contacts with prospective clients need to be limited only by the basic obligations of honesty, dignity, and commitment to the ideal that service is paramount to personal gain? If so, then the public should reap great benefit through easier access to lawyers, with little or no detriment to public or profession. If not, then how much real progress has there been?

2
Minimum Changes in
Restrictions on
Advertising and Solicitation

If the profession must accept the dreary conclusion that lawyers are not yet sufficiently professional to be given this kind of freedom to make their services truly available to people of moderate means, perhaps it can nevertheless take a few minimum steps to improve public access to lawyers. The following modest suggestions are illustrative of changes that might be made in present restrictions without in any way threatening lawyers' professionalism.

a
Advising clients of changes
in the law or in conditions

Lawyers should be given substantially greater freedom to advise persons they reasonably believe to be clients with respect to changes in the law or conditions and of the resulting need for further legal services. Present restrictions permit the giving of such advice only to a regular client, and then only in matters for which the client has regularly retained the lawyer (see *ABA Eth. Ops.*, No. 213; *ABA Inf. Eth. Ops.*, No. 809). This is much too restrictive. Even the occasional client tends to regard a lawyer he has consulted in the past as "his" lawyer. And clients appear to expect and want their lawyers to advise them of changes in the law or in conditions that may affect their interests, whether or not the advice is directly related to the matters for which they had previously consulted those lawyers.[23] Permitting lawyers to fulfill this expectation would seem to pose little danger to the public. Neither would it impair the professional milieu or reduce the capacity of lawyers to adhere to basic professional norms. But it would make lawyers' services more readily available.

23. The findings of the 1963 Missouri Bar Survey demonstrate the fact that in many situations clients think that their lawyers should volunteer such advice and that the lawyer is derelict in his duty if he does not do so (**220**:109).

b
Offering services
to other lawyers

Except for listings in law lists,[24] a lawyer who wishes to offer his services to other lawyers as a consultant or associate in a particular field of practice may do so in only one way. Canon 46 of the Canons of Professional Ethics of the American Bar Association permits him to notify other lawyers of his availability, provided that such notice is "in a form which does not constitute a statement or representation of special experience or expertness" (6, No. 46). The theory seems to be that as lawyers may not hold themselves out to the public as specialists, they may not include even in notices to other lawyers anything that might imply special ability.

This restriction has produced two notable limitations. First, a lawyer's notice to other lawyers that he is available to act as a consultant or associate in a "particular branch of the law or legal service" may not contain anything about his qualifications (see *ABA Eth. Ops.*, Nos. 184, 194; *ABA Inf. Eth. Ops.*, No. 440), as such information would imply some degree of special expertise. Second, a lawyer may not offer his services in any but those "particular branches of the law or legal service" approved by the American Bar Association Ethics Committee.[25] Approval seems generally to be based on the specificity with which the "branch" of practice is described—on the apparent assumption that the more narrowly and specifically it is described, the greater the implication of special ability.

This reasoning is not entirely satisfactory, however. It ignores the fact that *any* offering of services in a "particular" field, however broadly defined, implies some expertise, and the ques-

---

24. Because law lists also involve advertising to the lay public, they will be discussed separately *infra*.

25. It has been held, for example, that "assistance in writing briefs for the – – –[sic]Supreme Court" *is* "a particular branch of the law or legal service" (*ABA Inf. Eth. Ops.*, No. 454), while "legal research" is *not*(*ABA Eth. Ops.*, No. 145; *ABA Inf. Eth. Ops.*, Nos. 236, 907). See also *ABA Eth. Ops.*, Nos. 36,194,203,228; *ABA Inf. Eth. Ops.*, Nos. 231, 232, 233, 234, 235, 237, 238, 483, 489, 725, 763, and 765. Note that Informal Opinion No. 238 and the preceding Opinions dealt with "specialized legal services" under a former version of Canon 46, while subsequent Opinions speak in terms of "a particular branch of the law or legal service" in accordance with the present version of the Canon. The change in terminology seems to have effected no really significant change in the way the various services are viewed and handled, however. Cf. *ABA Inf. Eth. Ops.*, No. 236, with *ABA Inf. Eth. Ops.*, No. 907.

tion thus is really just one of degree—how much specialization or how much implication of special expertise is too much? Moreover, the rationale fails to reconcile all of the opinions; some of the approved "branches" are narrower and more specific than some that have been disapproved.[26] Thus, there appears to be no convincing explanation of why the offering of one's services in an *unapproved* "branch" of practice should be deemed to carry the forbidden implication of expertise, while the offering of services in an *approved* "branch" does not.

But there is a more fundamental question. In offering his services to other lawyers, why should not a lawyer be allowed honestly to represent himself as having special experience or expertness, to describe the offered service specifically, and to supply information about his qualifications? Is it because the lawyers to whom the notices would go are incapable of evaluating such information and therefore need protection?

Perhaps the reverse is true. Lawyers are generally knowledgeable and sophisticated, well able to evaluate the qualifications of fellow lawyers who offer their services. They would therefore benefit from having available precise descriptions of the services being offered and information about the qualifications of those who offer them. Their clients, and thus the public, would be the ultimate beneficiaries.

There are also geographic limits upon the distribution and publication of such notices. They may be sent to "local lawyers" only and be published in only "local legal journals" (6, No. 46).[27] While there may be some justification for preventing nationwide distribution or publication,[28] limiting distribution or publication to a single city and its environs seems much too narrow. This would seem especially to be so in an age when the interests and affairs of clients—and therefore the needs of lawyers for special assistance—are coming to be more and more widespread, geographically and otherwise.

26. See note 25 *supra*.

27. It has been held that the term "local lawyers" includes lawyers in the same city and in its immediate vicinity but not all the lawyers in a state (*ABA Inf. Eth. Ops.*, No. 765). Similarly, it has been held that publication of such a notice in a journal with nationwide circulation is improper (*ABA Inf. Eth. Ops.*, No. 489), as is publication in a state bar journal (*ABA Inf. Eth. Ops.*, No. 765).

28. It might be argued that nationwide publication of such notices should be restricted to the law lists, or some similar medium, where the task of policing will be fairly easy. It would seem, however, that the profession would be capable of policing the publication of such notices in those few journals or other publications of national circulation which lawyers would be likely to use to communicate with other lawyers.

More and better legal services would surely be made available to the public, then, with little danger of injury to either public or profession, if the restrictions on notices to other lawyers could be substantially relaxed.

c
Law lists

A comparison of the restrictions on notices to other lawyers with those on law lists may be revealing. As has just been pointed out, a lawyer may send to local lawyers, or have published in his local legal journal, notice of his availability to act as a consultant or associate of other lawyers in a particular field of practice, but may not say or publish anything in such notice about his qualifications or in any way intimate that he is skilled in the field.

If he can manage to get himself listed in a law list, however, he may have notice of his availability published and distributed nationwide, not only to other lawyers but to laymen as well. Furthermore, his advertisement in the law list may include a substantial amount of information about his qualifications.

Law lists have been characterized as "ethical advertising" (292). It would appear, however, that advertising in such lists is ethical only because the profession says that it is and not because of any reasoned theory as to ethical conduct. Indeed, it is difficult to conceive of any real reason, based solely on the intrinsic nature of the conduct involved, for condoning a lawyer's advertisement in a law list while condemning the same advertisement when sent as a notice to other lawyers or when published in a legal journal. The law list exception to the general rules against advertising and solicitation is therefore understandable only as a pragmatic rule, a historically developed product of utility.

Law lists had their beginning sometime around the end of the American bar's "era of decadence" (253:223-42). During this era, when state legislatures had virtually eliminated all requirements for admission to law practice (253:223-42) and when blatant advertising by lawyers was commonplace,[29] lay promoters

29. For example, The Greenville (South Carolina) Daily News for Saturday, December 7, 1889, reporting the death of Jefferson Davis, former President of the Confederate States

began to publish law lists as a profit-making enterprise and to distribute them to potential sources of legal business. These lists consisted simply of the professional cards (advertisements) of lawyers who had paid substantial sums for the privilege of having their qualifications thus made known to potential clients.

The American Bar Association Canons of Professional Ethics, which have consistently condemned advertising of various kinds, originally permitted the publication of "ordinary simple business cards" (**295**; **122**:266; **292**:123). Under this protection, law lists continued to flourish, and in 1928 the American Bar Association adopted Canon 43, specifically permitting the publication of "the simple professional card" in reputable law lists (**14**:130; **13**:75). By 1936 there were said to be some 300 law lists in existence (**13**:183), with the commercial lists alone forwarding an estimated 90 million dollars in business to subscribing lawyers during the year (**56**).[30]

With the publication of law lists largely uncontrolled, the situation appears to have become chaotic (**16**:843, 844). The need for some kind of regulation thus led to the American Bar Association's present rules and standards for law lists (see **15**:26; **17**:344-48, 349-50, 899-901, 1137-38; see also **20**:284; **21**:490).[31]

The law list exception to the general rules against advertising and solicitation, and the restrictions that have developed to govern law lists, are therefore less expressions of theory about ethical conduct than pragmatic attempts to curtail abuses in an established practice that had gotten out of hand. As such, they appear to represent an accommodation among the conflicting interests of the public, the bar, and the lay publishers of the law lists, premised perhaps on the conclusion that—at least at that particular stage of the bar's development—complete suppression of law lists would be impossible, even if desirable (**16**:842-45). In addition, regulation by the profession represents an implicit acknowledgment that law lists do perform a useful function in

---

of America, carries a number of advertisements by members of the Greenville bar, with such assertions as: "Prompt and careful attention given to all business"; "Collecting our Forte"; and "Money to Loan" (**143**).

30. It is said that in that same year lawyers paid approximately $1,500,000 for listings and for the purchase of directories (**56**; see also **221**).

31. The rules and standards, together with interpretations by the Law List Committee, are compiled in a "Mimeographed Compilation" published by that committee (see **292**:122, n.5).

making lawyer's services more readily available to those who need them.

The law list exception to the profession's general rules against advertising is sometimes justified on the ground that such lists are distributed only to lawyers and thus do not involve advertising to the public (*ABA Eth. Ops.*, No. 116). This is not so, however. They are distributed to nonlawyers as well as to lawyers. Indeed, some, particularly the commercial lists, are intended primarily for laymen and lay agencies, and even the general directories have some distribution outside the profession (26:672). Law lists should be viewed, then, as advertising to the public rather than as mere advertising among lawyers.

Distribution of law lists to the lay public is clearly useful, and such distribution does thereby enhance the availability of legal services. The exemption of law lists from the rules against advertising by lawyers would therefore seem to be justified, so long as the operation of the lists does not impair other important professional values or injure the public. The most serious problems seem to concern selectivity, the rating of lawyers as to ability, and the carrying of information — most notably, "branches of the profession practiced" — that may sometimes be misleading.

Selectivity is an inherent feature of law lists (292:123–24).[32] They exist because they provide reliable sources of reference to competent lawyers, and if they were not selective, they would have little or no utility. In addition, the rating of lawyers as to competence (148:35–36) is obviously useful to those who use the lists.

Both selectivity and rating raise the same problem — the problem of discriminating among lawyers. Even though such discrimination may be useful, it would not be tolerable unless done fairly and on the basis of appropriate criteria. Some of the lists select listees on the basis of legal ability, character, financial worth, and promptness in discharging obligations, determined through investigation of the prospective listee's reputation among other lawyers, local businessmen, judges, and court personnel (148:34–35). Ratings are also generally made on similar bases. Other lists carry the cards of only those lawyers who have been recommended by knowledgeable people or organizations;

---

32. Note that Sprecher distinguishes between "directories," which attempt to list all lawyers in the geographical area covered, and "law lists," which are selective.

for example, recommendations by legal representatives of insurance companies may be used in selecting listees for insurance lists (**148**:34). Some lists are said to rely upon the ratings prospective listees are given in other lists. In addition, a quota system is also sometimes used to restrict the number of listings (**148**:34). Typically, only one lawyer or firm will be listed in cities under a certain size, and the number of listees in larger cities is restricted according to population and other factors relating to the amount of legal business to be expected.

Are these criteria appropriate, and is the process of discrimination a fair one? Legal ability, character, financial worth, and promptness in discharging obligations have been held to be proper considerations (*ABA Inf. Eth. Ops.*, No. 171), but no effort has been made by the profession either to specify the level at which such standards are to be set or to supervise their administration. This is no doubt because the financial success of a law list depends upon the publisher's ability to satisfy those who use the list, and thus it is in the publisher's interest to list the best lawyers obtainable and to rate them accurately. This has probably been regarded as sufficient to insure generally the fairness of the procedure and to protect both the public and the profession. Experience would seem to indicate that it is. The system works well, and there have been comparatively few complaints about either selectivity or rating (**148**:36).[33]

Canon 27 also permits the publication in reputable law lists of brief biographical and informative data, including, among other things, "branches of the profession practiced" (**6**, No. 27; see also **292**:125; **148**:37–38). Until the recent promulgation of guidelines by the American Bar Association Law List Committee (**39**; see also **292**:125),[34] there were no effective standards governing representations in law lists about "branches of the profession practiced." A lawyer might list as many such "branches" as he wished, defined as broadly or as narrowly as he saw fit.[35] In the event of a question about a particular branch,

---

33. The number of complaints about law lists generally or about specific aspects of law lists is very small, according to the ABA Law List Department.

34. These guidelines specify that a "branch of the profession practiced" does not refer to work before a special tribunal, that "branches" practiced by individual members of a firm may not be specified in a firm listing, that "a 'branch' may not be stated in such a manner that it implies exceptional proficiency nor in such detail that it constitutes advertising," and that only those "branches" approved by the committee may be stated in law lists. There are presently fifty-eight such approved "branches" (**292**:126).

35. For a description of the abuses that had grown up, see Harnsberger (**148**:37–38).

the Law List Committee would decide the matter on an ad hoc basis. Present guidelines, however, limit such representations to "branches of the profession" that have been approved by the Law List Committee, although a lawyer may still show as many "branches" as he wishes.

Information about the branches of the profession a lawyer practices contributes toward the intelligent choice of counsel and is helpful to both the public and the profession. At the same time, such information is self-declared, and there is always the possibility that it will either deliberately or inadvertently misrepresent the facts about the lawyer's practice or imply more than it should about his qualifications.

Other kinds of biographical and informative material permitted in law lists may also be misleading, of course.[36] But there is a basic difference between the restrictions governing these other kinds of information and the regulations having to do with "branches of the profession practiced." The former seem to be directed primarily at preventing misrepresentation as such, whether or not the information implies anything about either the lawyer's general ability or about his proficiency in a particular field of practice. Thus, a lawyer may not show that he is a member of the ABA Section of Antitrust Law (*ABA Inf. Eth. Ops.*, No. 750), because such a representation may be taken as implying special proficiency in that field when in fact any lawyer may be a member of the Section, regardless of his proficiency or lack of it. On the other hand, he may show, as a "post of honor," that he is an officer of the Section (*ABA Inf. Eth. Ops.*, No. 915), even though such information might imply special proficiency. Presumably this is because most lawyers elected to such positions *are* probably expert in the fields of law or practice concerned. Thus, the danger appears comparatively small that the implication of expertness will be misleading.

The rules on "branches of the profession practiced," however, seem to be aimed not at misrepresentation but at any implication of exceptional proficiency, misleading or not. For example, while a lawyer may list contract law as a "branch of the profession practiced" (38:44) he may not list himself as a "consultant"

---

36. Restrictions have been found necessary to regulate the publication in law lists of: firm names; addresses; posts of honor; public and quasi-public offices; legal authorships; legal teaching positions; memberships and offices in legal and honorary fraternities and in legal, honorary, and scientific societies; references; and the names of clients regularly represented (see **292:126**).

in contract law (*ABA Inf. Eth. Ops.*, No. 214), or as practicing in the field of "policy and contract claims" (*ABA Inf. Eth. Ops.*, No. 215); the latter representations are said to imply "exceptional proficiency," while the former supposedly does not.

This approach to regulation assumes either that it is possible to publish the "branches of the profession" a lawyer practices without implying something about his ability in those branches, or that it is practicable to discriminate on the basis of the degree of expertness to be inferred from a particular formulation of a "branch of the profession practiced." Both are dubious assumptions. It is hard to see any real difference between showing "subrogation law" (one of the Law List Committee's approved "branches") as a "branch of the profession practiced" and the bald statement "I am an expert in subrogation law." Nor does there appear to be any significant difference between a lawyer's listing "drainage and levee law" (also approved) and asserting that he practices before the Claims Board of a local Sanitary District (an assertion he may not make under present rules).

Moreover, nothing would be gained by shortening the approved list and broadening the definitions of "branches of the profession practiced" as a means of reducing the implication of special expertise. The extent to which such an effort would succeed in removing the implication of expertness is precisely the extent to which "branches of the profession practiced" would cease to be useful for the only function for which they are included in law lists in the first place—enabling other lawyers and the public to make more intelligent selection of counsel. Put the other way around, if publication of a "branch of the profession practiced" helps toward the intelligent selection of counsel, it will necessarily imply expertness, and the more it implies, the more it helps—provided what it implies is true.

Perhaps the sensible way to regulate the publication of "branches of the profession practiced" in law lists, then, is to handle them in the same manner as the other biographical and informative data. The profession should stop worrying about whether or not—or the extent to which—"branches of the profession practiced" implies special proficiency; they should acknowledge that the implication is there and concentrate instead on ensuring that the implication is not misleading.

It would appear, then, that law lists are useful to both the profession and the public, and, with the minor exception of the problem of "branches of the profession practiced," that they do not unduly impair professional values or result in harm to the public. This is shown most clearly by thirty years of generally good experience under the American Bar Association law list program (148:33, 35–36). The public and profession would not continue to use law lists—generally without complaint—nor would lawyers continue to pay for listings or the publishers continue to prosper, if properly regulated lists had not been found to be useful and reasonably reliable sources of competent legal help. Indeed, perhaps law lists exemplify both the value and the feasibility of some relaxation of the general rules on advertising and solicitation. At the very least, the successful history of law lists suggests that the inconsistency between the present handling of law lists and the treatment of intra-bar communications under Canon 46 (notices to local lawyers) should be eliminated by substantial relaxation of the restrictions on notices to other lawyers.

d
Making known
special proficiency

It appears inevitable that the legal profession will undertake to recognize special proficiency in particular fields of law practice. If such recognition is to be of greatest benefit to the public, people must be given ready access to information that will enable them to find and make use of specialists. This means simply that the lawyer who is recognized as a specialist probably should be permitted to publish that fact wherever and whenever he is now allowed to publish the fact that he is a lawyer—including his shingle, his stationery, his professional card, his listings in classified directories, and the like. Permitting him to do so would in no way impair either the legitimate interests of the public or the bar's professionalism; but it would immeasurably enhance the availability of legal services by enabling people easily to locate lawyers who are qualified to handle their particular problems.

Consideration might also be given to the possibility of some relaxation of the restrictions on the media through which lawyers may make known the fact of specialized practice. If it is to help the public, such information must be made readily available to those who need it.

D
Conclusions

If there is anything significant in the foregoing discussion, it is probably not primarily in the suggestions for change in the profession's rules on advertising and solicitation. The significance of the discussion, rather, would seem to be in the broader point it makes—that availability of lawyers' services should be an important factor in decisions about what lawyers are to be permitted to do in offering their services to the public. For too long those decisions have been made on the assumption that the profession's own interests and traditions were the only pertinent considerations. They *may* be appropriate considerations, of course, provided they can be shown to have some direct and significant relationship to the interests of the public. But tradition is not, in itself, sufficient reason for professional restrictions that impair a lawyer's ability to fulfill his primary obligation of providing service to the public. It is surely time that the rules of professional conduct be evaluated from this broader perspective.

The
Lawyer Referral
Service

The organized bar's main response to the problem of making legal services more readily available to persons of moderate means has been the lawyer referral service. This plan is frequently mentioned as a practical alternative to group legal services (e.g., **254**; **99:69**; **96:95**; see also **102**; **275:288**).* One of the major recommendations of the California Group Legal Services Committee, for example, was that the bar undertake to meet the public's needs more fully through expanded and improved lawyer referral services (**89:703-707**).

The bar's confidence in lawyer referral may well be justified, inasmuch as the idea encompasses many sound principles that might be expected to increase the use of lawyers by the general public. At the same time, it must be acknowledged that the plan has thus far failed to live up fully to its promise. This may be due in part to the attitude of the bar toward lawyer referral. Lawyers have been generally indifferent toward the program, and in many communities they have been actively hostile to elements of the plan that are crucial to its vitality.

What can be expected from the lawyer referral plan? Is it, or can it be made, an effective legal service device? Is it a practical alternative to group legal services or other legal service arrangements? An examination of the program may suggest some answers to these questions.[1]

*Citations in boldface type refer the reader to the numbered "Works Cited" at 297-313; where numbers immediately follow the boldface references, the reader is referred to specific pages in that work.

1. Detailed descriptions of the plan may be found in: *Handbook on the Lawyer Referral Service* (**41**), and American Bar Association, Standing Committee on Lawyer Referral Service, *The Lawyer Referral Bulletin* (quarterly) (**42-46**). It should also be noted that much of this chapter is based upon information obtained from unpublished materials in the files of the ABA's Lawyer Referral Service Department and upon the

A
Essential
Elements of the
Program

The lawyer referral service is a method of bringing together
practicing lawyers and people with legal problems. Typically it
is operated by a local bar association, although in a few states it
is run by the state bar organization. The plan comprises three
basic elements: (1) a panel of lawyers who agree to serve clients
sent to them by the referral service; (2) some kind of referral
mechanism; and (3) some way of letting people know about the
service.

Beyond these basic elements, lawyer referral services vary
widely in structure and operation. Some function solely through
commercial telephone answering services: the prospective
client calls the referral service number and the answering service either arranges an appointment with a lawyer or gives the
caller the name and address of the next lawyer on the list. Other
referral services are operated in much the same manner but from
the bar association offices. Still others are run from separate
lawyer referral service offices, usually with somewhat more
elaborate procedures.

A considerable number of services, particularly those operated from separate offices or from the offices of the sponsoring
bar associations, make some attempt to screen applicants for
referral, ordinarily requiring them to come into the office for an
interview. The main objective is to determine that the applicant's problem really requires a lawyer's attention, although
where special panels of lawyers are maintained for specialized
fields of law, the screening process has the additional objective
of classifying the problem so that the client may be sent to a
lawyer specially qualified to handle it. A few referral services
attempt, at the referral office, to render advice or assistance on
minor problems that ordinarily would not be worthwhile or
attractive to practicing lawyers (138). Where this is done, of
course, the person giving such advice and rendering such services is a lawyer.

---

author's observation and examination of a great many lawyer referral services during
three years as Director of the ABA's Lawyer Referral Service Department. See also 252;
333; 204:517–18; 137:306–308, 316; 201:313–16; 93:317–21; 202:965–67.

The main objective of the referral procedure is to establish a lawyer-client relationship between the person with a legal problem and the panel lawyer to whom he is sent. It is contemplated that the relationship thus established should be substantially the same as that existing between the lawyer and his other clients. The plan does involve a few minor modifications of the traditional lawyer-client relationship, however. For instance, a modest predetermined fee for the client's initial consultation with a panel lawyer is made known to prospective clients in advance. While a lawyer's fee for his first consultation with new clients who come to him from other sources may vary all the way from his customary hourly charge down to no fee at all, he is obliged to charge a client sent him by lawyer referral no more than the fee set by the bar association for the first consultation. The usual charge is $5 for a half-hour consultation. Fees for subsequent services, however, are set by agreement between the lawyer and the client, as with other clients.

Another aspect in which the referral plan modifies the traditional lawyer-client relationship is the requirement that panel lawyers report to the bar association on cases referred to them. But though this requirement is typical, it is omitted or ignored in many communities. The disclosure of information about services performed and fees collected is regarded by some lawyers to be in conflict with traditional ideas about the confidences of clients. Perhaps more importantly, the making of reports is bothersome to most lawyers. There is probably also an element of covert resistance in lawyers' dislike of the reporting-back requirement, on the ground that it seems to have the effect—as indeed it does—of monitoring the adequacy and alacrity with which the referred matters are handled. In a few communities, panel lawyers are required to remit a portion of the fees earned in referred cases for the support of the referral service. Where this practice obtains, the sponsoring bar associations usually solicit follow-up reports more actively. Compliance with the reporting requirement appears to be somewhat better as a consequence.

Three other modifications of the traditional lawyer-client relationship in the lawyer referral plan may be mentioned: The first is the provision that, upon the client's request, fee disputes and other lawyer-client conflicts are to be submitted to arbitration. Resort to arbitration is apparently infrequent, however; indeed most referral services report disputes of any kind to be few

(41:10). The second is the use of special panels of lawyers to handle cases in particular fields of law practice. Special lawyer referral panels were first set up to handle matters falling within the fields of specialization recognized by American Bar Association Canon 27 — admiralty, patent and trademark.[2] Special panels now appear to have been extended to many other fields of practice as well. More will be said about this subject later. Finally, most bar associations operating referral services make some attempt to make their services known to the public through advertising or other means. Lawyer referral thus involves an element of solicitation that would be illicit under ordinary circumstances.

The lawyer referral movement is now more than 30 years old, having originated in Los Angeles in 1937 (137). That same year the American Bar Association established a Special Committee on Legal Clinics (10), which, after a series of name changes, became the Standing Committee on Lawyer Referral Service (25:121).[3] This Committee first endorsed lawyer referral in 1940 (18:225-62),[4] and most of its recent efforts have been devoted to promotion of the lawyer referral plan.

Under American Bar Association sponsorship, the plan has spread to over 200 communities (47). Referral services presently operate in all major cities and in many small ones. The 191 referral services responding to the American Bar Association's *1967 Annual Survey of Lawyer Referral Services* reported that the 22,794 lawyers on their panels had provided legal services to a total of 156,291 referred clients during the year (46:7, 10).[5]

This, then, is the lawyer referral plan. What may it realistically be expected to contribute toward solution of the problems of availability of legal services?

2. "It is not improper for a lawyer who is admitted to practice as a proctor in admiralty to use that designation on his letterhead or shingle or for a lawyer who has complied with the statutory requirements of admission to practice before the patent office to so use the designation 'patent attorney' or 'patent lawyer' or 'trade-mark attorney' or 'trade-mark lawyer' or any combination of those terms" (25:124).

3. Between 1937 and 1951 the Committee had been continued from year to year under a succession of different names, including: "Special Committee on Legal Service Bureaus" (18:409); "Special Committee on Low Cost Legal Service Bureaus" (19:148); "Special Committee on Low Cost Legal Service" (23:94); and "Special Committee on Lawyer Reference Service" (24:443). Note, however, that its charge has remained rather broad: "[To] study and report on methods of making legal service more readily available to persons of moderate means, and [to] encourage and assist local bar associations and other agencies to accomplish this purpose"(85).

4. Official ABA endorsement of the plan came in 1946 by resolution of the House of Delegates (22:109).

5. This represents a 23 percent increase in referrals over the previous year and an increase of 228 percent since 1954.

B
Evaluation

Again, perhaps the lawyer referral service idea can be evaluated in terms of the elements defined in chapter 1 as factors affecting the demand for lawyers' services.

1
Quality

Regardless of how legal services are dispensed or who renders them, their quality is of fundamental importance. If the advice is bad, if the instrument drafted is ineffective, if the advocacy is inept, then the system has little real utility, despite any efficiency in dispensing the services. The quality of the services provided through a lawyer referral service will depend upon the competence and integrity of the lawyers on the referral panels and upon the ability of the referral mechanism to match the lawyer to the client's need. The quality of the services offered through lawyer referral can be evaluated in part, then, by examining the methods by which panel lawyers are recruited, by studying the qualifications of those lawyers presently serving on panels, and by looking at the procedures by which a particular panel lawyer is selected to handle any given case. There is enough information presently available to make some assessments in these terms possible.

Generally, bar associations sponsoring lawyer referral services attempt to secure honest and competent lawyers for their referral panels in two ways: They seek to induce the better lawyers to serve, and they place restrictions on panel membership.

The usual method employed to induce good lawyers to join lawyer referral panels is to promote the program among members of the bar primarily as a public service activity, in the hope that only public-spirited lawyers will be attracted. This approach has some beneficial effects, although frequently it appears also to result in limiting support for the plan to a tiny segment of the bar, with consequent limitations upon the program's growth and vitality. At the other extreme, some bar associations promote the plan merely as a way to get business. This has the effect of repelling public-spirited lawyers and of attracting those who

want to develop additional sources of fees. Most bar associations
sponsoring the plan respond to this dilemma by grasping both of
its horns. On the one hand, they point out the potential benefits
to lawyers; on the other, they also emphasize the public service
aspect of the service. Probably these efforts cancel themselves in
net effect so that the result is the attraction of approximately a
cross-section of the bar.

Meaningful restrictions upon panel membership have not
been common. It is of course required that participating lawyers
be licensed to practice in the jurisdiction and be in good standing (41:39). Other restrictions are common but of little or no
apparent practical significance or effect. For example, many bar
associations restrict panel membership to members of the sponsoring association, while some require that panel members be
full-time practitioners. A few services require lawyers to have at
least one year of experience in practice before joining the panel
(46:10).

If licensure were completely reliable as evidence of competence and integrity, no further requirement would be needed
to assure the quality of a lawyer referral panel. (The problem of
matching the lawyer to the need would, of course, still remain.)
Unfortunately, a license does not invariably imply competence,
nor do the other commonly imposed restrictions contribute significantly to the protection of the public.

It is very difficult to estimate the range of competency and
integrity among the bar in any given community. There is reason
to suppose that it is wide in some places, narrow in others.
Common opinion within the bar in any locality is of only limited
help in this respect. In all major urban communities at least,
commentators can be heard to say that the bar does include
some incompetents but that on the whole the bar is pretty
capable. Within the limitations implied by these observations, it
seems safe—if unpleasant—to begin with the recognition that
not every member of a local bar association can be assumed to
be assuredly honest and competent, nor, for that matter, can
every full-time practitioner or every lawyer who has been in
practice longer than one year. Thus, even when combined, these
common restrictions on referral panel membership provide very
little additional assurance of integrity and competence beyond
that provided by licensure itself.

Few bar associations have been willing to impose more vigorous restrictions, however. The prevailing attitude is well expressed in a statement made several years ago by the American Bar Association Committee on Lawyer Referral Service: "When the courts of a state have admitted a lawyer to practice at the bar, a committee composed of his fellow members should be hesitant indeed before pronouncing him incompetent to serve on a legal panel" (42:2). This policy can hardly remain a final response to the problem if the bar is to take seriously the matter of more effectively providing legal services to the general public.

One minor but unbecoming by-product of the bar's reluctance to face the problem of the quality of lawyer referral panels has been the fairly common use of exculpatory clauses in the forms that applicants for referral are frequently required to sign. These clauses exonerate the sponsoring bar from legal liability for the mistakes or misconduct of panel lawyers.[6] The abundance of lawyerly caution that suggests the appropriateness of such clauses can be appreciated. At the same time, the recognition of the need for exculpation from legal responsibility is difficult to reconcile with the protestations that the panel members are adequately screened when their licensure has been verified. If the bar is not prepared to accept responsibility for the consequences of inviting a client to see any lawyer, it seems invidious to issue the invitation in the first place.

In a few communities, bar associations have begun to meet this issue squarely by attempting to see to it that only qualified lawyers serve on their lawyer referral panels. They seek to do so, as a rule, by requiring applicants for panel membership to be approved by a bar committee vested with discretionary power (41:39). Even here, the effect upon panel quality seems slight because criteria for qualification are vague and there is a tendency toward indulgence in their administration—the same factors, incidentally, that inhibit adequate professional discipline generally.

Clearly, most bar associations do little to insure that the lawyers on their lawyer referral panels are competent and honest. How good in fact, then, are present lawyer referral panels?

6. E.g., "I agree to make no claim nor file any court action against the _____ Bar Association or any officer thereof, or the Lawyer Referral Service or its officers or employees, at any time for any reason in connection with this matter, and understand that the Association and the Service, and their officers and employees make no representation concerning any attorney to whom the applicant is referred except that such attorney is in good standing in the legal profession and hence has satisfied the requirements of the authorities of this State as to his qualifications for practicing law" (41:54).

Would a person needing legal help be as well advised simply to pick a name from the classified directory?

From what has already been said, it would be surprising if panel lawyers were found to represent the "cream" of the profession, as the plan's proponents sometimes suggest. But are the program's critics right in charging that referral panels are only havens for the inexperienced and incompetent? Information is limited, but what is available indicates that the level of quality of most lawyer referral panels is about the average of the local bar generally.

It should perhaps be pointed out here that the actively practicing bar in the smaller communities is probably somewhat more uniform as regards competence and honesty than is the metropolitan bar. Common social and educational background, common law school background, similarity of practice, and close and intimate association among all members of the bar probably result in far less variation in professional characteristics than is to be found among the more heterogeneous bar in the larger cities (see generally **147; 92; 91**). But this fact is really only of limited significance in evaluating the honesty and competence of existing lawyer referral panels, as most of them are presently concentrated in the larger cities.

Some pertinent information in this respect is supplied by a 1965 study conducted by the American Bar Association's Committee on Lawyer Referral Service. This study undertook to develop a few basic facts about the lawyers presently serving on lawyer referral panels (**44:1**). Six referral services were selected as being fairly representative. They ranged from a new service in a city of 75,000 to an established program in a city of nearly 2 million. The six reflected a wide variety of other characteristics as well, including panel size, form of organization, referral procedures, and volume of cases handled.[7]

7. The following table shows some of the relevant characteristics of the referral services chosen for study:

Referral Service	Year Established	Population of Area	Bar Ass'n Membership	Panel Membership	Referrals in 1965
No. 1..	1961	75,000	300	68	150
No. 2..	1958	500,000	1700	302	1100
No. 3..	1950	1,500,000	3000	506	1300
No. 4..	1940	750,000	2000	241	1700
No. 5..	1950	300,000	650	209	400
No. 6..	1954	900,000	1300	136	750

Panel rosters were obtained, and each panelist's *Martin-dale-Hubbell* listing was examined to find, among other things: (1) his age; (2) the length of time he had been in practice; (3) his rating as to legal ability; and (4) his education.[8] For purposes of comparison, a similar check was also made of the *Martindale* listings of a sampling of lawyers selected at random from the entire bar in each of the same communities.[9]

Though the results varied somewhat among the six services, the figures were for the most part remarkably uniform. For this reason, the composite percentages — figured on the combined totals for all six services — seem to have a validity that could not be claimed were they simply averages of widely dissimilar individual totals. These composite percentages are informative.

With regard to age, the study shows a somewhat larger proportion of panel lawyers (67.1 percent) in the 30-50 year bracket than is the case among the entire bar in the same communities (48.9 percent).[10] And while the referral panels were similar to the bar as a whole with regard to the percentage of young lawyers (just over 7 percent for both), they have slightly fewer of the lawyers between the ages of 50 and 60 (15.9 percent as against 18.1 percent of the entire bar) and substantially fewer of the lawyers over 60 (9.4 percent of panel lawyers; 22 percent of the bar).

Much the same pattern prevails for years in practice, though in this respect the variations among the six referral services were slightly greater than they were with regard to age. Of the lawyers on referral panels, 11.9 percent had been in practice for fewer than 5 years, as compared with 13.0 percent of the entire bar; 21.9 percent of the panel lawyers had from 5 to 10 years of experience, compared with 16.1 percent of the bar; 36.5 percent of the panel lawyers had been in practice from 10 to 20 years, as against 25.9 percent of the bar as a whole; but only 29.7 percent of the panel lawyers had more than 20 years of experience, compared with 41.8 percent of the entire bar.

8. A note of caution, however: Except for the element of experience, the factors of age and length of time in practice are not entirely responsive to the issue of competence and not at all relevant to the question of honesty.

9. A subsequent check of certain statistics appearing in the *1964 Lawyer Statistical Report* for the entire bar in these same cities generally supports the validity of the figures obtained from the samples, though in an instance or two there were small variances that appear not to be significant for our purposes.

10. Of the panel lawyers, 39.2 percent were 30-40 years old, as compared with 27.6 percent of the bar as a whole; 27.9 percent of the panel lawyers were 40-50, while 21.3 percent of the entire bar were in that age group.

The pattern with regard to the *Martindale-Hubbell* rating of legal ability is also interesting.[11] The lawyer referral panels have slightly fewer of the lawyers given "a" ratings (7.3 percent) than does the bar as a whole (10.5 percent). This is to be expected because the panels have fewer lawyers with over 20 years' experience, and "a" ratings emerge partly as the result of longevity in practice. Similarly, because the referral panels have a greater proportion of the lawyers with under 20 years' experience, the fact that they have a greater proportion ot the "b" and "c" rated lawyers (23.1 percent) than the bar generally (13.8 percent) is also to be expected.[12] It is difficult, however, to arrive at a theory to explain why fewer of the panel lawyers were unrated (69.6 percent) than were members of the bar generally (73.1 percent), though perhaps a 3.5 percent difference is not sufficiently significant to require explanation.

The panel lawyers showed a slight edge over the bar as a whole in the matter of education, undoubtedly because many of the older lawyers—less numerous on lawyer referral panels— entered the profession at a time when admission to practice required a smaller amount of formal education than at present.[13] Again, the difference is not great enough to be really significant.

It would appear from this study, then, that lawyer referral panels represent a fair cross-section of the bar. Referral panels appear to be as good as—but not significantly better than—the bar as a whole. When a referral service sends clients to lawyers on a general panel in strict rotation, a potential client would have no better chance of getting a highly rated lawyer from the service than if he had simply taken a blind stab at the classified

11. The publishers of the *Martindale-Hubbell Law Directory* undertake to rate as many as possible of the lawyers listed therein, such rating being made on the basis of confidential inquiries directed to members of the bench and bar in the place where the lawyer practices. For an "a" rating, a lawyer's legal ability must be reported as "very high" and he must have been in practice not less than 10 years. For a "b" rating, his legal ability must be reported as "high" and he must have been in practice not less than 5 years. A lawyer whose legal ability is reported as "very high" and who has been in practice more than 5 years but less than 10 years is given a "b" rating. A lawyer whose legal ability is reported as "fair" or who has been in practice less than 5 years is given a "c" rating. As ratings have not been obtained for all listed lawyers, no implication is created by a lawyer's being unrated (**209** [1966]).

12. Of the panel lawyers, 18.4 percent had "b" ratings, as compared with 11.3 percent of the entire bar; 4.7 percent of the panel lawyers are "c" rated, as against 2.5 percent of the whole bar.

13. Of the panel lawyers, 92.4 percent had some college and 68.6 percent had college degrees, while 86.8 percent of the bar generally had some college and 65.1 percent had college degrees; 95.7 percent of the panel lawyers had LL.B. or equivalent degrees, compared with 91.6 percent of the entire bar.

directory. If he wanted an older, more experienced man, he *might* do slightly better with the "Yellow Pages"; if he wanted a younger and perhaps less expensive lawyer, his chances *might* be better if he used the lawyer referral service. But the difference would be small either way. In any case, of course, this kind of study reveals nothing at all about the absolute level of competence and integrity of the lawyer referral panels or among the bar at large.

One conclusion may be reached with some confidence from the existing evidence: Whatever else it may do, lawyer referral does not, in most places, appreciably improve the chances of a potential client to obtain capable legal services over the chances he would have by using a classified telephone directory. The organized bar has shown little inclination to perform any qualitative screening of lawyers for referral panels. Indeed, it is unlikely that most local bar associations could do so on a sustained basis. The internal conflicts and stresses that may be expected to arise if lawyers were to be excluded, except in the clearest possible cases, are probably too much for any loosely organized professional group to endure or perhaps even to contemplate. Moreover, presently existing bases for making qualitative assessments are dubious at best. Short of proving a case of malpractice, it is hard to imagine what evidence would suffice to justify excluding a lawyer from a panel. The bar has only limited access to reliable evidence on matters of competence, and the standards, other than those of simple fiduciary honesty, are elusive. In short, even if a bar association were determined to perform qualitative screening for general competence, it would be extremely difficult for it to do so in a just and satisfactory way—beyond applying such wooden standards as longevity in practice or law list ratings, which are based substantially upon hearsay. It appears unrealistic to suppose, therefore, that lawyer referral will improve significantly upon the selectivity of the Yellow Pages as far as the question of general competence is concerned.

This raises the question of how lawyer referral services go about matching the lawyer to the client's need. The problem of selecting a particular lawyer to handle a given case is really three problems. First, it is a matter of determining which lawyers are qualified to handle particular kinds of cases, a difficulty that is certainly compounded by the bar's reluctance to recognize and certify legal specialties.[14] Second, it is a problem of identifying and classifying the matters for which clients seek help. And third, it is a problem of devising a safe and fair—yet expeditious—selection procedure to match the lawyer to the case.

Bar associations sponsoring lawyer referral services have generally backed away from these three problems. This reticence is probably attributable to the same factors that produce the bar's reluctance to assess the competence of fellow lawyers. It is probably also attributable—particularly among bars that are new to the lawyer referral program—to fears of favoritism in the referral of lucrative cases under any but the simplest and most rigidly mechanical of systems.[15] Thus, though different systems are employed, only a few appear to be selecting a particular lawyer for a given case in a way that can be viewed as being of any real benefit to the public (see **269**).

One common system is to make referrals by strict rotation from a general panel, making no allowance for differences in the qualifications and interests of panel lawyers or in the needs of clients. This method successfully avoids all three of the problems mentioned above. But it does so at the cost of making it only accidental that cases are sent to lawyers best qualified to handle them, a result that can never be wholly satisfactory to either the public or the bar.

The system of making referrals by strict rotation from a general panel is modified in many referral plans to permit panel lawyers to designate in advance the kinds of cases they do not wish to handle.[16] When a lawyer's name comes to the top of the general list through the process of rotation, and the next case to be referred is of a kind he had declined to accept, he is passed over in favor of the next lawyer on the list who will take that kind of case. The first lawyer's name remains at the top of the list, however, until a case comes in that is not within the areas of practice he has excluded. This approach avoids the problem of determining the qualifications of panel lawyers, but it does not go far to assure that a given client will be sent to a qualified lawyer. The only real advantage is that clients are spared the

---

14. See chapter 3 *supra*.
15. See, e.g., the provisions in the "Statement of Policies and Standards" (41:37-38).
16. E.g., the sample "Rules and Forms" (41:38–44).

bother and unpleasantness of going to lawyers who do not want to serve them.

A variation of this system permits panel lawyers to select the fields of practice in which they will accept cases, with a limit—usually three or four—on the number of fields that may so be designated. This variation offers one advantage. A lawyer's affirmative designation of a field of law as one in which he wishes to receive cases implies that he deems himself to be qualified in that field, an implication far more positive than exclusion of fields in which he does not wish to receive cases. This variation does offer somewhat more—though perhaps still too little—assurance that the lawyers to whom clients are sent are actually qualified to handle the matter involved.

Permitting lawyers on a general panel to designate in advance the kinds of cases they will or will not accept raises the problem of classifying clients' cases. Some bar associations employ a lawyer to perform this task and require that prospective clients come to the referral service office for a personal interview before being sent to a panel lawyer. Others use a lawyer to classify the cases and make the referrals, but permit him to do so by telephone. Several allow experienced and trusted nonlawyers (typically, bar secretaries) to interview prospective clients, classify their cases, and refer them to lawyers. Again, some referral services require the clients to come to the office, while others allow the job to be done by telephone. A very few have entrusted this responsibility to carefully instructed telephone answering services (128). It would appear that a lawyer would do a better job of classification, while use of nonlawyers would be more expeditious and less costly. No studies of any kind have ever been made to determine whether this is so, however, and only speculation is possible. Where anything more than rough screening is involved, it is difficult to see how it could properly be done by anyone other than a lawyer or at least someone with experience and training in law office "intake."

Problems of the safety and fairness of the referral procedure are not raised, to any great extent, under these approaches because the procedure is essentially mechanical (158). In a few places, however, the person who makes the referrals is permitted to exercise a degree of discretion in selecting lawyers for particular cases and thus to vary from the regular rotation. A case involving some peculiar element and requiring some unusual qualification might be sent to a lawyer known to be particularly appropriate, even though the lawyer would not otherwise have received the case. Where this kind of discretion is allowed, the safety and fairness of the referral procedure must necessarily rest upon the integrity and judgment of the person who exercises it. It is perhaps some indication of the extent of intraprofessional tensions concerning "business-getting" that in only a few places is anything like liberal discretion vested in the referral secretariat.

In the absence of a system involving discretion, and as an alternative to lawyers' self-designation of areas of special competence, it has become fairly common in recent years to establish subpanels of lawyers to handle different fields of practice.[17] The typical arrangement is to use a general panel supplemented by one or more special panels. In at least one city, however, all the lawyers who have signed up to receive cases from the referral service are on special panels, and no general panel at all is maintained.[18] As with the systems already discussed, the subpanel system raises both the problems of classifying clients' cases and of insuring the safety and fairness of the referral procedure. The same array of attempted solutions is also found here, although it is probably safe to say that the services utilizing special panels tend more often to employ lawyers as referral officials and to vest discretionary power in them to a greater degree than those using only general panels.

The problem of determining the qualifications of panel lawyers becomes particularly acute when special panels are used. The effectiveness of a special panel system is ultimately determined by the quality of the lawyers on the panels, and, accordingly, meaningful limitations on panel membership are essential. Here again the approaches adopted by different bar associations vary widely. Some bars do not impose any limitations

17. In the 1967 Annual Survey of Lawyer Referral Services, conducted by the ABA Committee on Lawyer Referral Service, 51 lawyer referral services reported that they used special panels in one or more fields of law. The Patent Law field accounted for the greatest number of special panels (29). Others were: Criminal Law (15); Domestic Relations (14); Workmen's Compensation (13); Bankruptcy (12); Probate (11); Immigration (9); Military Law (9); Real Estate (9); Labor Law (8); Admiralty (7); Negligence and Personal Injury (7); Corporation (6); Tax (5); Veterans Rights (5); Commercial and Business Law (4); Mineral & Water Law (4); and over twenty other fields of practice (see 46:11).

18. The Legal Referral Service of the Association of the Bar of the City of New York and the New York County Lawyers' Association.

upon special panel membership, choosing simply to rely upon the self-evaluation of lawyers who wish to become members. Some protection may be afforded the public by virtue of the fact that most lawyers are honest and will not apply for membership on a special panel for which they are unqualified. At the same time, there are no doubt some lawyers who will claim special ability where none exists, and a great many more may tend to overestimate their own skills. Indeed, it seems a fair guess that the lawyers whose qualifications, whether general or special, are most dubious, are the ones most prone to exaggeration of their special competence. It would appear evident, therefore, that the public interest may require something more than the mere establishment of subpanels to insure the quality of lawyers offered through lawyer referral.

Where special panels are set up in fields of practice that are already limited to lawyers with special qualifications, the problem of determining the qualifications of applicants for panel membership is perhaps less difficult. Patent panels, for example, can be limited to lawyers admitted to practice before the U.S. Patent Office, and admiralty panels can be limited to those who have been admitted to practice as proctors in admiralty. The result may be a certain degree of assurance that the client with a case in one of these fields will be sent to a lawyer competent to handle it. Of course, although admission to practice before the Patent Office or as a proctor in admiralty may signify a certain minimum competence, there is no doubt considerable variation as to competence within these specialties. And, unfortunately, this solution can have no general application because these fields embrace but a tiny fraction of the cases handled by most referral services.

The most common way of monitoring special panel membership is to entrust the task to a bar association committee. Ordinarily, such a committee operates with only generally stated criteria for making its decisions and is empowered to accept or reject an applicant for membership on a particular special panel on the basis of the committee's informed evaluation of his qualifications. The factors apparently included in the assessment are formal training in the field of law involved, various kinds of special post-admission training, experience, interest, and perhaps other qualifications deemed important by the committee. In at least one instance, the bar committee accepts an applicant for special panel membership only when the members of the committee agree unanimously that the applicant is "particularly qualified" in the field of law involved.[19] It is reported that the setting of high standards has elicited many applications from the more experienced and highly respected lawyers in the community, who regard acceptance for membership on a special lawyer referral panel as something of an honor—a public recognition by their peers of their special abilities. This procedure and this experience appear to be unusual, however.

Perhaps a comparison between lawyer referral services and law lists would be enlightening. They are alike in that they involve the bringing together of clients and lawyers through the agency of a third party—the bar association in the one case and the lay publisher in the other. As has been seen, many bar associations operating lawyer referral services have been reluctant to be selective in any significant way, either in admitting lawyers to referral panels or in setting up special panels in particular fields of practice. They feel that they cannot go behind the lawyer's license but must assume that all lawyers licensed by the state are equally qualified. It is thus ironic that while bar associations refuse to be at all selective in choosing the lawyers they will offer to the public, the profession nevertheless condones and participates in the law list program, under which lay publishers, for a profit, may exercise an almost unrestricted selectivity in choosing the lawyers they will offer to the public. There is no less irony in the profession's acceptance of the rating of lawyers' legal ability by a lay business organization, while at the same time—because of the supposed impossibility of devising a workable method of evaluating lawyers' abilities—refusing either to set up lawyer referral panels on a specialized basis or to adopt a system for certifying legal specialties. But if a business organization can, for purposes of a law list, evaluate and rate the legal ability of a lawyer in a manner satisfactory to the legal profession, why should the profession itself be unable to do so for the purpose of certifying special proficiency or for making specialized referrals under the lawyer referral program?

It seems apparent that the lawyer referral system as it presently exists does too little to insure the quality of the legal services

19. The service is operated by the San Bernardino County (California) Bar Association. A similar system has also been adopted in Palo Alto, Cal.

dispensed to the public. At the same time it should also be apparent that some referral services are moving in the direction of determining standards and that methods do exist for developing all lawyer referral services into more reliable sources of quality legal services.

The suitability of a particular legal service for the problem to which it is being applied, i.e., matching the legal service to the problem, has another dimension beyond the question of lawyer competency. The task of directing a potential client to a lawyer who is competent to perform a particular service presupposes that providing some sort of service by a lawyer is the appropriate response to the client's problem. In many instances, however, this presupposition is not necessarily sound: It may be that in the particular circumstances, some type of service other than that offered by a lawyer is more appropriate or less expensive, or both. Does lawyer referral respond to this problem in any effective way?

This question in turn focuses on the question, "What *are* legal services?" Put differently, what do lawyers in private practice do and how do they do it?

Superficially, this question is remote from the problems of lawyer referral. To the extent that lawyer referral becomes a functioning operation, however, the question will become an insistent one: If lawyer referral services grow to the point where they are sending substantial numbers of cases of a similar kind to lawyers on a particular special panel, it would be reasonable to expect that these lawyers would give such cases the benefit of their already-existing expertise in this special field of law, and that the special needs raised by these cases would in time modify the ways in which these lawyers deal with them. The result might well be the development of new solutions tailored more clearly to the requirements of the problems of moderate-income people.

2
Price

As the lawyer referral plan presently operates, it makes only one significant contribution to the problem of the price of legal services. This is the almost universal practice of establishing a modest fixed fee for the first consultation with a new client sent by the referral service (41:13). Typically, this fee is well under the usual hourly rate specified in most minimum fee schedules ($5 for the first half-hour of consultation is most common).[20] Ordinarily this fee is made known to prospective clients in advance, and in many places it is publicized. Hence, persons coming to referral services for assistance with legal problems generally know beforehand what they can expect to pay for their first talk with a lawyer.

As a substantial number of lawyer referral cases apparently require only the one conference,[21] this initial fee may be the only fee involved. This may be regarded as a partial solution to the problem of price, though it is a solution worked out at the expense of the bar and not by reduction of the cost of rendering legal services. In any event, the fees charged by panel lawyers for further work done on behalf of clients sent to them by the referral service are not set or restricted in any way, but remain to be agreed upon between the lawyer and his new client. Thus, the lawyer referral service probably has little effect upon the problem of the price of major legal services or upon the problem of the near-indigent's inability to pay the price of even routine services beyond the initial consultation.

It is sometimes claimed by proponents of the plan that panel lawyers are somewhat more ready than are lawyers generally to adjust fees according to the client's ability to pay. There have been no studies of any kind to substantiate this claim. To the extent that any particular lawyer referral panel is made up primarily of public-spirited lawyers, the claim may well have some foundation in fact. A study of the fees charged referral clients by panel lawyers would shed light on this issue and is much needed.

Further development in the use of special panels might have the effect of inducing panel lawyers to adopt more efficient practice techniques. Perhaps this would eventually effect a gen-

20. Of the services responding to the 1967 Annual Survey, 87 reported that the fee set for the initial half-hour consultation with a panel lawyer is $5; 37 have set it at $10; 13 at $7.50; and other referral services reported a variety of practices with respect to the fee for the first consultation. These ranged all the way from $15 for a half-hour to no fee at all.

21. The dearth of reliable data about the results of sending clients to lawyers through the referral service makes it hard to tell just how many cases require only a half-hour consultation, however.

eral lowering of the cost of providing those particular legal services and, it is to be hoped, the fee.

There are at least two ways in which the lawyer referral plan might be modified to help bring the price of legal services within the reach of people of moderate means. One is to develop a "reduced fee schedule"—perhaps on some sort of graduated scale—for services performed for the near-indigent or for people of low or moderate income. Because of the present unsatisfactory economic status of a substantial segment of the bar, however, it seems unlikely that any such "reduced fee schedule" could be given general application to all lawyer referral panels. Perhaps one answer may be a separate voluntary panel, composed of lawyers who, as a public service, would be willing to provide needed legal services to near-indigent and low-income people at reduced fees. Indeed a few referral services already have something of this sort in special panels of lawyers who have agreed to accept "problem" cases—cases that for one reason or another are not readily referrable. Both these procedures, however, involve the reduction in price of legal services without any direct attention to reducing the cost of producing them. In this respect, assuming that regular fee schedules are reasonable in amount, special fee schedules simply transfer part of the cost burden from the client to the lawyer. Commendable and professionally honorable as this may be, it is not an economically sound solution to the problem.

Another line of approach is to consider more carefully the possibilities for reducing the real costs of providing certain types of basic legal services. This problem transcends lawyer referral as such, but the lawyer referral mechanism suggests some lines along which solutions might be developed. It might be possible, for example, for lawyer referral services to develop a kind of "clinic" function as a supplement to the referral process (see **287; 101**). A few referral services move in this direction by attempting to answer simple questions and to handle minor matters at the referral service office instead of sending them out to practicing lawyers. This practice might be expanded to include the handling of all "uneconomic" cases—i.e., those cases that practicing lawyers cannot handle profitably at fees that people of low or moderate means can afford to pay. This approach, too, might utilize a sort of "graduated reduced fee schedule," permitting the clients to pay what they are able toward the cost of the services they receive, the fees so collected going to help pay the expense of the operation. This clinic idea will be discussed more fully in the following chapter.

Beyond offering a moderate fixed fee for the client's first consultation with a panel lawyer, present lawyer referral plans do little to solve the problem of the price of lawyers' services. The plans could come eventually to have a significant effect upon the price of routine and relatively minor services. But they offer only slight promise of solving the problem of the price of major services.

3
Accessibility

A major objective of lawyer referral is to make services more readily accessible to the public. "Accessibility" is a complex concept, a fact not often recognized in the legal profession's discussions of lawyer referral. Accessibility in the broadest sense includes practically all the factors that go into recognizing and responding to a problem requiring legal services. Certainly it includes the question of public attitudes toward lawyers and legal services, but in a narrower sense accessibility refers to factors of physical proximity and convenience. It is this narrower problem to which reference is now being made.

Under the lawyer referral plan, legal services are performed by practicing lawyers in their own offices. In its typical form, therefore, the plan has little effect upon the proximity of the lawyers to the prospective clients.[22] Most lawyers are still concentrated in the centers of the cities in which they practice; in large cities most lawyers are officed in the relative seclusion of the upper stories of downtown office buildings. The person from the outlying neighborhood usually must travel into the city center to reach a lawyer whether or not he finds him through the referral service. And the lawyer must be sought at an office environment that many would-be clients no doubt find awesome or even frightening and — for people with regular working hours — he is available only at inconvenient times of day.

22. Note that the pioneer effort to get lawyers to practice in moderate-income neighborhoods was the Philadelphia Neighborhood Law Office plan (3). See also chapter 6 *infra*.

There are of course neighborhood practitioners in all cities, and operations are sometimes organized to reduce the problems of lack of accessibility. While many lawyer referral services make no provision at all for sending a client to a lawyer in his own neighborhood, even though neighborhood lawyers may be on their panels, others do provide that the client may be referred to a lawyer in his neighborhood if he specifically requests it. A few services refer clients to local counsel as a matter of course (75).[23] In those services that try to provide referral by geography and at the same time maintain separate panels for various fields of law, problems arise as to which criterion of referral is to take priority. At least one referral service takes the approach that special competence of the lawyer should prevail in case of conflict.[24] Be that as it may, there is room for improvement in most lawyer referral services with regard to this aspect of accessibility, though the potential contribution of the lawyer referral plan to the resolution of physical proximity problems is limited ultimately by the location of private lawyers.

Convenience is another matter. The lawyer referral plan can contribute immeasurably to the ease with which legal services can be obtained by making the process of obtaining a lawyer through the service as convenient and pleasant as possible. Unfortunately, not all the people who run referral services see this as a primary goal; other objectives are often given greater attention. A good example is the common practice of requiring all applicants for referral to come to the referral service office for an interview before being sent to a panel lawyer (41:10-11, 41). Several reasons are given for this requirement. Where special panels of lawyers are used to handle cases in certain fields of law, applicants are required to come in person to the referral service office to facilitate proper classification of the client's problem and referral to the right lawyer. Where special panels are not used, the requirement that clients come to the referral service office before being referred to a panel lawyer is usually justified on the grounds that it: (1) tends to discourage people who aren't serious about seeing a lawyer and thus conserves the time of the referral service personnel and reduces the number of

---

23. Note also that the Lawyer Reference Service of the San Bernardino County Bar Association permits and encourages referral on a geographical basis.

24. The Legal Referral Service of the Association of the Bar of the City of New York and the New York County Lawyers' Association.

unkept appointments with panel lawyers; (2) saves the time of
panel lawyers by screening out problems that need not be sent
to lawyers — problems that are not legal in nature, people who
are simply "lawyer-shopping," cranks, etc.; or (3) makes it possible, in a few places, for advice and service in minor matters to
be given at the referral service office, again conserving the time
of panel lawyers.

But the requirement that all applicants come for a referral
interview at the service office may operate as a formidable barrier between the potential client and the legal services he needs.
The prospect of spending half a day in some "agency" office is
distasteful at best. Such a prospect is no doubt especially forbidding to a client who has first gone to a legal aid office, only to be
found ineligible for free legal help, and who must then
go — sometimes clear across town — to a referral service office,
there to undergo another interview before making still a third
trip to the office of a panel lawyer. It is almost certain that a great
many people who really need legal services and who might
otherwise be inclined to obtain them through a lawyer referral
service are now deterred from doing so by the prospect of such
an ordeal.

The problem, obviously, is how to realize the legitimate objective of the referral office interview while minimizing the
inconvenience to the public. Varying responses to the problem
have been made. Some referral services simply ignore the public convenience and insist that everyone come into the office for
an interview. Others contend that referrals can be made satisfactorily by telephone. Some take a middle position, making referrals by telephone unless the telephone interview indicates the
desirability of having the prospective client come in for a personal interview. Still others, though they require most applicants
to come to the office, will make telephone referrals under special
circumstances. Where applicants are generally required to come
to the referral service office, a number of bar associations have
nevertheless made special arrangements with legal aid societies,
armed forces legal assistance officers, and, in at least one instance, with personnel offices of industrial employers, for more
expeditious referral of clients from those sources.

One referral service, for example, maintains a direct telephone line to the legal aid society. When a legal aid attorney
encounters a person who, in his judgment, needs a lawyer but

does not qualify for free service from the legal aid society, he calls the lawyer referral service, which makes an appointment for the client with an appropriate panel lawyer. This information is then relayed back to the legal aid attorney by phone, and the client is sent directly from the legal aid office to the office of the panel lawyer. Another, more direct, approach is to combine the operations of legal aid and lawyer referral in the same facilities; it has been suggested more than once that the two programs should be completely merged.

In addition, questions have recently arisen with respect to the relationship of lawyer referral to the neighborhood law offices for the poor, which are developing under the federal government's anti-poverty program. One proposal is that organizations other than bar associations should be permitted to conduct lawyer referral programs. The proposal is, of course, included in the broader issue of group legal services, to be discussed in chapter 7. A few observations may be appropriate here, however.

Because neighborhood law offices for the poor will turn up substantial numbers of people who need to be referred to private lawyers, it is important that local bar associations work closely with them in setting up adequate referral arrangements. Similar efforts with labor unions and other groups are also called for. Lawyer referral is properly a bar function, and one in which the bar ought to be involved wherever that function is performed. But if the bar refuses to provide adequately for the public's needs, then a referral service provided by a non-bar group is surely preferable to no service at all.

The variety of opinion on the subject of the merger of lawyer referral and legal aid and on the related subject of lawyer referral programs conducted by non-bar groups, together with the corresponding variety of approach to solving the problems involved, suggest an important point about the objectives of lawyer referral. It seems clear that lawyer referral has not been shaped with reference to any specific potential clientele. Rather, it has aimed to provide access to lawyers for an undifferentiated general segment of the community. The only common characteristics of this public that have been deemed significant are the modesty of their means and the fact that they do not have pre-existing professional relationships with lawyers. Beyond this, it has simply been assumed that the potential clientele is substantially uniform in outlook, in orientation to the law and lawyers, in occupational affiliation and, within broad limits, in the nature of their need for legal services. From this premise it has been concluded that a single "strategy" for providing lawyers' services is appropriate. Furthermore, these assumptions accommodate a "strategy" that involves minimal departure from traditional methods of establishing the lawyer-client relationship. It may be possible that these assumptions are true, although many considerations to the contrary suggest themselves. The bar has never systematically questioned them, however, and thus it has never had to confront the problems that would be presented should these assumptions in fact be erroneous. And if these assumptions are not well founded—as, indeed, seems likely—the extent of permissible departure from traditional methods of establishing the lawyer-client relationship and the nature of the appropriate "strategy" for providing lawyers' services might be seen quite differently: The program *should* provide a convenient and readily accessible response to the legal problems of those on the verge of indigency who go to a legal aid office for free service but are unable, for one reason or another, to get help there. It should also provide a referral procedure appropriate to the requirements of the person of some means who knows what he needs, who is willing and able to pay for it, and who wants simply to be put in touch with the right lawyer. And it should make suitable provision for the needs of all those members of the public in between, whatever their needs happen to be.

This implies that the ideal lawyer referral service ought to be a multi-faceted service rather than a "one-track" system. Simple telephone referral may be the best possible way of serving the knowledgeable person who simply wants to be put in touch with "a good real estate lawyer." Such an arrangement may be quite inadequate to meet the needs of the unsophisticated person who needs a great deal of help in order even to identify his problem. Similarly, while the operation of lawyer referral and legal aid through the same facilities may be a good way to facilitate the referral to private lawyers of people who had first sought free service from the legal aid organization, it is almost certainly not an acceptable approach to providing services to people higher on the economic ladder. Indeed, any program closely identified with a welfare-charity type institution such as legal aid is likely to have little appeal to the vast majority of Americans who do not regard themselves as "poor," and a merger of the two programs would likely have the practical effect of limiting the scope of the lawyer referral program to the "spillover" from legal aid.

The answer would seem to be a lawyer referral program employing a variety of approaches appropriate to the varied needs of the entire public. The program would include a telephone referral system to serve, in a most convenient way, those whose legal problems do not require a personal interview; it would include some kind of direct referral procedure to enable legal aid offices and the new neighborhood law offices being established under the war on poverty to make referrals directly for clients they are unable to serve but who need to be sent to private lawyers; it would include a separate lawyer referral office to serve those whose problems could not be handled adequately through a telephone referral; and it might include other kinds of arrangements, as experience may suggest.

The lawyer referral service is but a bridge between lawyers and the public, and, like any thoroughfare, the traffic it carries will be determined in large part by how conveniently and how expeditiously it does its job. Much can yet be done to make legal services more accessible to the public by making lawyer referral services more convenient for people to use.

4
*Public
Attitudes*

What effect does the lawyer referral plan have upon the public's attitudes about law, lawyers, and legal services, and what effect may it be expected to have in the future? People can be expected to make use of a service only if they know that it exists and that they may benefit from it. This is true of any program contemplating a public response. It is no less true of legal services, and a successful program for providing such services to the public will be one that communicates effectively.

The profession has traditionally been hostile toward any kind of advertising or solicitation of business by lawyers, insisting that a lawyer's practice should be built through the acquisition of a deserved reputation for competence and integrity. Though there are sound reasons for this position, it has caused the bar to see the matter of public communication almost entirely from the

lawyer's point of view—i.e., the obtaining of clients by lawyers—and virtually to ignore the public's need to know about
the law and the services lawyers can provide. Only in recent
years has the bar developed any significant concern about
bar-public communication, and even now the emphasis is on
"public relations" rather than on informing the public about
legal problems and the availability of legal services.

The lawyer referral plan potentially could serve these purposes. The American Bar Association Committee on Lawyer
Referral Service has long urged local bars to conduct adequate
public information and publicity programs on behalf of their
lawyer referral services (41:26–29, 55–65; 43), and the Association's Committee on Professional Ethics has upheld the ethical
propriety of such efforts (*ABA Eth. Ops.*, No. 227; see also Nos.
13, 179, 191, 205, and 291). Advertising on behalf of bar-
sponsored referral services has also been held proper by at least
one state supreme court (386). Despite this, the impact of the
lawyer referral service upon public knowledge and attitudes
about law, lawyers, and available legal services appears to have
been small.[25] The bar's traditional hostility toward advertising
and solicitation of business by individual lawyers has inhibited
the acceptance of publicity efforts on behalf of referral services,
and some bar associations attempt to operate lawyer referral
services without attempting to reach the public with any kind of
effective message. A few provide no publicly visible indicia of
their existence—no telephone listing, no office or sign, no cards
or brochures, nothing at all even to let the public know that the
service is available, much less to induce people to use it. Some
have an ordinary telephone listing and nothing more.

Perhaps the most widely accepted publicity device is the
listing in the classified telephone directory.[26] Practice varies
from an ordinary listing, buried in the middle of the "Attorneys"

25. Perhaps the best evidence of this fact is in the statistics of the lawyer referral
services themselves. The extent to which the public is induced to make use of the referral
service is a good indication of the program's effect upon public knowledge and attitudes.
It has been estimated by one authority (336:193-95) that an adequate system of properly
run referral services would refer over 1 million new clients to practicing lawyers each
year. Even more striking is the conjecture that if the entire population of the country
were being served by referral services as effective as the best one reporting in the 1964
Annual Survey, the total number of referrals could conceivably be as high as 4 million.
When compared with the 156,291 referrals actually made in 1967, these figures at least
suggest that lawyer referral services are having much too slight an effect upon public
knowledge and attitudes about law, lawyers, and legal services.
26. In the 1967 Survey, 160 services reported using this device.

section of the classified directory, to a quarter-page advertisement. This Yellow Pages listing is generally conceded to be the most effective publicity device employed by lawyer referral services. The reason, perhaps, is that it is the only one most of them use. Other approaches that have proved in a few instances to be unusually productive have not yet been widely tried.[27]

Pamphlets, distributed usually through banks and similar institutions, are sometimes used. The broadcast media—radio and television—are utilized in a few instances, almost all of which involve free public service programs. Much the same thing is true of newspaper publicity. A number of referral services receive free newspaper coverage through news stories, human-interest stories, feature articles, and editorials, but only rarely do they resort to paid advertising. Among various other publicity devices used by lawyer referral services, posters are fairly common, but the use of billboards is rare (see **258**). One suggestion yet to be tried is the use of a symbol of some sort to provide a means of graphic identification of the program, perhaps accompanied by a new eye-catching and more descriptive name.

Publicity programs in connection with lawyer referral services appear to have been effective in stimulating public awareness concerning legal services (see **257**). Individual referral services have noted the way in which changes in the publicity effort are reflected in the number of people who utilize lawyer referral to obtain legal services.[28] Furthermore, certain referral services that consistently devote time, thought, and effort to the task of

27. According to the 1963 Survey, those referral services that used no publicity whatever averaged only 1.29 referrals that year for each 10,000 of population; where the Yellow Pages were used, the average was 10.36 per 10,000; and where other publicity efforts were also employed, the average climbed to 15.86 per 10,000. This seems to say that while use of the Yellow Pages increased the average number of referrals nearly tenfold, the other publicity efforts raised the average by only 50 percent. Though these figures do demonstrate the value of the Yellow Pages listing, they are somewhat misleading with regard to the other publicity efforts, however, because in the great majority of cases these "other publicity efforts" consisted of no more than a few pamphlets left with social service agencies, a single small human-interest story in a newspaper, a few letters to local employers, or a single radio program in which the lawyer referral service was mentioned casually. In only a very few places have referral services been publicized in really comprehensive and intensive public information programs. But where this *has* been done, the results have been quite dramatic, and some of the other publicity efforts have been especially productive in certain localities. The San Bernardino County (Cal.) Bar Association, for example, supplements its Lawyer Reference Service's listing in the Yellow Pages with continuous paid newspaper advertising, and in 1967 the service made 63.6 referrals per 10,000 population. In Burbank (Cal.) the Lawyer Referral Service, publicized continuously through newspapers, posters, pamphlets, and contacts with employers in addition to the Yellow Pages listing, made 87.3 referrals per 10,000.

28. E.g., Columbus, Ohio, and Pittsburgh, Pennsylvania (see **42A**:2, **43A**:1).

reaching the public and stimulating it to use the service are making records that indicate something of the real potential of the plan. In the 1964 Survey, while the national average for all of the referral services reporting was only 10.7 cases per 10,000 population, 9 of the services reported referral rates of more than 50 per 10,000 population, 4 had rates of 100 referrals per 10,000 population, and 1 had a rate of 254 (44A:1-4). The enormous differences in traffic between the most active service and the national average indicates the breadth of the gap that intensive publicity might help to close. The potential effects of mass-audience publicity are also suggested by experience in the medical field: the single most important stimulator of awareness and concern about specific medical problems — heart disease and cancer, for example — is mass-media advertising and information (131:103-88).

One of the main obstacles to the use of the mass communications media is the great cost. The loosely organized bar finds it difficult to accumulate the kind of capital necessary to finance such programs. This difficulty can perhaps be at least partly overcome by greater efforts to obtain the cooperation and assistance of sympathetic business institutions.

Although the largely unexploited possibilities of mass-media communication seem important, more sharply focused programs of public information appear from experience to have even greater direct effects. Of particular significance is the success of efforts directed toward reaching people through the institutions with which they are connected — most notably through their places of employment but also through labor unions, churches, public agencies, and similar institutions. Experience seems to suggest that the most effective way to persuade people to obtain needed legal services is by working with and through these institutions (see 334:579-81). In passing, it might be noted that these are the same kinds of institutions that often develop group legal service plans, a fact that would not appear to be entirely coincidental. Only a few bar associations have even begun to explore this approach, however.

The lawyer referral plan's impact on public knowledge and attitudes is potentially great, but comparatively little is presently being done in this field. If lawyer referral is to realize its potential, local bar associations will have to undertake continuous and comprehensive public education programs designed to tell the public, in understandable language, when a lawyer's help is needed, why it is needed, and how to go about getting the help. And a substantial portion of this effort must be devoted to reaching people through the institutions with which they are associated.

C
Conclusions

Even though the lawyer referral plan is bringing legal services of one kind or another to more than 100,000 people each year, the inadequacy of the plan as it presently exists in most communities is apparent. "Reaching" 100,000 people out of an adult population of over 100 million is a minuscule effect—less than 1 in 1,000. Moreover, with rare exceptions, lawyer referral does almost nothing to insure that clients will be sent to lawyers competent to handle their particular cases. It has no discernible effect upon the suitability of lawyers' services to the problems of people of moderate means. It has only a minor bearing upon the price of the services provided. Though in some places it does make lawyers' services more convenient and accessible to the public, in far too many places the plan is a mere gesture toward introducing the public and the profession to each other. And, generally speaking, it contributes little toward public knowledge and attitudes about law, lawyers, and legal services.

If the magnitude of the potential were seriously grasped by the bar and traditional inhibitions modified so that more effective programs could be worked out, lawyer referral could have great promise. Through the use of special panels, appropriate restrictions upon panel membership, and rational methods of selecting the panel lawyers to handle particular cases, the plan could insure that the legal services it offers to the public are of high quality. With large numbers of cases of a similar kind being sent to the lawyers best qualified to handle them, the plan might thus contribute to developing the kinds of legal services best suited to the problems of people of moderate means. In the same way, the plan might well come to have some beneficial effect upon the price of at least routine legal services. Through the adoption of more convenient and expeditious referral procedures and through consistent effort in public education and publicity—particularly effort exerted through the institutions with which people of moderate means are connected—the plan could reasonably be expected to reach and serve many times the number of people now receiving legal help. In short, the plan can be infinitely more effective than it now is.

What accounts for the present gap between the plan's performance and its apparent potential? What is the prospect that the gap can be closed and the lawyer referral service made a really effective mechanism for providing legal services to the public?

The principal cause of the plan's failure to live up to expectations must surely be the bar's traditional conservatism and resistance to change. This conservatism has been sustained by the absence—until very recently—of the kind of dramatic events that would give compelling urgency to the bar's efforts to serve people of moderate means. The typical attitude has been, "It may be all right in places where they need it, but people in our community have no problem finding a lawyer." It has taken the recent clamor over group legal services to arouse even a small segment of the bar to the seriousness of the problem of unmet legal needs.

Another factor is the bar's failure to commit significant resources to the promotion of lawyer referral and a lack of consistency in promotional efforts. The American Bar Association Committee on Lawyer Referral Service has championed the cause with vigor, but only recently has the Association begun to commit any significant portion of its financial resources to promotion of the plan.

It may also be observed that the American Bar Association's approach to promotion has thus far been relatively diffident. The emphasis has been on trying to sell the *idea*, leaving the details of its implementation almost completely to the local bar associations. The Association Committee has only suggested general principles, supplemented by information about the alternatives being employed in different communities. As a consequence, bar associations accepting the plan have usually undertaken the least effective alternatives, for the simple reason that these choices least disrupt the status quo and require the least in funds and effort. Paradoxically, however, experience suggests that many local bar associations, when they become newly interested in the plan, do not want alternative plans from which to choose. They appear to prefer a "model" plan—with detailed rules and forms already prepared—that needs only to be adopted and put into effect. After 30 years of experience, someone should now be able to say, "This is the way it *should* be done, and here are the details of how to do it." One hopeful sign has been the report on the subject by the American Bar Association Committee on Availability of Legal Services (28:580) and the resulting action of the American Bar Association Lawyer Referral Committee in formulating and promulgating a specific and progressive "Statement of Standards and Practices for Lawyer Referral Services" (29:189). Whether this will prompt local bar associations to take the desired action remains to be seen.

Among the state bars, the leader in promoting lawyer referral has been the State Bar of California, which in recent years has provided a professional staff to push its development. And, as noted earlier, one of the recommendations of the California Group Legal Services Committee was that the bar should experiment with expanded and improved lawyer referral services. It is not surprising then, that the movement is strongest in California. Other state bar organizations have generally been far less vigorous in promoting the plan. Similarly, reception of the plan at the local bar level has been disappointing.

Aside from problems of promotion, one further reason for the lawyer referral plan's generally disappointing performance must surely be lack of adequate critical study. No one—either at the national level or at the local level—has ever known just how well or how poorly the plan has been functioning. It is true that surveys of lawyer referral services have been made from time to time in the past, but only in recent years have they been made in sufficient detail and with sufficient consistency to permit use of the data for anything but the broadest of generalizations about the plan. And even now, conclusions about the effectiveness of the lawyer referral program from the public's point of view can be little more than guesses, pending careful follow-up studies of referral cases and clients. In the absence of adequate information, proponents of the plan have simply assumed that it is working well, an assumption that effectively dampens any impulse toward change or improvement.

Finally, beyond the need for better information is the need for more adventuresome experimentation. Indeed, the effectiveness of the lawyer referral plan could be increased substantially through the intelligent and vigorous application of those ideas that have already been advanced or tested in use. Even such modest "experimentation" would be an improvement, and the use of real imagination might yield truly gratifying results.

Lawyer referral is a modest program, disturbing cherished traditions far less than some of the more radical transformations that may one day be forced upon the legal profession as a result of its failure to adapt to changing public needs. The plan can be effective, but it will become so only through a substantial commitment—of resources, of course, but above all a commitment to change itself—at all levels of the organized bar. This is the kind of commitment that would cause lawyer referral to become truly effective as a method of making lawyers' services available to people of moderate means.

VI

Special
Law Offices
for People of
Moderate Means

Discussion of the problems of making lawyers' services more readily available to people of moderate means has thus far centered upon the rendition of services through traditional law practice. It leads naturally to a related question: Might legal services be better provided to people of moderate means through some special kind of facility, such as a low-cost legal service bureau or something of the sort?

The question is not new. Karl Llewellyn commented in 1938 about the need for a facility to provide legal help to people who can pay something, but not full fees, for the services they require (194).* The same idea was discussed in 1947 by Reginald Heber Smith, who, like Llewellyn, saw a possibility that such agencies might grow out of bar-sponsored lawyer referral services (287). In more recent years, Louis M. Brown has called for the development of special low-cost law offices within the framework of private practice (80). And one type of special legal service facility, the Philadelphia Neighborhood Law Office, has actually been in existence for thirty years.[1]

Might one of these arrangements, or some other nontraditional form of law practice, have promise as a method of dispensing legal services at reduced cost to people of moderate means?

_____

*Citations in boldface type refer the reader to the numbered "Works Cited" at 297–313; where numbers immediately follow the boldface reference, the reader is referred to specific pages in that work.

1. For a description of the Philadelphia Neighborhood Law Office Program, see Abrahams (3).

A

The Objectives
of a Special
Legal Service Facility

Perhaps it would be well to begin by reviewing the objectives appropriate for a special legal service facility. The goal of such a facility should be to provide legal services to people of moderate means as effectively as possible. To do so, it would have to deal successfully with those factors defined earlier as the elements affecting the public's use of lawyers' services—quality, cost, accessibility, and public knowledge and attitudes.

It is no doubt possible, as a matter of pure theory, to design a special legal service facility that would respond with complete effectiveness to all of these factors. But those schemes that have thus far been either tried or proposed have—even when offered by someone as imaginative as Llewellyn—fallen short of being complete responses. Generally, the problem of quality is addressed only indirectly. The cost problem is only partly solved. And while some proposals would seem to promise at least partial effectiveness in making lawyers accessible to the public, none of them would go the whole way in bringing lawyers and clients together.

The reason must be that speculation about low-cost legal service facilities makes sense only when it takes into account the very real practical obstacles involved. Thus, the various proposals are not expressions of theoretically ideal ways of dispensing low-cost legal services to people of moderate means, but rather they are estimates of what might be reasonably effective and feasible.

So, too, with this present examination of the concept of low-cost legal service facilities. The potential effectiveness of such facilities will be considered in the context of the problems that thus far appear to have inhibited their growth.

B

Conflicting
Interests

Why have special low-cost legal service facilities thus far

failed to develop in any effective form, even though the idea appears to make such eminent good sense? The answer probably lies in conflicting values and interests, for while the concept does seem responsive to the essential issues, it also brings significant interests into conflict. Perhaps these conflicting interests can best be examined by looking separately at two different approaches to low-cost legal service. One is based upon what is essentially a private practice model, although not traditional private practice, while the other encompasses an institutionalized model.

1
Private Low-cost
Law Offices

Professor Brown advocates an essentially private practice approach. It would involve independent lawyers who would assume the risks and receive the rewards of private practice (see, generally, 80). The model differs from traditional private practice in three ways, however. First, it would have a different orientation and different objectives from those of most traditional law practice arrangements. It would be directed specifically toward the problems of people of moderate means, thus concentrating primarily on small matters for which only small fees could be justified. In theory, at least, the lawyers who participated would not be principally concerned, as many private practitioners now seem to be, with attracting and keeping the "better" business or the "better" clients. Rather, the main objective would be the efficient handling of a large number of small matters. Second, the volume handling of small cases at a profit would probably require the adoption of techniques and procedures quite different from those of traditional private practice. Division of labor, routinization of procedures, standardization of forms and materials, use of nonprofessional personnel—all would have to be brought to a high state of development if private law offices were to be able to offer these kinds of legal services at acceptably low cost while providing reasonable financial rewards to the lawyers. And third, some deviation from traditional professional restrictions would be necessary, particularly with respect to activities by which clients are obtained.

The Philadelphia Neighborhood Law Office program has thus far been the profession's most notable effort to develop private low-cost law offices. It would seem to offer an ideal setting for a discussion of the values and interests challenged by the private practice approach to low-cost legal services.[2]

Under the Philadelphia plan, Neighborhood Law Offices are private law offices intended to make competent legal services available at modest cost to people of moderate means in the neighborhoods where such people live, work, and shop. A lawyer may establish an approved Neighborhood Law Office only with the permission of the Philadelphia Bar Association, which inquires into such matters as the suitability of the neighborhood and the qualifications of the lawyer. If approval is given, the lawyer must agree to charge clients no more than five dollars for the first half-hour consultation and base other fees upon the Bar Association's minimum fee schedule. In addition, he must agree to keep his Neighborhood Office open at least fifteen hours a week and abide by certain other rules regarding records, reports, and similar matters.

In return the Bar Association permits the lawyer to display an illuminated sign to identify his office as a Neighborhood Law Office. He may also be listed in the classified telephone directory under a separate Neighborhood Law Offices listing. The fee schedule and a certificate showing good standing in the program may also be displayed in the office. In addition, the Philadelphia Bar Association provides a limited amount of institutional-type advertising on behalf of the program.

In keeping with the objectives of the plan, Neighborhood Law Offices are located in well-traveled areas near the centers of business in the neighborhoods. Both for economy and to avoid any of the client-inhibiting effects of ostentation, a conscious effort is made to keep the furnishings, decor, and general appearance of the offices unpretentious and harmonious with their surroundings.

The Neighborhood Offices are independent of each other. They are also independent of both legal aid and lawyer referral. Although downtown lawyers may take part in the program, they

2. The following information comes largely from the *Manual of Instructions for Neighborhood Law Offices*, published in 1964 by the Philadelphia Bar Association, and from the author's own observations, made during a visit to Philadelphia in May 1965. See also Abrahams (2); Committee Report (118); Abrahams (1).

may not operate Neighborhood Offices as branches of downtown firms. A few lawyers practice full time in Neighborhood Law Offices, but most of those who participate appear to do so only on a part-time basis. Of special significance is the fact that the Neighborhood Offices have never been subsidized. The lawyers who operate them take all the risks and reap whatever profits there are. While some offices have succeeded, others have failed.

In the most recent year for which reports are available (1968), twenty-one Neighborhood Law Offices performed legal services for 4,042 clients. Of these cases, approximately 54 percent required nothing more than a short consultation.[3] It is estimated that one case in eight is profitable to the lawyer, the occasional profitable cases paying the way for those that are not (see 3:730). Since the program's inception, well over 100,000 clients have received legal services from Neighborhood Law Offices (3:728).

The Philadelphia Neighborhood Law Office program has been at least modestly successful as a method of making lawyers' services more readily available to people of moderate means. Its most notable impact seems to have been in the field of accessibility: It has put lawyers where the people are. It has no doubt also had some effect upon the quality of the services available, primarily through careful selection of the lawyers who are permitted to practice in the Neighborhood Offices. In addition, although the Bar Association's continuing supervision over the operation of the Offices has been directed mainly at things other than the quality of the services rendered, the mere fact of supervision probably has some beneficial effect upon quality. As will be discussed more fully, the program has also taken some small steps toward solving the cost problem and has made some minor concessions to the need for publicity and other measures for bringing lawyers and clients together. At least modest success in all this is suggested both by the program's longevity and by the number of cases that Neighborhood Law Offices have handled over the years.

At the same time, it would also seem fair to say that the program's achievements have been somewhat short of optimal. The cumulative figure — 100,000 cases since the beginning of the

---

3. Statistics from a report prepared by Isadore Winderman, Attorney-in-Charge of the Philadelphia Lawyer Reference Service, who is also administrator of the Neighborhood Law Office Plan.

program — sounds impressive, to be sure. But 4,000 cases a year do not constitute an overwhelming response from a total population of nearly 5 million (317:19), particularly when this performance is compared with the nearly 35,000 cases handled in 1967 by agencies providing legal services to the poor in Philadelphia.[4] Moreover, there would seem to be some significance in the fact that the program has not been adopted anywhere else in the country, despite the favorable comment it has received both in legal periodicals and in the popular press.[5]

There appear to be a number of reasons for the program's failure to achieve more than this limited success. All have to do with the values and interests that would be brought into conflict by the measures that would be necessary to make the program really effective.

One factor seriously limiting the success of the Neighborhood Law Office program is the apparent inability of such small general-practice law offices using traditional procedures to effect any significant reduction in the price of legal services. Economies in rent and other overhead expenses make it possible for Neighborhood Offices to offer an initial half-hour consultation with a lawyer for only five dollars, an amount well below what half an hour of service would cost under the time charges of most lawyers. This is not entirely inconsequential, as over half the matters brought to Neighborhood Offices are problems requiring no more than this brief consultation.

But the program appears to have less effect on fees for services beyond the initial consultation. Some observers have privately expressed the belief that the fees charged by Neighborhood Law Offices are generally lower than those charged by lawyers not under the program who practice in similar localities, but there have been no studies to verify this. The differential, if any exists, is probably small, limited as it is by the inexorable economics of traditional law practice.

Nor is there evidence that the Neighborhood Offices have in fact developed any special techniques for the efficient and profitable handling of small cases that would make possible any substantial reductions in fees. Traditional law offices in almost

4. The Philadelphia Legal Aid Society handled 11,502 cases in 1967, while the Community Legal Service program handled 21,932. See ABA Committee on Legal Aid and Indigent Defendants (48).

5. See note 2 supra. Among national magazines that have carried articles on the program are Saturday Evening Post, Atlantic Monthly, and Coronet (see 2.729).

every sense, they appear to have produced no real cost-reducing innovations. Indeed, it is not even claimed that the efficient handling of small cases is the basis for the program's economic viability; rather the Neighborhood Offices are economically successful because one case in eight is substantial and, in a low-overhead operation, able to pay the way for the seven that are not profitable even at regular fees. Moreover, because the fees of Neighborhood Law Offices are tied to the Bar Association's minimum fee schedule, there are close limits on the extent to which economies in practice are likely to be passed on to clients in the form of lower fees, even if such economies were achieved.

The relative lack of success of Neighborhood Law Offices in the poorer neighborhoods tends to support the conclusion that they have not achieved any significant price breakthrough. They seem to thrive in solid middle-class neighborhoods where, presumably, they are least needed, but they appear marginal at best in the poorer localities where the need for a low-cost legal service agency would seem to be greatest.[6]

It is not a foregone conclusion that any system would be able to dispense legal services profitably at fees that could and would be paid by clients on the verge of indigency. But a low-cost legal service facility that benefited only the upper middle class and left the near-poor without service could hardly be counted a complete and genuine success.

Assuming for the moment that some kind of private practice system *could* provide low-cost legal services at a profit, why hasn't such a system developed, even in as favorable a setting as that provided by the Philadelphia Neighborhood Law Offices program?

The conflict seems to turn on what is essentially a matter of style. The profitable handling of small cases for low fees, if possible at all, would probably require a greater change in the style of law practice than most lawyers are willing to accept. Any routine, mass-production style of practice would be unacceptable to nearly all lawyers, even when undertaken for the laudable purpose of providing legal services to people who could

6. There have been no statistical studies to show just where the program is successful and where it is not. The one real authority on the program, however, acknowledges that not all Neighborhood Offices are successful and that one factor in success or lack of it seems to be the economic status of the neighborhood (2:729). The author's own observation of the Neighborhood Offices confirms this conclusion by Mr. Abrahams.

not otherwise obtain legal help. The entire lawyer ethos, the dream that drives young men though law school and sustains older lawyers in what are often difficult practice situations, is something far removed from the mass production of routine remedies for trivial cases. Instead, both the lawyer and the prospective lawyer tend to see themselves in much grander roles — not as mechanical purveyors of routine services in mundane and inconsequential cases, but as defenders of life and liberty and as counselors to the nation's great and vital businesses. As a result, real low-cost law practice could not be expected to appeal to most lawyers or potential lawyers, nor could any but the most inconsequential changes in the style of law practice be expected to find acceptance — unless, perhaps, the low-cost legal service program could somehow acquire the crusade spirit of legal service programs for the poor, along with the economic underpinning that makes a crusade possible. The Philadelphia Neighborhood Law Office experience suggests that, while young idealistic lawyers may be found to provide legal services to people of moderate means in a near-traditional style, neither their idealism nor the tolerance of the older members of the bar extends to the kind of innovations in practice that would make such offices genuinely low-cost facilities.

A second major conflict involves possible measures for bringing lawyers and clients together. Substantially increasing the availability of lawyers to people of moderate means probably requires more than simply putting lawyers in the neighborhoods; affirmative measures seem necessary to apprise people of the service and convince them of its value. Philadelphia's Neighborhood Law Office program acknowledges this fact in providing some collective advertising for approved Neighborhood Offices and in permitting individual offices to use illuminated signs and be listed in special classified telephone directory listings. While these measures seem far from adequate to educate people about their needs for legal services and to bring them together with lawyers, even this modest relaxation of professional restrictions raises a thorny question: Does the benefit derived by the public from Neighborhood Law Offices justify giving the lawyers who practice in them this kind of competitive preference over lawyers who are not under the program but who practice, or might wish to practice, in the same neighborhoods?

Approval as a Neighborhood Law Office is, in fact, a kind of exclusive franchise; only approved offices may call themselves "Neighborhood Law Offices," and only one such office is ever approved for a given neighborhood. Furthermore, there are some neighborhoods where the official Neighborhood Law Office competes directly with other private law offices not under the program. But so far, the competitive preference given to Neighborhood Offices seems not to have caused unbearable friction. This is no doubt because the slight degree to which professional restrictions have thus far been relaxed has not permitted the Neighborhood Offices to employ effective measures for getting clients; and fear of friction is probably the primary reason that Neighborhood Law Offices have not been allowed to use effective means of reaching the clients they are supposed to be serving.

This, of course, is a conflict implicit in any private-practice approach to low-cost legal service. Do the benefits offered to the public by private low-cost law offices justify giving one group of lawyers the competitive advantage they will almost surely need to reach the clients they are to serve? So far, the legal profession has been extremely reluctant to grant such competitive advantage to any segment of the privately practicing bar for any purpose. This issue would have to be met squarely before any private low-cost law office scheme would have any chance of real success.

2

*Low-cost
Legal Service Bureau*

The approach envisioned by Llewellyn and Smith follows an institutional model, more nearly analogous to institutionalized legal aid than to private law practice. Indeed, Llewellyn anticipated an ultimate merger of the legal aid and low-cost legal service functions (194:122-25).[7] The distinctive characteristic of the idea is the use of salaried lawyers in an institutional setting

---

7. In effect, the merging of legal aid and low-cost legal service functions would simply mean raising the legal aid elegibility standards to include people of moderate means as well as the poor and requiring the recipients of service to contribute to the cost according to their means.

to perform low-cost legal services for people of moderate means. Moreover, both Llewellyn and Smith seem to have assumed that the cost of providing competent service would exceed the amounts clients would be able to pay, despite economies and efficiencies in practice. Thus, the model seems also to contemplate some kind of subsidy from the bar, from charity, or from some other source.

Llewellyn put his finger on the essential problem with the institutional model when he warned that some procedure would be necessary to insure that occasional profitable cases went to practicing lawyers (194:124). Clearly, a low-cost legal service bureau's handling of cases that private lawyers might handle at a profit would conflict directly with the economic interests of part of the practicing bar. Fear that paying clients would thus be diverted from private lawyers no doubt accounts for much of the resistance to the low-cost legal service bureau idea. Indeed, this fear is sometimes even a source of opposition to legal aid for the poor.

But perhaps the problem is more pervasive even than Llewellyn suggested. There are lawyers — marginal, to be sure, but lawyers nevertheless — to whom even the "uneconomic" case is desirable. When a lawyer is underemployed, with more time than clients, even the smallest fee is profitable. After all, it is better to be doing something for a small fee than to be doing nothing for no fee. Thus, the interests of a segment of the bar — the underemployed — conflict with any low-cost legal service bureau idea that would handle even the smaller and less remunerative cases.

But there is more to it than this. The client of moderate means is important to the underemployed private lawyer not simply for the small fee to be earned from a little problem, nor solely for the chance that occasionally the case will be a sizable one. Such a client represents, in addition, the private lawyer's source of exposure to a wider potential clientele. A steady stream of moderate-income clients through the office of a practicing lawyer means not only a steady stream of small fees and an occasional large one, but also the possibility of getting referred cases — including, perhaps, some of the "better" business — from the families, friends, and acquaintances of this original moderate-income clientele. Today's client in a trivial traffic case may have an uncle who tomorrow will be looking for a lawyer to incorporate a new business that may one day grow into a big business. Any low-cost legal service bureau that cuts off the flow of moderate-income clients thus impairs the growth potential of the lawyer's practice, and in doing so it conflicts seriously with the lawyer's economic interests.

Of course, we are here talking about only a segment of the bar. Lawyers whose practices are well established and who are busy with substantial and profitable legal business usually have little time to spend on small matters on the mere chance that they will bring in more "good" business. But there are still lawyers who do have the time and who genuinely need the smaller cases, both to sustain them in practice and to sustain their hopes for growth. This conflicting economic interest has surely been a large factor in preventing the development of low-cost legal service bureaus in the past, and it will no doubt continue to stand as an obstacle to the development of such agencies in the future.

The problem of advertising and publicity, on the other hand, would not appear to be nearly so difficult in the institutional approach as in the private practice approach. The experience of both legal aid and lawyer referral suggests that reasons deemed weighty enough in the first place to justify the institutionalization of a portion of the legal services distribution system will probably also be sufficient to justify at least some relaxation of restrictions on client-getting activities (356; 386). Or perhaps it is simply that once the practicing bar relinquishes its claim to serve a particular clientele and turns it over to an institutionalized service mechanism, it is no longer so intensely concerned with competitive advantage as regards that clientele and therefore is less concerned with traditional inhibitions on client-getting activities.

Similarly, practice style seems also to be a less pressing concern where the need for institutionalization has been accepted. No one seems unduly bothered, at any rate, by the fact that the style of practice in legal aid offices may be somewhat different from the traditional style of private practice. Again, perhaps the reasons that support institutionalization also support acceptance of the necessary changes in style. Or, possibly, it is simply that lawyers who enter institutionalized practice are no longer seen by other lawyers as being "real" lawyers. Thus, because their fellows no longer fear injury from identification with them, in-

stitutional lawyers tend to become partially exempt from requirements of style.

Maybe this all boils down to a simple dichotomy. On the one
hand, a special low-cost law office on the private practice model
runs into difficulty with the lawyer's conception of himself as a
professional and of what it means to be a lawyer. The model
cannot become reality so long as the lawyer sees himself and his
role in a way that will not permit the changes in practice necessary to provide truly low-cost service or in the business-getting
methods necessary to reach the desired clientele. On the other
hand, a special legal service office based on the institutional
model—a low-cost legal service bureau—encounters problems
with conflicting economic interests. As long as a legal service
bureau would conflict with a significant economic interest of a
consequential segment of the bar, it could become a reality only
if it offered some counterbalancing advantage to the bar or if its
social value were to come to be seen as so great and compelling
as to justify sacrificing the conflicting economic interests of particular lawyers.

C
Some
Possible Answers

1
The Private Practice
Approach

One possibility for an effective low-cost legal service facility
on the private practice model involves a subsidy. If the handling
of small matters cannot be made profitable except through
changes in practice style unacceptable to the bar, then perhaps a
system in which part of the cost is borne by someone other than
the recipient of the services would provide a workable answer.

This is the approach taken in the English Legal Aid and
Advice Schemes, described in chapter 2. Lawyers provide
services in the traditional manner to the poor and to people of
moderate means; the recipients pay for the services received
according to their means; and public funds are used to com-

pensate the lawyers for the difference between adequate fees and what the clients are able to pay.

Much the same thing is done in this country in the so-called Judicare experiments under the OEO Legal Services program. Utilized primarily in rural areas, the Judicare programs reimburse private lawyers for services provided without charge to the indigent. However, as these programs are limited to the poor, they make no provision for contribution by the recipient of the service (see **255; 274**).

It may be feasible to use the subsidy idea in developing low-cost legal service facilities on the private practice model. For example, some kind of subsidy arrangement might enable facilities like the Philadelphia Neighborhood Law Offices to offer services at greatly reduced fees. Or, a Judicare program might be expanded to cover the services of traditional private practitioners not only to the poor, but also to people of moderate means on a contributory basis. Either approach would make possible the furnishing of truly low-cost services without drastic changes in practice style.

The subsidy idea is not without problems, however. As such a program would involve private practitioners, it would no doubt encounter the profession's customary reluctance to relax restrictions on client-getting activities or give one lawyer competitive advantage over another. Thus, the program might have difficulty in reaching the people intended to be served. A serious policy question would also be raised. Is it an acceptable use of public funds to subsidize the rendition of legal services in the traditional manner if the same services might be rendered at substantially less cost in some other manner? This is the issue being posed by those who oppose Judicare because of its high cost per case as compared with the cost per case in institutionalized legal service offices (e.g., **163**:429; **207**:12; **274**:1003). When resources are inadequate, it is hard to justify their use merely to preserve the style of traditional law practice. For the present, then, a subsidy to private lawyers for the providing of services to people of moderate means seems to be a fairly remote possibility.

But a recent development is encouraging as a possibility for development of low-cost legal service facilities on a private practice model. One large metropolitan law firm in Baltimore has opened a branch office to provide free legal services to the poor.[8] The expenses of the office, the costs of litigation, and the salaries of the lawyers who staff the office are being paid by the firm. Moreover, all of the firm's resources will be available to its poverty law office. This notable manifestation of dedication to the ideal of public service could be the beginning of a dynamic new concept of professionalism. If the concept included not only free services for the poor but also reduced-fee services for those able to pay part but not all of the cost of needed services, and if it also embraces the view that the lawyer has a duty to take effective steps to reach out and bring in those people who need his services, it may result in the best of all possible low-cost legal service facilities. The experiment will certainly bear watching.

2

The Institutional Approach

There seem to be two possibilities for development of low-cost legal service facilities on the institutional model. The first is the one discussed at length in the following chapter—group legal services. Lay groups or organizations may undertake to supply legal services to their members as a benefit of membership, either without charge or at reduced fees. Such programs appear to offer advantages of cost, quality, and accessibility. A group program is also likely to enjoy the confidence of potential clients to a significant degree because of trust in the sponsoring institution.

Group legal services do conflict with the economic interests of some segments of the practicing bar, but their chances of success nevertheless appear good. There are two main reasons. First, they offer the bar a counterbalancing economic benefit. They promise an over-all increase in the utilization of legal services by people of moderate means; thus, while they may take legal business away from some lawyers, the net result to the bar as a whole should be economic benefit. And second, the question of

8. This is the Baltimore firm of Piper and Marbury. See Office of Economic Opportunity (320). Note, however, that one of the members of the firm who helped to work out the program was E. Clinton Bamberger, first permanent director of the OEO Legal Services program. This would seem to be a special incentive not enjoyed by most firms. On the other hand, desire to demonstrate public spirit equal to that of Piper and Marbury may well prompt other firms to follow the Baltimore firm's example.

the social value of group legal services as weighed against the economic interests of some lawyers is no longer for the legal profession to answer. The groups operating such programs have concluded that such arrangements do have social value sufficient to justify the sacrifice of any conflicting economic interests of lawyers. And the Supreme Court of the United States seems to agree (**392; 364; 409**). The only real question remaining for the profession appears to be the question of limits. Will there be any limitations on the manner in which group programs provide legal services, and where will those limits be set? The issue is yet to be resolved.

Another possibility for the development of low-cost legal service facilities on the institutional model is found in the governmentally supported programs providing legal services to the poor (see **163:429; 207:12; 274:1003**). Such programs might ultimately be extended to provide services to people of moderate means, with the recipient of the service contributing to payment of the cost according to his means.

It is a bit of a jump, of course, from an institutional program providing free legal services to the poor to one that also provides services to people of moderate means on a contributory basis, and any attempt to so extend governmentally supported legal service programs can be expected to encounter a good deal of resistance. Resistance might be ideological—aversion to extension of governmental activity. Or it might have an economic basis. Indeed, there are occasional complaints even now that legal service programs for the poor take paying clients away from private lawyers. Such complaints do not appear to reflect the thinking of either the organized bar or the courts, however, both of which seem committed to the position that the social value of legal service programs for the poor justifies any economic loss they may cause to practicing lawyers—at least as long as cases generating substantial fees are sent to practicing lawyers **27:140-41**; see also **11**). That this forbearance would extend to a program furnishing services for people of moderate means in fee-generating cases seems highly unlikely, however.

While there may be resistance, one element of institutionalized legal service programs might ultimately produce pressure for their extension beyond the limited field of service to the indigent. Unlike such services as medical treatment, which usually is of concern to no one but the patient and his family, legal services typically do involve people other than the recipient of the service. When the services of a lawyer are furnished without charge to a poor person, the objective is likely to effect a result detrimental to the interests of someone else. And when that "someone else" is a person of moderate means, he is apt to begin to wonder why *he* must bear the burden of expense in protecting or asserting his interests while his opponent is getting a "free ride" from the government. It may well be that pressure will thus in the future develop for comprehensive legal service programs that do not discriminate among different segments of the public. If so, then the extension of institutionalized legal services programs to include not only the poor but also the moderate-income group on a contributory basis might be a natural development. With present resources inadequate even to satisfy the demand for legal services among the poor, however, such an extension does not appear imminent.

3
A Hybrid Approach?

There may be reasons, quite apart from matters of style or economic interest, for wishing to preserve the practicing lawyer's involvement in the rendition of legal services to people of moderate means, even in an institutional setting. There are those who contend that legal services can be performed properly *only* by a professional practicing privately. And even many of those who accept the institutional model feel that there is some special social benefit—benefit to both clients and lawyers—in having poor people and people of moderate means come in contact with private practitioners (77). Assuming that this is so, is there any way to preserve the involvement of practicing lawyers in the rendition of legal services to the poor and to people of moderate means, even though special low-cost legal facilities were to develop on the institutional model?

One possibility is simply for practicing lawyers to participate more extensively in institutionalized legal service programs. Some of the larger law firms now make it a practice to grant leaves of absence to younger lawyers who wish to spend six months or a year working in a legal service agency for the poor, with the firms in some instances continuing to pay the salaries of the young men who take leaves for this purpose. Of course, there is no reason that this should be limited to young lawyers. As a practical matter, however, it probably will be largely so limited, mainly because young, idealistic lawyers are the ones most likely to want to work in legal service agencies and because the cost to a law firm for a young lawyer to do so is less than it would be for an older one.

It has also been suggested that practicing lawyers might volunteer to work in legal service agencies one day or so a month, much as doctors sometimes volunteer small amounts of time on a regular basis in free medical clinics. The utility of this kind of arrangement for legal services is questionable, however. Part-time legal aid lawyers would probably be less than completely effective because of lack of knowledge about the fields of law and procedures involved. Moreover, while a lawyer who volunteers once a month at a legal service agency may be genuinely useful in working on cases that require no more than one-time consultation and advice, he might not be so useful on cases that require extended services.

All in all, greater individual participation by practicing lawyers in institutionalized legal service agencies would not appear to be the most effective method of providing such services. And the social benefits would seem limited; poor and near-poor clients would be exposed to a fairly narrow range of privately practicing professionals — primarily young lawyers employed by large firms — while the benefits of exposure to poor and near-poor clients would accrue primarily to the same limited group of lawyers.

One other possibility for involving practicing lawyers in institutionalized legal service activities has been suggested. This is the possibility that law firms might undertake, on a contract basis, to furnish legal services to the poor and to people of moderate means as a part of the governmentally financed legal services program. Such a scheme, in essence a subsidized version of the Baltimore firm's experiment, would be a mixture of the private practice and institutional models. Under it, a law firm would contract with the appropriate government agency to operate a special legal service facility in a specified neighborhood. The law firm would operate this special facility much as a

branch office might be operated, but as a part of the institutionalized legal services system.[9]

A number of advantages might be claimed for such special
legal service facilities. They might make available to poor and
moderate-income clients the expertise and the resources of successful law firms. They would seem to offer substantial assurance of quality and integrity. They would give the bar—albeit a
segment of the bar that is already economically secure—an economic benefit that might to some extent compensate for any
economic disadvantage to those lawyers who might lose paying
clients to such facilities. And, because the services would be
rendered at neighborhood locations remote from the regular
offices of the firms, innovation designed to make the handling of
small cases more efficient and less costly might be more likely to
develop than at already established law offices. It has even been
suggested that special legal service facilities operated on contract by law firms might be a source of employment for many of
the lawyers now practicing on a marginal level in the poorer
neighborhoods. The thought is that the firms would provide the
facilities, the organization, and the supervision while the bulk of
the lawyer manpower would come from the presently marginal
practitioners.

There are some difficulties with this interesting idea, however. To begin with, there is the question of the willingness of
lawyers presently practicing independently in poorer neighborhoods to subject themselves to the supervision of law firms, even
for the sake of higher and more secure incomes. Perhaps many
would be willing to do so. But urban solo practitioners seem to
be the kind of independent-minded individualists who would
find even the thought of working under the supervision of a law
firm most repugnant. Perhaps more importantly, there would
also seem to be some question of whether the independent and
individualistic methods by which these lawyers now practice
law are sufficiently amenable to modification and innovation as
to enable such lawyers to function adequately in this special
kind of institutional setting and under the supervision of law

9. Such facilities would differ from the poverty law office described at note 8 *supra* in
that they would be part of the institutionalized legal services system, while the Piper and
Marbury office appears to be an independent effort.

firms. It is doubtful that they would either be interested in this kind of practice or be able to do very well in it.

Another difficulty concerns the legal manpower to be supplied by the law firm. It seems doubtful that many of the lawyers practicing in firms — not many of the senior or more solidly established members, at any rate — could be induced to undertake to practice in special low-cost legal service facilities, or even to supervise such facilities.

This observation leads to what is probably the most serious difficulty with the idea. Is there any compelling incentive for law firms to undertake the operation of special neighborhood low-cost legal service facilities? Viewed as an income-producing activity, such an undertaking would not seem nearly so attractive as the activities in which law firms are regularly engaged. Put crudely, they could make more money "doing their own thing" than they could make in operating a low-cost legal service facility. Thus, involvement in such a program might be expected only as an expression of public spirit. And it is possible that many law firms would prefer to manifest their public spirit in ways that would not subject them to the unique responsibilities and extra effort that would be required for the operation of a special low-cost legal service facility on a contract basis. The example of the Baltimore firm,[10] however, perhaps suggests that there may be firms willing to embark on such an innovative and adventuresome experiment.

D
Conclusions

These, then, are what appear to be the most likely possibilities for development of special low-cost legal service facilities: (1) Some kind of subsidy that would enable private law offices, either in their traditional form or patterned after the Philadelphia Neighborhood Law Offices, to furnish the services of lawyers to people of moderate means at reduced fees; (2) combination poverty–low-cost legal service offices operated independently by large law firms as a public service; (3) com-

10. See note 8 *supra*.

bination poverty–low-cost offices operated by established firms on a contract basis as part of the institutionalized legal services system; and (4) group legal service programs. The first three possibilities would seem to possess sufficient merit to justify at least serious experimentation. The last, at once both the most controversial and the most likely of the possibilities, will be discussed in the following chapter.

Group
Legal
Services

The lawyer-client relationship has traditionally been the foundation of law practice. This highly personal relationship involves elements of fidelity, confidentiality, individual responsibility, and professional independence. A cherished tradition, it is an effective arrangement for rendering legal service while providing a high degree of protection to the interests of the individual client. Indeed, the lawyer-client relationship may properly be viewed as a vital element in the lawyer's functions as counselor, advocate, and champion of individual rights.

It is not surprising, then, that one of the ways in which the legal profession has given expression to its "spirit of public service" (253:5)* has been through efforts to preserve the lawyer-client relationship. Certain of the profession's ethical standards, for example, are designed chiefly to insure that those who provide legal services to the public are committed to the lawyer-client relationship and to the high personal obligations it requires.[1] Laws restricting the practice of law to licensed attor-

*Citations in boldface type refer the reader to the numbered "Works Cited" at 297–313; where numbers immediately follow the boldface reference, the reader is referred to specific pages in that work.

1. Among the Canons of Professional Ethics of the American Bar Association are a number that deal primarily with the obligations of the lawyer-client relationship: Canon 4 (When Counsel for an Indigent Prisoner); Canon 5 (The Defense or Prosecution of Those Accused of Crime); Canon 6 (Adverse Influences and Conflicting Interests); Canon 9 (Negotiations with Opposite Party); Canon 10 (Acquiring Interest in Litigation); Canon 11 (Dealing with Trust Property); Canon 12 (Fixing the Amount of the Fee); Canon 13 (Contingent Fees); Canon 14 (Suing a Client for a Fee); Canon 15 (How Far a Lawyer May Go in Supporting a Client's Cause); Canon 16 (Restraining Clients from Improprieties); Canon 21 (Punctuality and Expedition); Canon 32 (The Lawyer's Duty in Its Last Analysis); Canon 34 (Division of Fees); Canon 35 (Intermediaries); Canon 37 (Confidences of a Client); Canon 38 (Compensation, Commissions and Rebates); Canon 42 (Expenses of Litigation); and Canon 44 (Withdrawal from Employment as Attorney or Counsel). In addition, most of the remaining Canons relate either directly or indirectly to

neys, as well as the bar's efforts to prevent the unauthorized practice of law, are also directed in large part toward this objective.[2] So, too, have been the profession's efforts to prevent deviation from the forms and procedures of traditional law practice.[3]

The legal profession has also long recognized that differing circumstances and changing conditions may sometimes call for different forms of organization in law practice, for modified law practice methods, or for differences in the arrangements by which people obtain lawyers and pay for their services. The growth of large law firms in response to client need was a deviation from the traditional pattern of solo practice, for example. Indeed, there was at one time some fear that large firm law practice endangered the lawyer-client relationship. Experience has shown this fear to have been unfounded, however. The risk to the lawyer-client relationship from large firm practice is slight and is offset by the many advantages of such practice. As Harrison Tweed has observed, the client may obtain from the large law firm "precisely the close and confidential counselling which is in the best tradition of the Bar" (312:13).

Similarly, legal aid, long accepted and fostered by the bar, frequently involves substantial deviation from the forms and procedures of traditional private law practice. It is common, for instance, for the lawyer providing free legal services to the poor to be a salaried employee of a nonprofit corporation, such as a legal aid society. This deviation from traditional patterns has caused relatively little concern within the bar.[4] Undoubtedly,

the obligations of the lawyer-client relationship. See American Bar Association, *Opinions of the Committee on Professional Ethics* 15–197 (1967) (13). [Hereinafter Formal Opinions of the Committee will be referred to as "ABA Eth. Ops." Informal Opinions will be referred to as "ABA Inf. Eth. Ops."]

2. There is a substantial body of law and literature on this subject. For comprehensive bibliographies see Bass (70). See also Chicago Bar Ass'n v. Quinlan & Tyson, Inc. (367); Bar of Fairfield County v. Dacey (357); State *ex rel.* Florida Bar v. Sperry (403).

3. The bar has opposed numerous arrangements involving the intervention of lay intermediaries between lawyer and client. E.g., People *ex rel.* Courtney v. Ass'n of Real Estate Taxpayers (397); *In re* Maclub of America, Inc. (389); Dworken v. Apt. House Owners Ass'n (377). And it has prohibited various kinds of conduct by lawyers, including communication directly with an adverse party represented by counsel and representation of conflicting interests without disclosure and consent. See *ABA Canons of Professional Ethics*, Nos. 9 (Negotiations with Opposite Party) and 6 (Adverse Influence and Conflicting Interests) (6). See also *ABA Eth. Ops.*, Nos. 10, 16, 26, 30, 33, 34, 37, 39, 40, 49, 50, 55, 58, 60, 64, 66, 70, 71, 72, 75, 77, 78, 83, 86, 95, 99, 101, 102, 103, 104, 108, 110, 112, 118, 124, 125, 128, 129, 132, 134, 135, 136, 142, 160, 165, 167, 177, 178, 181, 192, 200, 218, 220, 222, 224, 231, 235, 242, 243, 245, 247, 261, 262, 271, 272, 275, 278, 282, 287, 288, 296, 306, 315.

4. "Charitable societies rendering aid to the indigent" are given specific exemption from the prohibitions of Canon 35 (Intermediaries) by the Canon's declaration that such agencies are not deemed to be intermediaries. Until recently, no reported cases involved

this is because the social value of an organized and effective method of providing legal services to indigent clients far outweighs any risk of diluting or impairing the lawyer-client relationship. In addition, experience indicates that the lawyer-client relationship can be adequately preserved in legal aid programs.

Among other accepted deviations from the traditional forms and procedures of law practice have been the public defender program,[5] the armed forces legal assistance programs (*ABA Inf. Eth. Ops.*, No. 567), and arrangements by which claims against insureds under liability insurance policies are defended by lawyers provided by the insurer (*ABA Eth. Ops.*, No. 282).

In recent years, much interest has arisen concerning arrangements for providing legal services on a group basis. These arrangements, which also deviate from traditional law practice, are known generally as "group legal services." Current interest in such arrangements has grown out of a series of notable events.

One such event was the decision of the Supreme Court of the United States in *National Association for the Advancement of Colored People v. Button* (hereinafter called *Button*) (392). This case upheld, against prohibitory state law, an activity of the NAACP which provided the services of staff lawyers to its members and others in cases involving racial discrimination. Another was the Supreme Court's decision in *Brotherhood of Railroad Trainmen v. Virginia ex rel. Virginia State Bar* (hereinafter called *BRT*) (364)[6] upholding a union activity in which injured members of the union were advised of their need for legal counsel and referred to lawyers selected by the union. Both activities were sustained on the ground that the statutes prohib-

---

challenges to legal aid activities conducted by charitable organizations. A recent case has approved such activity, however. Azzarello v. Legal Aid Society (356). Since inauguration of the Legal Services Program of the federal Office of Economic Opportunity, a number of cases have been brought by lawyers or bar groups challenging the propriety of certain of the local projects funded by the OEO. Most of those that have thus far been decided have approved the programs involved. E.g., In re Community Legal Services, Inc. (372); Stanislaus County Bar Ass'n v. California Rural Legal Assistance, Inc. (402). But see In re Community Action for Legal Services, Inc. (370).

5. Benjamin v. Legal Aid Society (358), a companion case to Azzarello v. Legal Aid Society (356), approved a private defender program, but no case has been found dealing with public defenders. The public defender movement has not been entirely without opposition, however; e.g., "Cleveland Bar Opposes Public Defender Plan" (107:141-42).

6. On remand, the Chancery Court of the City of Richmond entered an injunction that prohibited the solicitation of business for attorneys but permitted the recommendation of attorneys. Holding that the mandate of the U.S. Supreme Court did not permit the drawing of such a distinction, the Virginia Supreme Court of Appeals remanded with instructions that the order be modified accordingly. Brotherhood of Railroad Trainmen v. Virginia ex rel. Virginia State Bar (366).

iting them violated rights guaranteed under the First and Fourteenth Amendments to the Constitution of the United States. The discussion generated by these decisions was intensified by the 1964 Progress Report of the Group Legal Services Committee of the State Bar of California. This report recommended amendment of the California Rules of Professional Conduct to permit the operation of group legal services (89).[7]

Then, in *United Mine Workers of America, Dist. 12 v. Illinois State Bar Ass'n* (hereinafter called *UMW*) (409), the Supreme Court held that constitutional protection also extended to an arrangement by which a labor union provided the services of a salaried lawyer to assist individual members in workmen's compensation matters. Shortly after this decision, a report of the American Bar Association Committee on Availability of Legal Services added to the discussion by recommending that group legal service arrangements be recognized as a method of enhancing the availability to the public of competent legal services and that such programs be permitted to operate subject to specified safeguards (29:231; 518).

The California State Bar again took up the issue in May 1969, when its Board of Governors approved a proposed change in the Rules of Professional Conduct to permit the operation of group legal services in certain limited circumstances and subject to specified safeguards (172:319). These proposed new rules will become operative if they are adopted by the California Supreme Court.[8]

These events have produced much ferment and discussion within the profession, and they have been analyzed from many different points of view. Because of the importance of group legal services to the question of availability of legal services, it would seem appropriate that they also be considered from this perspective.

Previous analyses of the subject have generally taken one of two approaches. The California GLS Report, for example, focuses most directly upon the aspects of need and utility, seek-

---

7. The 1964 Progress Report of the Group Legal Services Committee of the California State Bar (89) will hereinafter be referred to as the "California GLS Report." It should be noted that subsequent action of the Board of Governors of the State Bar of California approved certain of the Report's recommendations but disapproved the recommendation that the California Rules of Professional Conduct be amended to permit the operation of group legal services (170). The Committee was later discharged (178:478-80).

8. At this writing, action by the California Supreme Court is still pending.

ing to demonstrate the benefits offered to the public by group legal services (89).[9] Other discussions, particularly law review articles, have tended to dwell mainly upon the constitutional issues raised by the *Button, BRT,* and *UMW* cases and to speculate on the problem of reconciling the rights of the states to regulate law practice with the constitutionally guaranteed individual rights involved in at least some group legal service programs.[10]

This chapter will take a third approach. Unfilled needs for legal services and the utility of group arrangements for filling them will not be discussed at length. The group device is unquestionably useful, and it does fill needs (89:662-68). By educating group members about their legal problems and by making them aware of the availability of legal help, the group device encourages the assertion of individual rights and claims that may not otherwise be asserted. By making lawyers readily accessible and by facilitating contact with them, it encourages the use of lawyers by people who would probably not otherwise seek their help. By utilizing the purchasing advantage enjoyed by a group to obtain the services of lawyers particularly competent in the fields of law of concern to the group, the group device enhances the quality of the legal services available to group members. And by lowering the cost of legal services—through reducing the cost of rendering the services and spreading the cost among all members of the group—it is able to bring legal services to many people who would not otherwise be able to afford them.

But the utility of the group device is not the central question before the legal profession. Nor is the constitutional issue. Although crucial to the cases in which it is raised, the question of infringement of individual rights by state regulation of law practice is not necessarily the measure of the bar's obligations to the

9. See especially chap. 2, "The Unfilled Need for Legal Services" (pp. 654-59), and chap. 3, "The Functions of Group Legal Services" (pp. 660-69) in Cal. GLS Rep. (89).

10. For articles commenting on the constitutional issues raised by the *Button* case see: 294; 63; 79; 95; 124; 150; 218; 289; 322; 324; 325. For articles commenting on the constitutional issues involved in the *BRT* case—or in *Button* and *BRT* together—see: 234; 236; 233; 94; 217; 330; 159; 303; 306; 323; 326; see also 415:1206-19. A few articles predating the *Button* case treated a somewhat broader range of issues. (See 194; 242; 342; 341; 109; 190; 237; 117.) A few of the law review articles appearing since the *Button* decision go beyond the constitutional issues to discuss such topics as the utility of group legal services in relation to the interests of both the public and the profession. For especially noteworthy articles see 351; 100, 275; 97; see also 74; 283, 205; 311; 240; 116; 114. For more recent articles including comment on the *UMW* case see 302; 235; 115; 215; see also 103.

public. The legal profession has responsibilities that go far beyond the mere avoidance of unwarranted interference with constitutionally guaranteed rights. They embrace positive duties of service to the public, duties founded upon the basic commitment of the profession to the public interest. One of the most fundamental of these responsibilities is the duty to make competent legal help readily available to all who desire it.

The central issue before the legal profession, then, is not whether group legal services are useful, nor whether present restrictions on the obtaining of legal services through group arrangements conflict with individual rights guaranteed by the Constitution, but whether such restrictions unnecessarily impair the ability of lawyers to discharge their primary obligation to the public. The objective of this analysis will be to explore that issue.

A
Review of
Intermediary Arrangements
for Providing Legal Services

1
Definition

The term "group legal services" is an abbreviated designation for a complex subject. Like many shorthand labels, it at once says both too much and too little. For example, it is sometimes taken to connote the grouping of lawyers in law firms, clinics, or other aggregate-practice arrangements, instead of the grouping of recipients of legal service.[11] These are, of course, two quite dissimilar matters. Conversely, the term is sometimes understood to refer only to a narrow category of programs for providing legal services to certain specific groups, such as members of labor unions or automobile clubs. Such a limited view tends to overlook other programs that have substantially similar characteristics and objectives.

There is in fact no commonly accepted definition for the term

11. The distinction between the grouping of recipients and the grouping of lawyers is discussed in Cheatham (99:70).

"group legal services."[12] Moreover, many discussions of the subject proceed upon implied definitions that really beg the important questions. One purpose of categorizing a legal service arrangement as a "group legal service" is to render it subject to restrictions designed primarily to prevent interference with the professional judgment of participating lawyers, for example. To include a particular arrangement within the term *as a matter of definition*, then, is to presume the facts that govern the very point at issue — the tendency of the arrangement to interfere with professional judgment.[13] An analysis based on such a definition would not be especially helpful.

Thus, it may be advisable to forgo use of the term "group legal services" and to speak instead of "intermediary arrangements." Use of this latter term may tend to avoid the presumptions, preconceptions, and emotional responses associated with the label "group legal services" and focus instead on the really crucial element. A new term may also be defined as broadly or as narrowly as may be necessary for meaningful analysis.

12. Perhaps the nearest thing to a commonly accepted definition of "group legal services" is the one quoted in the California GLS Report:

> Legal services performed by an attorney for a group of individuals who have a common problem or problems, or who have joined together as a means of best bargaining for a predetermined position, or who have voluntarily formed, or become members of an association with the aim that such association shall perform a service to its members in a particular field or activity, or through common interests it appears that the organization can gain a benefit to the members as a whole.
>
> Examples of such organizations are labor unions, employer organizations, trade associations, teachers' groups, civil service employees or any body politic, members of a social club or of an automobile club, fraternal organizations, and numerous other such associations. Included also may be groups who associate themselves for the purpose of establishing a plan of prepaid legal services to be rendered to individual members thereof, whether or not the members have a common interest in a certain field of activity (89:661).

Note, however, that although this definition undoubtedly intends to cover legal services performed for *individual members* of a group, as is suggested in its later parts, at the outset it speaks of legal services performed "for a group of individuals," which is quite a different thing.

The term "group legal services" has also been characterized simply as having "to do with lay groups which want to furnish lawyers to their members" (96).

13. E.g., Canon 35, which specifically excludes from the term "intermediary" all charitable societies rendering aid to the indigent, despite the fact that such charitable organizations do indeed intervene between lawyer and client and may direct the performance of the lawyer's duties. Conversely, it specifically forbids lawyers to accept employment "from any organization, such as an association, club or trade organization" to render "legal services to the members of such an organization in respect to their individual affairs." This specific application of the principles articulated in the previous portion of the Canon presumes that every arrangement by which a lawyer accepts employment from an organization to render legal services to its members will result in interference with professional judgment; it permits no inquiry into the facts of any given case to see whether such interference does actually take place.

For the present discussion it would appear desirable to formulate a definition that embraces all legal service arrangements having relevant similarities, whether or not they might be included in any popular or professional conception of what are or are not "group legal services." From such a broad base it may be possible to discover relevant differences to support the drawing of rational distinctions. Therefore, the term "intermediary arrangements" will be used to mean all arrangements in which legal services are rendered:

1. To individual members of an identifiable group (identifiable in terms of some common interest, even though it be nothing more than a shared desire or need for legal services)
2. By a lawyer or lawyers provided, secured, recommended, or otherwise selected by
   a. The group, its organization, or its officers, or
   b. Some other agency having an interest in obtaining legal service for members of the group

It should be emphasized that this definition has been formulated solely for purposes of this analysis and is not proposed as a general definition or for use in any other context. Furthermore, this definition is in no way meant to imply either approval or disapproval of any of the legal service arrangements it embraces, nor to suggest that the various arrangements embraced are necessarily to be equated in any way beyond the fact that they do possess certain relevant common characteristics. Rather, the definition is meant simply to bring within the ambit of examination all legal service arrangements that, because of common characteristics, may appropriately be looked at together.

It should be noted that the "group" portion of the definition is especially broad. It is meant to include arrangements that have similar characteristics but that might otherwise escape attention under a narrower view of what the word "group" usually connotes. Also noteworthy is the fact that the definition excludes arrangements in which the lawyers rendering the services are merely paid by, but not provided, secured, recommended, or otherwise selected by the organization or agency.[14]

Perhaps it should also be pointed out that the definition and

14. A lawyer selected by the client himself but paid by someone other than the client may, under certain circumstances, tend to come under the control of the person or organization paying the fee. For example, in a case involving extended litigation, the lawyer's fees may be paid periodically as the services are performed rather than in one lump sum at the end of the litigation. In such a circumstance it is conceivable that the person or organization paying the fees may seek to direct the litigation as it progresses. It

all of the following discussion are limited specifically to legal services *provided by lawyers*. The rendition by laymen of services that relate to legal problems, whether on an individual or a group basis, is a separate topic, raising quite different issues.[15] Furthermore, although this analysis deals with legal services and with intermediary arrangements for their rendition, the primary concern throughout will be with the relationship of lawyers to such arrangements and with what lawyers should be permitted to do with respect to them.

2
Examples of Intermediary Arrangements[16]

For the purpose of analysis, intermediary arrangements may be classified into four main categories. First, there are programs

---

was thought, however, that such circumstances would be rather infrequent, and the susceptibility of lawyers to the exercise of such control so slight, that this analysis could be limited to situations where someone other than the client plays some role in the *selection* of the lawyer. Note that it has been held not to be unethical for an employer to pay the legal expenses of its employees, for an association to do the same for its members, or for a labor union to do so for its members, so long as the organization does not select the lawyer (*ABA Inf. Eth. Ops.*, No. 469).

15. The rendition of legal services by laymen is a question of the kinds of services that should be performed exclusively by lawyers, while the topic discussed in this paper involves the question of the ways in which people are to be permitted to obtain lawyers' services. Some arrangements by which organizations provide lawyers' services to their individual members or to others may also involve the rendition of legal services by laymen unsupervised by lawyers, of course. To the extent that this may be so in any given case, therefore, the arrangement may be subject to disapproval as a device for the unlawful practice of law by laymen, quite apart from the question of its priority or impropriety as a method of providing *lawyers'* services. And, of course, a group program may provide legal services solely through laymen, a pure matter of unauthorized practice. See Hoffmeister v. Tod (383); *Re* Unauthorized Practice of Law in Cuyahoga County (408); Annotation (414).

16. For additional examples of intermediary arrangements, see 89:669-89. It should be noted that no attempt is made, either in this review of intermediary arrangements or in the subsequent analysis of the restrictions on such arrangements, to differentiate between court cases and the opinions of bar association ethics committees. Although ethics opinions are not law, there would seem to be some justification for equating them with court decisions as determiners of proper conduct for lawyers. Indeed, judicial decisions do not appear to play a major part either in developing ethical concepts or in affecting lawyers' behavior. Many ethical doctrines have been more fully refined and amplified in the opinions than in the cases, and a lawyer concerned about a questionable point of ethics is more likely to seek the answer in an opinion of a bar association ethics committee than in a court decision. Moreover, the decisions tend often to be based largely on doctrines formulated in ethics opinions. Thus, because ethics opinions are at least as important as are cases as statements of ethical norms and as determiners of professional conduct, no attempt is made here to differentiate between the two. The reader should always bear in mind, however, that this discussion of "rules" and "restrictions" does not deal with what the *law* is, but rather with the norms — both positive law and intraprofessional interdiction — that help to determine the professional conduct of lawyers.

operated by civil rights organizations, charitable organizations, or government agencies. Such programs are usually concerned with securing and preserving the constitutional rights of individuals or with providing lawyers' services to the poor or to individual members of other disadvantaged groups. Second, there are the programs by which membership organizations seek to provide legal service benefits to their individual members. Such groups include labor unions, professional and trade associations, auto clubs, and a variety of other kinds of membership organizations. The third category comprises programs by which business or profit-making organizations provide lawyers' services to individual members of particular groups. These arrangements may involve some genuine community of interest between the organization and the group — the providing of lawyers' services to employees by employers, for example. Or they may be essentially commercial arrangements, where the main community of interest between the agency seeking to provide the services and the group of intended recipients is an apparent demand on the part of the group, which the agency seeks to supply, either at a profit or as a means of facilitating its regular business. And finally, there are the insurance programs, typically commercial in nature but possessing other characteristics that require separate consideration.

These four categories cover intermediary arrangements that have been accepted by the bar and approved by the courts, arrangements that have been prohibited, and some that are merely proposals for legal service programs. The following examples do not purport to be exhaustive.

a
Charitable and
public service programs

This category includes legal service programs provided by organizations devoted to the securing of constitutional rights for their members or others, those conducted by charitable organizations primarily for the benefit of the poor, those provided by government either for the poor or for other groups with special needs, and those provided by the bar itself.

(1)
Civil rights programs

The intermediary arrangement that gave rise to *Button* (392) is perhaps the most noteworthy example. The Virginia State Conference of NAACP Branches, an unincorporated association of local groups affiliated with the National Association for the Advancement of Colored People, Inc., undertook to provide legal assistance to Negroes aggrieved because of racial discrimination. This assistance, offered without charge to members and nonmembers alike, consisted of representation in both civil actions brought to attack various forms of racial segregation and criminal cases containing questions of possible racial discrimination. For this purpose the Conference established a staff of lawyers, elected at its annual convention. None of the staff received a salary or retainer; rather, per diem fees were paid by the Conference for professional services rendered in particular cases. The Supreme Court of the United States held this activity to be a form of political expression, protected by constitutional guarantees of free expression and association.[17]

An earlier program with a somewhat similar objective but with a substantially different ideological cast was conducted by an organization called the American Liberty League (see 348:70-78). The Liberty League was an association formed in the early New Deal days and dedicated to the protection of constitutional rights against what was seen as a threat from certain New Deal legislation, particularly the then new National Labor Relations Act. A National Lawyers Committee, made up of lawyers who were members of the League, offered to represent without charge indigent citizens who felt that their constitutional rights were being violated.[18]

17. Other programs in this field of activity include the Lawyers' Committee for Civil Rights Under Law (see Tweed [314]) and the Lawyers' Constitutional Defense Committee, Inc., which was established under the auspices of the American Civil Liberties Union and which has been given ethical sanction by the American Bar Association Ethics Committee. See Honnold (157); *ABA Inf. Eth. Ops.*, No. 786. See also *In re* Ades (353); Powell v. Alabama (399).

18. In *ABA Eth. Ops.*, No. 148, the American Bar Association Committee on Professional Ethics held this activity to be a proper one for lawyers under Canons 4, 27, and 28. The activity was regarded as a form of legal aid to the indigent and therefore acceptable. The Committee dealt with Canon 28 (Stirring Up Litigation) by saying: "It will be noted that the offer made in the [radio] address is to defend citizens against threatened infringement of their constitutional rights. So far as we are able to anticipate, no *substantial* increase in litigation is likely to result from the expressed willingness of these men to

(2)
Legal aid and
charitable programs

The traditional legal aid agency is a charitable or nonprofit corporation created for the purpose of providing lawyers' services to indigent persons with civil legal problems and, in some instances, to indigent persons accused of crime.[19] The poor within the geographical area served by a particular legal aid organization clearly constitute an identifiable group. Their legal problems tend to be concentrated in certain fields, such as landlord-tenant relations and consumer credit (**291;** see also **337:6-41**), and they have a common interest in certain kinds of legal problems because they share the condition of indigency. The arrangement between the organization and the lawyers who provide the services varies. In many places the lawyers are full-time employees of the agency. In others they are volunteers to whom legal aid cases are referred. The indigent clients ordinarily pay no fee — or, at most, token fees — for the services they obtain.[20]

Not every intermediary arrangement involving a charitable

---

serve in such capacity. All that they have offered is their experience and skill 'if and when any American citizen, however humble, is without means to defend his constitutional rights in a court of justice.' " (Emphasis added.) In thus giving approval to a *little* "stirring up," the opinion comes in direct conflict with the doctrine underlying the Canon — that the judicial machinery is designed solely to adjudicate controversies which the parties deem of sufficient importance to assert voluntarily, without any encouragement. The concluding paragraph perhaps suggests the real basis of the opinion: "The question presented, with its implications, involves problems of political, social and economic character that have long since assumed the proportions of national issues, on one side or the other [of] which multitudes of patriotic citizens have aligned themselves. *The issues transcend the range of professional ethics.*" (Emphasis added.)

19. For a general treatment of legal aid see Brownell (**84**).

20. A recent proposal for a group program of a legal aid type but involving a narrow field of law practice has come from the nonprofit National Association for Retarded Children, Inc. This proposal contemplates an array of "law consultants," whose primary function would be to provide consultative service to private lawyers representing members of the association with respect to legal problems concerning mental retardation. The proposal provides that these staff law consultants might also supply free legal services directly to indigent clients with respect to this limited field of practice. It further specifies that the staff law consultants would be permitted to accept employment directly from individual members of the association only in their "private capacities." See *ABA Inf. Eth. Ops.*, No. 888.

Another proposal contemplated the formation of a charitable agency to utilize salaried attorneys as well as volunteers to provide lawyers' services without charge to prospective immigrants. The attorneys would assist in obtaining information and in preparing necessary papers to facilitate immigration. See Ass'n of the Bar of the City of New York, Committee on Professional Ethics, *Opinions*, No. 444 (**227**). [These opinions will hereinafter be cited as *NYC Eth. Ops.* Their texts may be found in William Nelson Cromwell Foundation, *Opinions on Professional Ethics* (1956). Citations here will be to the opinion numbers only and not to the page numbers.]

organization entails free legal services to the indigent, however. It has been held, for example, that a lawyer-member of the board of directors of a social welfare agency might properly give advice to the agency at reduced fees in the hope that the agency would refer paying clients to him, provided there was no agreement to that effect between the lawyer and the social welfare agency (*ABA Inf. Eth. Ops.*, No. 929). On the other hand, it has been held improper for a lawyer who is a full-time employee of an educational institution or church which is engaged in soliciting gifts and bequests from prospective patrons either to draft wills for them without charge or to have wills providing for such bequests drafted by other lawyers at the institution's expense (*ABA Inf. Eth. Ops.*, No. 831; *NYC Eth. Ops.*, No. 608).[21] A hospital's referring of patients entitled to workmen's compensation benefits to a particular lawyer for representation before a state labor department and in court has also been held to be improper (*NYC Eth. Ops.*, No. 409).[22]

(3)
Governmental programs

A number of governmental activities may be appropriately viewed as intermediary arrangements. The legal service programs funded by the federal Office of Economic Opportunity are operated by a variety of local agencies, both governmental and nongovernmental (see **277; 335**). In substance these programs are arrangements by which the public, through the government, provides lawyers' services to members of disadvantaged groups. Generally speaking, these programs provide a comprehensive range of legal services, and there are a great many different arrangements between the agencies operating the programs and the lawyers who provide the services. That the "group" being provided service is defined only in terms of income level and residence within the agency's service area makes the arrangements no less a service to a group.[23]

---

21. The ABA Ethics Committee did say, however, that prospective donors who did not have their own lawyers might properly be referred to other lawyers, provided that the institution did not pay the fees.

22. Although the hospital was a nonprofit organization, its expressed intent in supplying lawyers to patients with workmen's compensation claims was "to see to it that the hospital's claims are protected."

23. The Criminal Justice Act of 1964 also set up what may be in substance a kind of intermediary program. Here, the service offered is representation to members of that

Another intermediary program operated by many local governments is the public defender system, providing, at public expense, representation of indigent criminal defendants in both the state and federal courts (see **149; 206**). Here the lawyers who provide the services are typically salaried employees.

The legal assistance programs of the Army, Navy, Air Force, and Coast Guard constitute yet another type of intermediary arrangement. Under these programs, legal-assistance offices, maintained at most large military installations and staffed by lawyer-officers, provide legal help to servicemen, dependents, and certain others connected with the armed forces (see **347**). Such help is limited, however, to advice and some other services in noncriminal cases that do not require advocacy. Noncriminal matters requiring advocacy and criminal cases to be tried in civilian courts are sent to local private attorneys — sometimes, but not usually, through a local bar association lawyer referral service. These legal assistance programs are quite independent of the military justice system, in which defendants in courts martial are represented by assigned military counsel. The military justice assigned-counsel system can also be viewed as an intermediary arrangement, however.[24]

(4)
Bar association
programs

Bar associations participate in many of the programs described above. For example, many local bar associations take part in the support and operation of legal aid programs. State and local bar associations also participate in a substantial number of the legal service projects that have been funded by the federal Office of Economic Opportunity, and the American Bar Association has provided significant assistance in the development of this pro-

---

group of people who are indigent and who are defendants in the federal courts. Three alternative arrangements are open to adoption by individual federal district courts. The act authorizes local plans to provide for representation (1) by private attorneys, (2) by attorneys furnished by bar associations or legal aid agencies, or (3) through some combination of the two (see **430**).

24. The supplying of lawyers to servicemen in matters of legal assistance and courts martial has been held to be proper, as analogous to the assignment of counsel to represent civilian defendants in criminal courts and the supplying of free legal aid to indigents, with the clients free to get their own lawyers if they wish. *ABA Inf. Eth. Ops.*, No. 567.

gram. The bar also works with the armed forces in carrying out that portion of the Legal Assistance program involving the use of civilian counsel.

One intermediary arrangement operated entirely by bar associations is the Lawyer Referral Service. Under this program, persons needing legal help are referred to practicing lawyers by bar-operated referral offices.[25]

b
Membership
programs

The distinctive characteristic of the intermediary arrangements in this category — which includes those arrangements operated by labor unions, trade associations, professional associations, automobile clubs, and membership groups formed for the accomplishment of specific purposes — is that they focus especially on interests common to members of a particular group. This is not to say that every member of a group will be interested in the objectives for which the group creates a legal service program, but only that the subject is of sufficiently common concern to most of its members that the group, as an entity, might be thought of as having a collective interest in the subject.

(1)
Labor unions

Intermediary programs conducted by labor unions fall generally into two main types, although there are a great number of variations within these types. Perhaps the best known is a referral program such as that operated by the union in the BRT case (364; see also 363; 382; 393; 401; 376; 352; 385; 369). Under it, the union selects "regional counsel" in the various regions of the country. Injured workers and families of workers killed on

25. Although the clientele of a lawyer referral service may be somewhat broader than the "group" idea is customarily thought to embrace, and although a bar association is not a "lay agency," lawyer referral services are nevertheless "intermediary arrangements" in the sense that they involve the selection of lawyers for individual clients by someone other than the clients. Lawyer referral services have been approved in Jacksonville Bar Ass'n v. Wilson (386). See also Gunnels v. Atlanta Bar Ass'n (381).

the job are contacted through the union's Department of Legal Counsel, which advises them of their need for counsel and recommends to them that they consult the regional counsel. The union also provides assistance in the investigation of such claims. In the past, regional counsel had been required to remit to the Brotherhood a portion of the fees earned in cases referred to them under the plan. This feature of the program appears now to have been eliminated (364:5). In the *BRT* case, the U.S. Supreme Court has upheld the right of the union—under First and Fourteenth Amendment guarantees of free speech, petition, and assembly—to engage in such activities despite objections that the plan constitutes the unauthorized practice of law and the solicitation of legal business for participating lawyers.

The other principal type of union-conducted intermediary arrangement provides members the services of staff lawyers. In the Mine Workers program, for instance, the union provides representation to its members in workmen's compensation cases through a lawyer who is a full-time salaried employee of the union (see **409**). The arrangement involved in *Button* (392:420) is also of this type, with the legal services being provided by staff lawyers who are, however, compensated on a per diem basis. Another program of this type is conducted by a state employees' association, which maintains a legal staff to assist members with respect to employment problems. Legal counseling is made available to all members, and in some instances the association's staff lawyers represent members in litigation.[26] There are many variations on these two basic themes, of course.[27]

26. Representation is not available: (1) to members who were not members at the time the problem arose; (2) where the action required is contrary to the policy of the organization; (3) where the basic question involved is a question of fact; (4) in workmen's compensation matters; (5) in appeals from reports of performance; (6) in appeals from rejection during a probationary period; or (7) where the basic issue is severity of punishment enforced and where the penalty is within reasonable limits. In exceptional situations, however, representation may be provided in such matters if it is determined to be in the best interests of the organization as a whole.

27. Some unions offer members the services of their own counsel, often under a very informal arrangement. In one instance, counsel for a small local was known by members to be available to give advice on personal legal problems. No fees were charged, either to the union or to the individual recipients of advice, although some of these clients were said to leave a few dollars on the lawyer's desk as a gratuity. It may be assumed that any legal employment resulting from this service would be at the lawyer's regular fees. See also *ABA Inf. Eth. Ops.*, No. 970, involving the drafting of wills for union members by union attorneys.

At least one union has retained a firm of private practitioners to devote a substantial amount of time to the representation of members in workmen's compensation matters, although this has been held improper as a violation of Canon 35 and of state law. *NYC*

(2)
Professional and
trade associations

The intermediary arrangements in this category are generally similar to those in the programs operated by labor unions, although there are some further interesting variations. A large teachers' association, for example, makes its employed counsel available to confer with members on "professional" problems — problems having to do with retirement, certification, contracts of professional employment, salaries, leaves and tenure (see 89:675-76). The plan contemplates that the association member will obtain his own lawyer in the event that extensive representation is required, in which case the legal fund of the association pays a substantial portion of the cost. If the individual member cannot or does not wish to get his own lawyer, however, the association's counsel will represent him.[28]

Eth. Ops., No. 513. The same sort of arrangement has been used with unemployment compensation cases and in the prosecution of individual claims for prevailing wage rates under a state labor law. This latter arrangement was held improper by *NYC Eth. Ops.*, No. 773. See also *ABA Inf. Eth. Ops.*, No. 470, which distinguished between arrangements in which a lawyer is supplied to employees to represent them in small unemployment compensation cases involving identical issues (held unacceptable) and multiple representation or representation on a "test case" basis where there is no intermediary involved and no solicitation by the lawyer. These latter arrangements were compared to the class suits permitted under the federal rules.

Another similar arrangement provides legal services in housing, garnishment, consumer fraud, and tax matters (142; 141). Note, however, that this arrangement also involves the use of laymen as advisers at neighborhood service centers. See also *NYC Eth. Ops.*, No. 763.

Workmen's compensation cases have also been handled by means of an arrangement under which the union retains private lawyers to represent injured workmen only in the negotiations with the employer prior to the filing of claims with the state industrial accident board. If negotiation is unsuccessful and a claim must be filed, the prospective claimant may then employ the same lawyer to handle it — at reduced fees — or seek out a lawyer of his own choosing. Another variation is a combination of salaried-counsel and retained-counsel systems, where the union-employed counsel provides advice and representation in the state in which the union office is located, with matters arising in other states being referred to locally retained lawyers. This arrangement was held improper by *NYC Eth. Ops.*, No. 799.

In still another variation, a union retains private counsel on an ad hoc basis to handle multiple individual claims arising out of a single set of circumstances. In one instance, a lawyer was retained to represent a large number of individual claimants with small unemployment compensation claims arising out of a single work stoppage. This was approved in Dorsey v. E.S.C. (375). Social security claims are also said to be the subjects of union legal service programs of one type or another. See also *NYC Eth. Ops.*, No. 176.

28. In another variation, having similarities to both civil rights and union programs, a national education organization has recently made an arrangement with a national civil rights organization for the representation of individual Negro teachers with respect to dismissal, discipline, and other professional problems. The civil rights organization provides the lawyers and the education organization pays the cost.

Associations of landlords and apartment house owners have provided the services of lawyers to individual members, primarily in rent collection and eviction cases. E.g., *NYC*

(3)
Membership groups
formed for
special purposes

A common type of intermediary arrangement involves the organization formed for the chief purpose of conducting a campaign of political or economic action. Providing lawyers' services to individual members of the organization is frequently an indispensable part of such a campaign. Although the rights of individual members may be asserted in such action, it is essentially "test case" litigation, intended to establish principles important to all members of the group. One example is an Association of Real Estate Taxpayers, formed a number of years ago in Illinois to work for equitable taxation of property. This organization provided a salaried lawyer to represent individual members in proceedings to contest taxes on real estate and to protect such property against forfeiture and tax sale during the pend-

---

Eth. Ops., Nos. 118, 770; Dworken v. Apt. House Owners Ass'n (**377**). Cf. New York County Lawyers' Ass'n, Committee on Professional Ethics, *Opinions*, No. 261 (**227**). [Opinions hereinafter cited as *NYCLA Eth. Ops.* Their texts may be found in William Nelson Cromwell Foundation, *supra* note 20]. A state farmers' organization at one time proposed that a lawyer be retained to handle probate matters for individual members (*disapproved*, ABA *Eth. Ops.*, No. 56). Among other trade or professional groups that have sought to provide lawyers' services to their members are hairdressers (*disapproved*, NYC *Eth. Ops.*, No. 753), and an association of city attorneys that has retained counsel to represent individual municipalities in treble damage suits against suppliers of goods and services who violate antitrust laws in their dealings with the municipalities. The program of the maritime industry, described in *Cal. GLS Rep.* (89:683–85), is another example. See also *NYC Eth. Ops.*, No. 359.

The intermediary arrangement has also been used in the field of debt collection, where groups of creditors have attempted to retain lawyers to represent individual members in the collection of debts. This was held improper in *ABA Eth. Ops.*, No. 35. But see *NYCLA Eth. Ops.*, No. 47, part III, which held a similar arrangement to be proper, stating: "We assume, of course, that the lawyer's retainer by the association leaves him free to follow his own conscience. The Committee sees no impropriety in the course suggested, provided that [the association] is a bona fide organization formed by its members for their own benefit, is not engaged in a regular business of collecting accounts of non-members for profit and that it is the actual interest of the organization which prompts its solicitation, and provided the plan is not merely a cover for the solicitation of business by the attorney." Perhaps the conflict between these two opinions may be at least partly explicable on the basis of the dates on which they were given. The ABA opinion was rendered in 1931, the New York County Lawyers' Association opinion in 1914.

Another debt collection plan involved a nonprofit membership corporation composed of charitable hospitals. In order to facilitate the collection of debts for hospital care, the individual hospitals formed a nonprofit corporation, which in turn employed attorneys on salary to handle collections for the individual members. The individual member hospitals for whom collections were made paid fees for the services rendered to them by the organization's attorneys, but these fees were set at a level sufficient only to cover the cost of the service, with no profit accruing to the organization. This was held to be the unauthorized practice of law in Hospital Credit Exchange, Inc. v. Shapiro (**384**).

ency of litigation.[29] Other examples of this kind of program are those providing lawyers' services to members of ad hoc tenants' associations[30] and property owners' associations formed for specific purposes (89:687–88).[31]

(4)
Automobile clubs

Automobile clubs, which may or may not be nonprofit, are membership organizations whose general objective is to provide a wide range of services related to the ownership and use of automobiles, including towing services, theft protection, trip planning, insurance, bail-bond service, and some kinds of legal services. The legal services have usually been provided in one of four ways. In the first, the association has provided services to its members directly through its own staff of employee lawyers, retaining local counsel in areas where its staff attorneys are not readily available.[32] In the second, the association has private lawyers on retainer to provide specified services to members.[33] In the third, the association recommends to its members certain lawyers selected in communities around the country:[34] The

29. People *ex rel.* Courtney v. Ass'n of Real Estate Taxpayers (397) held such activities to be the unauthorized practice of law.

30. This was disapproved in *NYC Eth. Ops.*, No. 714.

31. One further variation is the employment of lawyers by an existing membership association on an ad hoc basis for a particular group of cases. An example of this is a private membership association made up of certain members of the armed forces, which retained counsel to advise and represent the survivors of members who had been killed in a particular air crash. A lawyer was retained by the association to investigate the crash and to represent any prospective litigant who wished his services. Prospective litigants were encouraged to employ him or, if they had their own lawyers, to request that the organization-selected lawyer be associated with their own lawyer in the litigation. Apparently the association paid the lawyer's fees and the other costs of investigation and general preparation, but the information available did not make clear whether additional fees were to be paid by the individual litigants for the handling of their respective cases.

32. Among cases holding this kind of program to be the unauthorized practice of law are People *ex rel.* Chicago Bar Association v. Motorists Association (396); People *ex rel.* Chicago Bar Ass'n v. Chicago Motor Club (395); Rhode Island Bar Ass'n v. Automobile Service Ass'n (400); Automobile Club of Mo. v. Hoffmeister (355).

33. This was held improper in State *ex rel.* Seawell v. Carolina Motor Club (405). See also *ABA Eth. Ops.*, No. 8.

34. See *In re* Maclub of America, Inc. (389), holding such activity to be the unauthorized practice of law. But see *In re* Thibodeau (407), holding that essentially the same activity was not unauthorized practice. The court attempted to distinguish between these two cases on the ground that the organization in Thibodeau undertook only to pay the fees of lawyers selected by members from its recommended panel, while the organization in Maclub purported to undertake to furnish legal services. It appears, however, that in fact the two organizations were doing precisely the same thing—paying the fees of lawyers selected by members from approved lists provided by the association. See also 418:548-49.

member who needs legal services consults one of these lawyers
and is reimbursed for the legal fees involved. The member is
customarily free to select some other lawyer if he so desires,
however. Because these three arrangements have been held to
be the unauthorized practice of law, automobile clubs appear to
have limited their legal service activities in recent years to a
fourth—the providing of a simple indemnity to pay legal fees in
certain kinds of matters.[35] One such club, for example, agrees to
reimburse members for the cost of a lawyer's appearance in
court, up to a maximum of $475, according to a schedule allow-
ing $275 for trial and $200 for appeal of a manslaughter charge,
$85 for trial and $75 for appeal of a reckless driving charge, and
$30 for trial and $30 for appeal of other charges. This approach
is, of course, simply a limited form of legal expense insurance,
and, because it does not involve selection of the lawyer by
someone other than the ultimate client, it does not properly
come within the "intermediary" definition formulated above.

c
**Programs conducted by
profit-making
organizations**

This category includes a wide variety of arrangements. A
distinction may be drawn, however, between the employer programs, which involve a fairly substantial community of interest
between the employer and the employee group being served,
and the various other programs in which the community of
interest between the profit-making organization and the
recipients of the legal service is not so clear.

(1)

Employer programs

The interest of the employer in the legal well-being of employees is, of course, essentially the same as his interest in their
health—to maintain employees as productive workers. When an

35. E.g., the "American Oil Motor Club," a motor club-type service contract being
promoted by the American Oil Company. Note that the legal service benefits now being
offered by the Chicago Motor Club are also of this type.

employer does provide lawyers' services, it is generally because the employer feels that the amount spent in helping employees solve legal problems will be more than compensated by savings in time and productivity. Thus, employers sometimes seek to provide lawyers' services to employees in fields where the problems involved are most likely to interfere with productivity or the employment relationship. One employer, for example, provides debt counseling and, when appropriate, legal representation to employees threatened with wage garnishment.[36] Another provides assistance with income tax returns.[37] Of course, corporation legal departments are frequently approached by individual employees seeking legal help, and rendition of such service on an informal basis appears to be quite common, especially in smaller corporations.[38]

(2)

Other programs of
profit-making organizations

The intermediary arrangements included in this subcategory are of a number of different types. All are intermediary arrangements within the definition formulated above, for they involve the providing of services to individual members of groups (gen-

36. This is a function which has grown out of some ten years of experience in the administration of payroll deductions resulting from garnishment proceedings. This employer has about 22,000 employees. At any given time, approximately 2000 pay checks are subject to deductions to satisfy garnishments (a fairly consistent 10 percent), and the company pays out over $500,000 annually in garnishment payments. The major function of the garnishment program is bookkeeping: to ascertain whether an action has been filed, to determine the amount of the debt, and to keep records of payments made. In discharging this function, the administrator of the program has become something of a general financial consultant. Furthermore, where a particular case appears to involve problems which indicate that a lawyer's services might be helpful to the employee, the case is referred to the corporation's counsel, who will contest the garnishment or render other appropriate services. See 183.

37. Lawyers employed by the company are brought into the plant at income tax time, and employees are urged to consult with them if they need help with their tax returns. At one time, at least one industrial employer is reported to have hired attorneys for the purpose of providing a complete range of legal services to employees (see 89:679-81). This program is no longer in operation, however, and nothing else of quite this magnitude has been discovered.

38. The ABA Ethics Committee has held that where the attorney is freely selected and compensated by the employee and is directly responsible to him, and where no conflict of interest exists, the mere fact that the attorney also represents the employing corporation does not prevent him from representing an employee (*ABA Inf. Eth. Ops.*, No. C-476). Whether such approval may be extended to cover the situation where the employer undertakes to make known to employees the availability of its counsel, or even to encourage employees to use him, is not clear.

erally, particular customer groups) by lawyers who have been provided, secured, recommended, or otherwise selected by someone other than the ultimate client.[39]

One arrangement involved a corporation engaged in the business of investigating and adjusting claims for insurance companies. This corporation employed lawyers on a case-by-case basis, not only to conduct investigations and to adjust claims, but also, where necessary, to represent individual insurance companies in litigation. The fee arrangement is not entirely clear, but apparently the lawyer's fees for the investigation and adjustment services were paid by the corporation, which in turn charged the individual insurance companies for the service. It would appear, however, that the individual insurance companies paid the lawyers directly for representation in litigation.[40]

Some banks, savings and loan institutions, trust companies, real estate brokers, and other similar commercial enterprises provide lawyers' services to their customers — generally in matters in which the providing of legal services will facilitate or expedite their primary businesses.[41] One example is an in-

39. E.g., a management engineering firm that provided, among other services relating to labor relations, legal advice and representation (held improper by *NYC Eth. Ops.*, No. 678); a firm of engineering contractors that, on behalf of owners of property adjoining a projected subway, undertook to supervise construction to avoid damage to adjoining property, to procure repairs for damaged property, to represent property owners in the adjustment of compensation therefor, and to provide legal representation in suits for damages (held improper in *NYCLA Eth. Ops.*, No. 296); a corporation service organization that offered customers a full range of lawyers' services with respect to the organizing of corporations (lawyer participation held improper in *ABA Eth. Ops.*, No. 31); a realty management corporation that offered the assistance of lawyers in the drafting of leases and in the institution, prosecution, and defense of actions involving the managed properties (lawyer participation held improper by *NYC Eth. Ops.*, No. 551); an insurance brokerage corporation that, for a single annual fee, offered to its insurance customers comprehensive legal services to be provided by a lawyer employed by the corporation on an annual salary (*disapproved* by *NYC Eth. Ops.*, No. 733); a mercantile agency that offered, through an advertisement in a trade journal, to provide those engaged in the trade with general legal services (*disapproved* by *NYC Eth. Ops.*, No. 294); and a patent protective service that offered to provide investigation services and legal representation in patent infringement cases (*NYC Eth. Ops.*, No. 576 held this arrangement to be improper if it is merely a cloak for solicitation, but proper "if the lay agency's purpose is to serve its patrons and not to get business for the lawyer"). Cf. Vitaphone Corp. v. Hutchinson Amusement Co. (**410**), which upheld a copyright infringement action brought by a Copyright Protection Bureau, a common agent of eight motion picture companies, for the investigation and prosecution of copyright infringements. See also *NYCLA Eth. Ops.*, No. 47, part III.

40. See *ABA Eth. Ops.*, Nos. 96, 198, approving this arrangement.

41. See Kentucky Bar Ass'n v. First Federal Savings & Loan (**388**); *ABA Inf. Eth. Ops.*, Nos. 508, 544, 643; *NYC Eth. Ops.*, Nos. 22, 192. Perhaps it should be noted that a great deal has been done to delineate the limits of permissible activity in certain of these fields through interprofessional conferences. Representatives of the American Bar Association and various business and professional groups have worked together to produce a number of statements of principles defining the proper spheres of activity of the respective

vestment firm that, as an adjunct to its investment-counseling activities, offered advice relating to the legality and the tax consequences of investment programs prepared by the firm for its clients.[42] It is said that some accounting firms are employing lawyers for similar purposes. Some investment bankers, bond houses, and others engaged in buying state, municipal, and school district bonds for resale also offer to provide legal services to the issuers with respect to the issuance of such bonds.[43] It also appears to be quite common for mutual funds, insurance companies, and others to provide predrafted trust forms and other forms to their customers, although this would be better viewed as the providing of "legal services" than as the providing of "lawyers' services."

Because the collection of commercial claims so often requires legal action, it is common for lay collection agencies to forward claims which they have been unable to collect by other methods to preselected lawyers for the filing of suit. This, too, is a kind of intermediary arrangement.[44]

Finally, from time to time lay agencies have offered lawyers' services for sale to the public as a profit-making enterprise, unconnected with any other business or service offered by the agency.[45] One example is an "Estate Organization Service," offering the services of lawyers in setting up and administering *inter vivos* trusts designed to avoid probate. These arrangements can be viewed as intermediary arrangements because they involve the selection of lawyers by lay agencies outside the direct lawyer-client relationship, although the group involved—the

professions and businesses. Presently existing statements of principles deal with the activities of accountants, banks with trust functions, collection agencies, insurance adjusters, life insurance underwriters, publishers, realtors, and social workers. A Conference of Lawyers and Casualty Insurance Companies has not yet adopted any statement of principles. See 209:vol. 3, 214A-229A.

42. *NYC Eth. Ops.*, No. 484, disapproved this as a violation of Canon 35.

43. ABA Committee on Unauthorized Practice of Law, Informative Opinion A (53); Missouri Bar Advisory Opinion, No. 101 (219).

44. Under the various ethics opinions, it is generally regarded as permissible for a lawyer to represent individual creditors referred to him by a lay collection agency, provided that the direct lawyer-client relationship exists between the lawyer and the creditor-client, and provided that the lay agency does not interpose itself as an intermediary to control the activities of the lawyer. Arrangements in which the lay agency receives any part of the lawyer's fee, or in which the lawyer is in reality an employee of the agency, are viewed as improper. See *ABA Inf. Eth. Ops.*, Nos. C-735, 794; *NYC Eth. Ops.*, Nos. 480, 562, 731. See also Midland Credit Adjustment Co. v. Donnelley (390).

45. *In re* Co-operative Law Co. (374); State v. Merchants Protective Corp. (404); People v. Merchants Protective Corp. (398); People v. Cal. Protective Corp. (398).

purchasing public — probably stretches the concept of an "identifiable group" to the limits of workable utility.[46]

d

Insurance programs

(1)

Liability insurance

There is a strong community of interest between a liability insurer and its insured, arising from the fact that when the insured is found liable for damages on a claim covered by liability insurance, the company is also liable to the extent of the coverage. Standard contracts of liability insurance therefore typically give the company both the right and the duty to defend such claims, a practice that has been held to be permissible under the American Bar Association Canons of Professional Ethics (*ABA Eth. Ops.*, No. 282). Title insurance similarly provides for the representation of insureds by insurers on claims covered by the title policy. Both of these arrangements may properly be viewed as intermediary arrangements because they involve the providing of legal services to individual members of a group (the insureds of a particular insurer, especially where the insurance is marketed on a group basis) by lawyers selected and paid for by the insurer. The fact that employment of the attorney is occasioned by a claim requiring defense of a joint interest of the insurer and the insured does not obviate the fact that the insurer alone selects the lawyer who is to represent not only its own interest but that of the individual insured as well.

Another example is teachers' on-the-job liability insurance.[47] The insurance contract provides for liability coverage with respect to claims arising out of the insured teacher's professional activities. It also gives the insurer both the right and the duty to defend such claims. Thus it is an intermediary arrangement under the definition being used here. It also provides, however, that a teacher who requires legal representation in criminal

46. Note that the rendition of such services by laymen rather than by lawyers presents purely unauthorized practice questions and is entirely outside the scope of the present discussion.

47. One such program is offered by the Teachers' Insurance Association through state teachers' associations.

actions arising out of employment, in actions or proceedings for dismissal, or in actions involving specified professional interests may be reimbursed by the insurer for a portion of the fee paid to a lawyer chosen by the insured—provided that the final verdict or final decision is not against the insured. This part of the coverage is not an intermediary arrangement, of course, because the client selects the lawyer. Rather, it is in substance a pure legal service insurance arrangement.

A number of medical associations—at least one of them being a statewide organization—have set up intermediary arrangements to deal with their members' exposure to malpractice claims. These are essentially liability insurance programs in which the insurer selects the lawyer.[48]

(2)
Automobile club benefits
as insurance

Legal service benefits currently being offered by automobile clubs in traffic cases (dollar indemnities for representation in

48. In one such arrangement, the medical association arranges with a commercial insurer for the issuance of liability coverage to its members, negotiating the limits, scope of coverage, and premium schedule. (Individual doctors are free to obtain coverage elsewhere, but in fact the overwhelming number do so through the association plan because of its cost advantages, convenience, and auxiliary services.) All malpractice claims against the covered member doctors are referred to the insurer, which in turn has retainer arrangements with a law firm.

The medical association has established a medical review committee composed of its own members. The review committee passes independent judgment—usually based on a searching no-holds-barred inquiry—on the merits of all malpractice claims against covered members. If the committee deems a claim to be meritorious, the insurer is advised either to settle or, where the damages claim is regarded as excessive, to contest only on the question of damages. If the committee concludes that the claim is unjustified, the insurer is advised to refuse settlement and to fight the claim. The advice, which may be reviewed or augmented by the retained law firm, is systematically followed by the insurer.

In any event, all defense of claims against covered doctors are handled by the retained law firm, except where local counsel is retained or associated ad hoc in cases filed away from the retained firm's base of operations. The law firm is compensated for its services by the insurer according to standing arrangements for per diem and hourly fees. The costs of legal defense are added by the insurer to its cost of underwriting the liability exposure and its administrative and overhead costs in servicing the policy.

Each year or so, the costs of the coverage—claims, overhead, and costs of defense—are reviewed by the medical association and the insurer, and the rates paid by individual doctors are adjusted accordingly. In effect, the arrangement is a malpractice defense mutual, serviced by, and backed by the reserves of, an insurance company. And, because the lawyer is selected by the insurer, it is an intermediary arrangement within the definition being used here.

So far, these arrangements appear not to have been viewed as group legal services—or, more specifically, as either intervention between lawyer and client by the medical association or the channeling of cases to a single law firm.

specified kinds of cases by a lawyer of the member's own choosing) have also been mentioned previously.[49] They too are essentially legal service insurance rather than intermediary arrangements — insofar as the organization has nothing to do with selecting or recommending the lawyer. The older types of auto club legal services, where the club provided or assisted in the selection of the lawyer, might appropriately be viewed both as insurance and as intermediary arrangements.

(3)
Legal expense
insurance proposals

The above examples, are, of course, forms of prepaid legal expense insurance, but they may also be intermediary arrangements, depending upon the role played by the insurer in the selection or recommendation of a lawyer to render the services. Proposals have been made from time to time for the establishment of comprehensive legal service programs similar to the medical insurance now so prevalent. As a result of a feasibility study conducted under the auspices of the American Bar Foundation, the American Bar Association is now in the process of setting up experimental insurance programs.[50] Any such insurance plan that contemplates either the selection of the lawyer by an agency other than the individual to be represented, or the recommendation of particular lawyers by such agency, should be regarded as an intermediary arrangement.

3
Present Extent of
Intermediary Arrangements

It is probably safe to generalize that intermediary arrangements, within the definition formulated above, are extensive and spreading.[51] The vast expansion of efforts to provide lawyers'

49. See note 35 *supra.*
50. See chapter 2 *supra.*
51. The foregoing examples of intermediary programs tell us nothing at all about the extent to which such programs are now in operation or about the number of cases they handle, of course. Some of the examples are presently existing programs, and others are merely proposed programs. Still others are arrangements that the courts have passed

services to the poor, for example, is common knowledge (see 239:805-50), as is increased activity in the field of protecting and asserting constitutional rights.[52] The military legal assistance programs are well established and provide services to substantial numbers of people. For instance, the Army Legal Assistance program alone handled over a million cases during the fiscal year from July 1,1965, to June 30,1966.[53]

The present extent of labor union activity in the providing of lawyers' services to union members is largely unknown. One study was undertaken about fifteen years ago under the auspices of the Survey of the Legal Profession.

The report of the study states:

> Most labor lawyers report that they are called upon and expected to do considerable free work. This includes not only public appearances at meetings, conferences, and legislative bodies, but also personal legal work for the officers of the union, personal advice to some of the members, and work for small affiliated local unions.

> More than three-quarters of the lawyers report that they do personal legal work for union officials, while seven out of eight labor lawyers state that they do general legal work for individual members of the union. Approximately one-quarter of these lawyers report that they are paid for this work by the union while the remainder are paid directly by the individual members of the union. Generally, the lawyers report, this type of work is non-lucrative when it consists of personal and telephone advice or even written opinions.

> The work for the individual union members covers a wide variety of fields. Legal problems relative to wills and estates are most prevalent, closely followed by real estate and tort cases. Industrial accident and unemployment compensation cases, which are closely allied to labor work, come next and occupy more than half the labor lawyers. Tax work and social security problems are handled by slightly less than half of the labor lawyers.

---

upon. Moreover, information about intermediary programs is difficult to obtain. Many arrangements are of an informal nature and are thus hard to identify. In addition, the legal profession's long-standing disapproval of certain kinds of intermediary arrangements undoubtedly prompts the organizations engaging in them to be somewhat secretive, at least where the inquirer is a lawyer or represents a legal organization.

52. This activity is reflected in the decisions on the right to counsel in criminal cases: Gideon v. Wainwright (380); Escobedo v. Illinois (378); Miranda v. Arizona (391). See also, with respect to right to counsel in juvenile proceedings, Kent v. United States (387); *In re* Gault (379).

53. Information supplied by George J. McCartin, Jr., Lt. Colonel, JAGC, Chief of Legal Assistance Division, Office of the Judge Advocate General, Department of the Army.

The fact that a labor union has an attorney who does some work for individual members is no guarantee that the union members have adequate individual legal services. In fact, many labor lawyers report that because of their labor specialty and label as a 'labor lawyer,' the individual union members often do not turn to them for individual legal problems, including probate, tort, real estate, criminal, and other legal work. In addition, because of the pitfalls of internal union politics involving officials, the union attorneys in many cases do little legal work for individual union members. The limitations of the Code of Legal Ethics also prevent many labor lawyers from actively soliciting the legal business of the individual members of the labor organization. There seems to be a definite need for education of union members as well as possible reinterpretation of the Code of Legal Ethics in this field to make available to the individual union member more adequate legal services.[54]

Nothing indicates that union activity in providing lawyers' services to members has decreased in the interval since this study. Indeed, present indications are that such activity has grown. Of special interest is a recent resolution of the International Longshoremen's and Warehousemen's Union urging locals to utilize union counsel in providing legal services to union members.[55]

54. The study was conducted by a committee composed of Robert M. Segal, counsel for the Massachusetts Federation of Labor; J. Albert Woll, then general counsel of the American Federation of Labor and presently general counsel of the AFL-CIO; and Arthur J. Goldberg, then general counsel of the Congress of Industrial Organizations (276). But note that the Blaustein and Porter digest of the Segal report has only the following to say about service to individual members by labor union lawyers. "Because of the rapidly shifting internal political situations in many unions, most labor lawyers find it inadvisable to do legal work for individual members. The stereotype designation of 'labor' lawyer is another factor preventing service to the rank and file, since few members consider their organization's counsel competent to deal with their personal problems" (73:51–56). It might be suggested, however, that these observations somewhat misstate the conclusions of the Segal report.

55. The text of the resolution is as follows:
    PROVIDING LEGAL SERVICES FOR OUR UNION MEMBERSHIP
    WHEREAS: The International Union has long been aware of the difficulties its members experience in matters requiring legal representation, the most serious of which is in the area of on-the-job injuries involving compensation claims or third party actions; and
    WHEREAS: A recent decision by the U.S. Supreme Court in a case involving the Brotherhood of Railroad Trainmen has held that a union has a constitutional right to refer its members to union attorneys on matters within the area of the union's concern; and
    WHEREAS: There are various practices prevailing in the ports in the handling of industrial injury cases, and men injured off (sic) the job often engage the first attorney or other persons they can get hold of, with the results that frequently they recover far less than they should due to high fees, inadequate services and quick settlements; and
    WHEREAS: The attorneys for the International and the Locals have

An extensive independent survey would be required to obtain any kind of reliable quantitative estimate of present intermediary arrangements. It is apparent, however, that collective effort to achieve common goals is increasing in all fields of social, political, and economic endeavor, and it is a virtual certainty that such activity in the field of legal services will also continue to grow.

B
An Examination of
Present Restrictions

1
The Legal Profession's
Responsibilities to the Public

The legal profession holds an exclusive license to provide legal services to the public. Exclusive license carries with it great responsibility. Because only lawyers may render legal services, the profession must see that adequate legal services, performed by honest and competent lawyers, are readily available to all who want them.

In carrying out these exclusive functions, the profession's role is somewhat unusual. Because of its tradition of self-regulation based upon ethical principles, because of its privity to—and in many states affiliation with—regulatory authority, and because of the close relationships of individual lawyers with legislatures and courts, the profession has a preponderant if not decisive

represented the union in every major struggle and have demonstrated their devotion, integrity, competence and willingness to establish a fair and reasonable basis of compensation for their work; and

WHEREAS: Arrangements between the locals and their attorneys could result in reducing contingency arrangements in industrial injury cases to 25% applied to the net recovery (without deduction for investigation expense) rather than the gross amount, thus assuring the injured worker a substantially larger recovery than is now possible; and

WHEREAS: Virtually all of our members lack adequate means to afford preventive and remedial legal protection in all kinds of areas affecting their lives, liberties and their assets;

THEREFORE BE IT RESOLVED: That each local or area seek an arrangement for the benefit of the members, with its attorneys already on retainer to handle industrial injury cases and other legal matters for its members. [Resolution # 20-A, submitted and carried. International Longshoremen's & Warehousemen's Union, Longshore, Shipclerk & Walking Boss Caucus, San Francisco, California, April 4, 1966.]

influence in determining how its exclusive license is to be exercised. Thus it has a decisive influence in determining how the public interest is to be served with respect to lawyers' services. This is a demanding role, calling for continuous self-examination by the profession to make sure that its determinations are sound and truly in the public interest.

The legal profession has generally performed this role well. There can be little question that genuine concern for the public interest has been the bar's primary motive in establishing and administering most of the rules and restrictions under which its exclusive license is exercised. As noted earlier, a primary objective of the profession's ethical standards is to preserve the traditional lawyer-client relationship, an objective unquestionably in the public interest. Moreover, independent and individualistic though lawyers may be, the voluntary compliance of most lawyers with the profession's ethical code attests to their fundamental commitment to the spirit of public service. This fact does not, however, relieve the profession of the continuing duty of self-examination to make sure that its exercise of this exclusive license remains attuned to the public interest.

One theory sometimes urged for the profession's guidance in determining how its exclusive license is to be exercised is the idea that no deviation from traditional forms or procedures of law practice or from traditional methods of dispensing lawyer's services should be permitted without some conclusive demonstration of a great public need, presently unfilled and unfillable through traditional forms and methods (283:327, 336-38; 315). This theory may be motivated by concern for the public interest, but it is not a sound basis for true professionalism. First, the theory erroneously presumes that the profession's past determinations about public interest and about the exercise of the bar's exclusive license are infallible and immutable. Proper respect for tradition and for the wisdom of the past may require that past decisions be given consideration and due deference, but they do not preclude reexamination of yesterday's answers to see if they fit today's problems. Indeed, the legal profession's position of influence in the determination of public interest demands continuous and searching reexamination. Second, the theory deprives the public itself of any meaningful part in determining what is in its own interest. The fact that the public wishes to obtain lawyers' services through an arrangement that deviates from traditional forms of law practice does not necessarily mean that such an arrangement is actually in the public interest. But the fact of public demand is relevant to the question of public interest and should not be ignored.

It appears significant in this regard that the profession's approval of the military legal assistance programs (and, at least by implication, of legal aid programs) was based in part upon the fact that prospective recipients of the services remained free to obtain their own lawyers if they wished (*ABA Inf. Eth. Ops.*, No. 567). Thus, military legal assistance programs are deemed acceptable at least partly because the serviceman with a legal problem has the option of using the intermediary arrangement or obtaining private counsel. Much the same principle is involved in Canon 6, which permits a lawyer to represent clients with conflicting interests, provided he makes full disclosure to the clients and obtains their express consent. The clients thus have the option of seeking other counsel or continuing with the same lawyer despite the conflict. In both the military and the private practice situations the decision is the client's, although an honorable lawyer would no doubt decline to represent conflicting interests, even with the consent of the parties, if he felt that he could not represent them fairly and faithfully. With respect to certain intermediary arrangements, however, the public is denied any choice at all — the arrangements having been completely prohibited without any regard for the wishes of the segments of the public that would have been served. Such denial is difficult to justify.

In presuming the infallibility and immutability of existing restrictions and in ignoring expressed desires of the public, this theory clearly misplaces what, in a litigation context, would be called "the burden of proof." In an economic and social system based on free enterprise and free association, those who would restrict enterprise by legal controls in the name of the public good have a burden of proof, and a heavy one. This is especially so where the power to impose restrictions rests with those who have been given exclusive license to engage in the enterprise being restricted. So it is where the public — or a particular segment of the public — wishes to obtain lawyers' services through an arrangement that it finds to be useful or beneficial but that is not deemed permissible under traditional restrictions on law practice. The public is not obliged to prove its need; the legal profession is obliged to justify the restrictions.

2
Objectives and Application of Present Restrictions

a
Public interest objectives

Legal and ethical limitations on the obtaining of lawyers' services through intermediary arrangements involve interests of both the public and the profession. Because the public interest is the main concern of this study, the following discussion will consider primarily what appear to be the principal public interests at stake. The interests of the profession will be left to be discussed briefly at the conclusion of this chapter.

As they existed prior to the *Button, BRT,* and *UMW* decisions, and as many lawyers would still have them continue, the profession's restrictions on the obtaining of lawyers' services through intermediary arrangements might be summarized as follows: All intermediary arrangements, except those – like legal aid – that have been exempted by definition and those – like casualty insurance arrangements – that the profession has chosen not to look at as intermediary arrangements, are completely prohibited as the unauthorized practice of law, and lawyer participation in them is regarded as unethical.

This restrictive position derives principally from Canon 35 of the Canons of Professional Ethics of the American Bar Association.[56] The main objective of this Canon, which deals with the intervention of intermediaries in the lawyer-client relationship, seems to be to preserve the lawyer's independence in the exercise of his professional judgment and in the discharge of his professional obligations to his client. The Canon seems to accomplish this by eliminating, or at least reducing, the possibility of outside control over the lawyer by lay intermediaries.

56. Canon 35 (Intermediaries) is quoted at 265 *infra.* See also 13:156–64.

Several other Canons are also pertinent, although the relationship is less direct. For example, the purpose of Canon 34,[57] which prohibits the splitting of fees with laymen, is customarily viewed as being the prevention of "exploitation" of lawyers by laymen. The preventing of "exploitation" involves a number of interests of the profession, including economics, status, and image. As far as the public is concerned, however, there would seem to be just one real interest. So long as the lawyer's performance is not affected, and as long as the fee is reasonable in relation to the service performed, the client and the public generally have no real interest in who gets a cut of the fee. The public's interest would seem rather to be primarily in the possible effect of fee-splitting upon the lawyer's performance. Thus, the public-interest objective is again to preserve the lawyer's independence in the exercise of his professional judgment. The reasoning is simple: A layman or lay agency with a pecuniary interest in the rendition of a legal service is likely to seek to exercise some control over the lawyer who renders it. And, if the layman's pecuniary interest results from a *quid pro quo*—such as an agreement to refer clients to the lawyer—the lawyer may be susceptible to being influenced or controlled. To avoid this possibility, the Canon prohibits the lawyer from permitting laymen or lay agencies from acquiring any pecuniary interest in his services.

Canon 47 [58] forbids lawyers to assist in "the unauthorized practice of law by lay agencies," a term which state laws typically define as including both the rendition of legal services and the furnishing of lawyers.[59] This broad prohibition is often based

57. Canon 34 (Division of Fees): "No division of fees for legal services is proper, except with another lawyer, based upon a division of service or responsibility" (13:148–55).

58. Canon 47 (Aiding the Unauthorized Practice of Law): "No lawyer shall permit his professional services, or his name, to be used in aid of, or to make possible, the unauthorized practice of law by any lay agency, personal or corporate" (13:193-97).

59. Typical of state laws prohibiting the practice of law by corporations is the Illinois statute, which says:

> § 411. Unlawful for corporation to practice law. It shall be unlawful for a corporation to practice law or appear as an attorney at law for any reason in any court in this state or before any judicial body, or make it a business to practice as an attorney at law for any reason in any court in this state or before any judicial body, or make it a business to practice as an attorney at law for any person in any said courts or to hold itself out to the public as being entitled to practice law or to render or furnish legal services of any kind in actions or proceedings of any nature or in any other way or manner to assume to be entitled to practice law or to assume, use and advertise the title of lawyer or attorney, attorney at law, or equivalent terms in any language in

on the idea that a corporation or other artificial entity is not a
"natural person" and is therefore incapable of participating in
the highly personal lawyer-client relationship.[60] Such reasoning
may be sound where the lay organization provides legal services, whether they be predrafted legal forms, legal tasks performed by lay employees, or legal services rendered in some
other manner not involving direct service to a client *by a lawyer.*
It is not appropriate, however, where the services are rendered
directly to the client by a lawyer and where the involvement of
the group or lay agency is solely in providing, securing, or
recommending the lawyer. Lawyers are capable of engaging in
the personal lawyer-client relationship, even though introduced
or even furnished to the client by some outside agency. Thus,
where the services are rendered by a lawyer, it is the lawyer
who is practicing law and not the intermediary agency (192).

Unauthorized practice laws that prohibit the furnishing of
lawyers, as distinguished from the furnishing of legal services,
must therefore rest on a different rationale. Once again, the
objective seems to be to eliminate or reduce the possibility that

---

such manner as to convey the impression that it is entitled to practice law, or
to furnish legal advice, furnish attorneys or counsel, or to advertise that
either alone or together with, or by or through, any person, whether a duly
and regularly admitted attorney at law or not, it has, owns, conducts or
maintains a law office or an office for the practice of law or for furnishing
legal advice, services or counsel [421].

60. The Committee on Unauthorized Practice of Law of the American Bar Association
has put it this way:

A corporation can neither practice law nor hire lawyers to carry on the
business of practicing law for it, and whether it is a corporation or a voluntary association operating under a trade name, which employs the lawyers, is
unimportant.

The right to practice law attaches to the individual and dies with him. It
cannot be made the subject of business to be sheltered under the cloak of a
corporation because the relationship of attorney and client is personal. Only
a natural person may practice law.

It is unlawful and against public policy for a corporation to maintain a
legal department or hire attorneys and advertise their services for the use of
others.

Automobile clubs organized, among other things, for the purpose of furnishing legal services to its (*sic*) members have been held to be engaged in
the practice of law as to such services.

The relationship of attorney and client is that of master and servant in a
limited and dignified sense, and it involves the highest trust and confidence.
It cannot be delegated without consent, and it cannot exist between an
attorney employed by a corporation to practice law for it and a client of the
corporation, for he would be subject to the directions of the corporation and
not to the directions of the client. There would be neither contract nor
privity between him and the client and he would not owe even the duty of
counsel to the actual litigant [53:46–47; see also 417:1364–78].

a lay agency might exercise control or influence over the professional activities of the lawyer. And the principal public interest involved seems to be the lawyer's independence in the exercise of his professional judgment and the performance of his professional functions for the client.

Although rarely mentioned in the cases and opinions dealing with intermediary arrangements, Canon 6 is nevertheless related to the question of control or influence over the lawyer by someone other than the client being served.[61] It prohibits the representation of conflicting interests except upon full disclosure and by the express consent of all concerned. Thus, it is addressed to one of the elements—conflict of interest—that is involved in any threat to the lawyer's independence of professional judgment from intermediary legal service arrangements. One objective of the Canon, therefore, is clearly to keep the lawyer's exercise of his professional judgment free from compromising influences and to make sure that the interests of someone other than the individual client do not affect the lawyer's professional performance—even when that someone else is another of the lawyer's clients.

61. Canon 6 (Adverse Influences and Conflicting Interests):
   It is the duty of a lawyer at the time of retainer to disclose to the client all the circumstances of his relations to the parties, and any interest in or connection with the controversy, which might influence the client in the selection of counsel.
   It is unprofessional to represent conflicting interests, except by express consent of all concerned given after a full disclosure of the facts. Within the meaning of this canon, a lawyer represents conflicting interests when, in behalf of one client, it is his duty to contend for that which duty to another client requires him to oppose.
   The obligation to represent the client with undivided fidelity and not to divulge his secrets or confidences forbids also the subsequent acceptance of retainers or employment from others in matters adversely affecting any interest of the client with respect to which confidence has been reposed [see 13:22–39].
Thus, Canon 6 explicitly and unqualifiedly permits the representation of interests that are genuinely in conflict, provided that full disclosure is made to, and consent obtained from, all concerned. The ABA Ethics Committee has several times refused to recommend deletion of the clause which permits such representation (see *ABA Inf. Eth. Ops.*, No. 296). Nevertheless, certain of the opinions of the Committee (e.g., *ABA Eth. Ops.*, Nos. 112, 245) have condemned the representation of conflicting interests in particular circumstances, even with the consent of the parties. Opinions which thus modify the Canon appear to rest on two grounds. First, the spirit of the Canon—complete fidelity to the client—is viewed as precluding the representation of conflicting interests in circumstances where fair and faithful representation of both parties appears to be impossible, even with disclosure and consent. Second, the representation of conflicting interests in some circumstances looks too bad to be permitted, even though the lawyer may in fact be able to represent both parties fairly and faithfully. Most of the opinions, however, do follow the Canon in permitting representation of conflicting interests where there has been disclosure and consent.

Canons 27 and 28,[62] which deal with advertising and solicitation of legal business by lawyers, frequently have a part in
cases and opinions on intermediary arrangements. This is because they proscribe indirect advertising and the solicitation of
business for lawyers by agents, and intermediary arrangements
have frequently been looked at as being nothing more than
advertising and solicitation by or on behalf of the participating
lawyers. It is submitted, however, that this may not be the most
meaningful way in which to view intermediary arrangements, as
it ignores the real character of such arrangements and focuses
instead upon a merely incidental characteristic. For in nearly all
the cases and opinions, the proscribed intermediary arrangements have been essentially group efforts to obtain competent
legal services on acceptable terms for individual members, with
the benefit to the participating lawyer—in the form of the channeling of legal business or of outright employment—being nothing more than an incidental byproduct of the arrangement.

Moreover, as observed in chapter 4, there is some doubt
about the extent to which all of the profession's present restrictions upon the business-getting activities of lawyers are really
called for by the public interest. This being so, it is hard to
justify the extension of those restrictions to proscribe absolutely
arrangements that are not essentially business-getting activities
on behalf of lawyers, but rather lawyer-getting activities on behalf of groups of potential clients. Perhaps there is some justification for restrictions that would prevent lawyers from participating in intermediary legal service arrangements that use dis-
honest or misleading advertising and solicitation methods. And
lawyers probably should not be permitted to participate in arrangements that use business-getting measures so extreme that
the legal profession is brought into such disrepute as to impair
its ability to discharge its own important responsibilities to the
public. In addition, of course, where an intermediary arrange-

62. Canon 27 (Advertising, Direct or Indirect):
    It is unprofessional to solicit professional employment by circulars, adver-
    tisements, through touters or by personal communications or interviews not
    warranted by personal relations. Indirect advertisements for professional
    employment such as furnishing or inspiring newspaper comments, or procur-
    ing his photograph to be published in connection with causes in which the
    lawyer has been or is engaged or concerning the manner of their conduct,
    the magnitude of the interest involved, the importance of the lawyer's
    position and all other like self-laudation, offend the traditions and lower the
    tone of our profession and are reprehensible; but the customary use of
    simple professional cards is not improper.

ment *is* nothing more than a business-getting scheme for lawyers, then proscription may be justified—depending upon the view taken by lawyers generally of advertising and solicitation. But to go beyond this and completely proscribe intermediary arrangements just because they happen to produce employment for lawyers cannot be justified on public interest grounds.

One further possible public interest consideration is sometimes raised. Although the idea has not been given explicit formulation in the Canons, it is sometimes argued that the public does have an interest in the quality of legal services it obtains, and that the intermediary arrangement will inevitably tend to cause participating lawyers to lower the quality of the services they render. It is contended that because the lawyer has been employed or selected by someone other than the individual recipient of his services and need not, in many instances, look to

---

Publication in reputable law lists in a manner consistent with the standards of conduct imposed by these canons of brief biographical and informative data is permissible. Such data must not be misleading and may include only a statement of the lawyer's name and the names of his professional associates; addresses, telephone numbers, cable addresses; branches of the profession practiced; date and place of birth and admission to the bar; schools attended, with dates of graduation, degrees and other educational distinctions; public or quasi-public offices; posts of honor; legal authorships; legal teaching positions; memberships and offices in bar associations and committees thereof, in legal and scientific societies, and legal fraternities; the fact of listings in other reputable law lists; the names and addresses of references; and, with their written consent, the names of clients regularly represented. A certificate of compliance with the Rules and Standards issued by the Special Committee on Law Lists may be treated as evidence that such list is reputable.

It is not improper for a lawyer who is admitted to practice as a proctor in admiralty to use that designation on his letterhead or shingle or for a lawyer who has complied with the statutory requirements of admission to practice before the patent office to so use the designation of patent attorney or patent lawyer or trade-mark attorney or trade-mark lawyer or any combination of those terms [13:74-129].

Canon 28 (Stirring Up Litigation, Directly or Through Agents):

It is unprofessional for a lawyer to volunteer advice to bring a lawsuit, except in rare cases where ties of blood, relationship or trust make it his duty to do so. Stirring up strife and litigation is not only unprofessional, but it is indictable at common law. It is disreputable to hunt up defects in titles or other causes of action and inform thereof in order to be employed to bring suit or collect judgment, or to breed litigation by seeking out those with claims for personal injuries or those having any other grounds of action in order to secure them as clients, or to employ agents or runners for like purposes, or to pay or reward, directly or indirectly, those who bring or influence the bringing of such cases to his office, or to remunerate policemen, court or prison officials, physicians, hospital *attaches* or others who may succeed, under the guise of giving disinterested friendly advice, in influencing the criminal, the sick and the injured, the ignorant or others, to seek his professional services. A duty to the public and to the profession devolves upon every member of the Bar having knowledge of such practices upon the part of any practitioner immediately to inform thereof, to the end that the offender may be disbarred [13:130-31]

the individual recipient for the fee, he will not have any incentive to maintain the quality of his services. The argument is sometimes varied to assert that the handling of a large number of cases of the same kind will impair the quality of the lawyer's performance.

These arguments are not persuasive, however. To begin with, the contention that the handling of large numbers of similar cases will induce a lower standard of performance may be countered by the contrary assertion that concentration of effort in a limited field of practice will produce a higher level of proficiency than would otherwise be developed. Moreover, while the cases and opinions are full of allegations that intermediary arrangements will result in low-quality services, they contain a dearth of hard evidence that such arrangements actually have impaired the quality of the services rendered.

More importantly, these arguments contradict one of the most fundamental premises of the legal profession. The essence of a profession is dedication to the ideal of service before personal gain. But if a lawyer will lower the quality of the services he renders merely because he was employed or selected by someone other than the individual recipient of the service, or because he must look to someone other than the recipient for his fee, is his claim to "professionalism" anything more than hollow pretension?

Even if it could be shown that the services rendered through intermediary arrangements are inferior in quality to those offered by private practitioners, and even if this discrepancy could be squared with the lawyer's claim to "professionalism," there would still be the question of why the public interest should require that such arrangements be proscribed. It can be argued that a state may legitimately require a minimum level of competence of those it permits to practice law. And the profession would seem to be acting legitimately in providing lawyer referral services and other devices for assisting clients to select better lawyers. Indeed, it might even be argued that a state could legitimately set up special classes of law practice, with higher qualifications required for the performance of some kinds of legal functions than for others. But could it be argued that one person or class of people could legitimately be required to obtain a given legal service from a special class of lawyers while other people were permitted to get the same service from any lawyer? And where, as under the present system, only a minimum level of competence is required for law practice, and where most people are permitted to obtain their legal services from any lawyer, could either the profession or the state justify requiring a particular class of people to obtain their legal services from large Wall Street law firms or prohibiting that group from getting services from general practitioners on the ground that the large firms can provide better service?

The point, of course, is that where the profession and the state have undertaken only to require a minimum level of proficiency for licensure as a lawyer, the client himself should probably be the one to determine the level of quality—above the minimum—that he will purchase. One might contend that the minimum level is too low, or that the provisions for maintaining the level are inappropriate or imperfectly applied. But one could hardly contend that measures to remedy such deficiencies should be applied to some lawyers and not to others or to some prospective clients and not to others. Restrictions that seek to improve the quality of the legal services obtained by members of groups by limiting the manner in which such people may secure lawyers do precisely that. They say, in effect, "You cannot act collectively to purchase a level of quality that you and others would be completely free to purchase individually." The person who acts in concert with others to obtain individual legal services should have the same alternatives, with respect to the quality of the service to be purchased, as the person who acts individually. Thus, the quality of the services offered through intermediary arrangements is not a major public interest consideration.

It is apparent, then, that present restrictions on the obtaining of lawyers' services through intermediary arrangements are directed primarily at a single public interest objective—preserving the lawyer's independence of professional judgment and action.[63] There can be no doubt that this legal profession value is extremely valuable to the public. Indeed, perhaps the most important qualities that lawyers offer to the public are undivided allegiance to the interests of each individual client and independence from outside control over the performance of their

---

63. It is worth emphasizing that the public's interest is in the protection of the lawyer's independence of professional judgment and not in the protection of the independent lawyer's professional practice, two matters often confused by the bar.

professional tasks. If the lawyer is a true professional, then securing his freedom from outside control or influence should, as a matter of course, secure for the public all those values usually claimed as benefits of professional service. The lawyer's independence of professional judgment and action, the key to the entire subject of group legal services, will therefore here be regarded as the prime objective of restrictions on intermediary legal service arrangements.

b
Application of
present restrictions

Some intermediary arrangements are clearly not in the public interest, and the restrictions that prohibit them and forbid lawyers to participate in them are unquestionably sound. The most obvious are the commercial arrangements that seek to offer lawyers' services to the public for a profit. Similarly, many of the intermediary arrangements that have been given approval by the profession, arrangements such as legal aid and the military legal assistance programs, are just as clearly in the public interest, and the public good is served by their existence and by the participation of lawyers in them.

There is a middle ground, however, where the present application of restrictions on intermediary arrangements is vulnerable to criticism. Arrangements having similar characteristics are too often distinguished from each other on grounds that bear no reasonable relation to the demands of the public interest. As a result, many intermediary arrangements which the public finds useful and wishes to utilize are presently prohibited, even though some of them appear to pose no greater threat to the professional independence of the lawyer than do many of those that are permitted. This may occur when intermediary arrangements are either permitted or prohibited simply by definition, with their essential characteristics being overlooked or ignored. Or it may result from simply presuming the facts that should determine the central question—whether the arrangement does in fact pose a significant and unavoidable threat to the lawyer's independence of professional judgment and action.

The difficulty arising from the approval or disapproval of intermediary arrangements by definition, without regard to the

essential characteristics of the particular arrangement, stems
from Canon 35 itself. It begins with a statement of broad principles:

> The professional services of a lawyer should not be con-
> trolled or exploited by any lay agency, personal or corporate,
> which intervenes between client and lawyer. A lawyer's re-
> sponsibilities and qualifications are individual. He should
> avoid all relations which direct the performance of his duties
> by or in the interest of such intermediary. A lawyer's relation
> to his client should be personal, and the responsibility
> should be direct to the client.

The Canon then, by definition, excludes legal aid programs:
"Charitable societies rendering aid to the indigent are not
deemed such intermediaries." Finally, the Canon makes specific
application of the broad principles by stating:

> A lawyer may accept employment from any organization,
> such as an association, club or trade organization, to render
> legal services in any matter in which the organization, as an
> entity, is interested, but this employment should not include
> the rendering of legal services to the members of such an
> organization in respect to their individual affairs.

The basic principles proclaimed in the first paragraph of the
Canon are sound, but the attempts at particularization create
problems. It is not clear, for example, why charitable societies
and the lawyers employed by them to render legal aid to the
indigent should not be subject to those fundamental principles.
Indeed, it is not inconceivable that a charitable society might,
under some circumstances, seek to intervene between the lawyer and his client and seek to control the lawyer's services. And
no good reason appears for relieving the legal aid lawyer of his
basic professional responsibilities to his client. Similarly, the
second paragraph forbids a lawyer to accept employment from
an organization to render services to its individual members,
ignoring the possibility that there might be situations in which
such an employment arrangement would not in fact violate the
basic principles stated in the first paragraph.

Hospital Credit Exchange, Inc. v. Shapiro (384) is an example
of the prohibition by definition of a legal service arrangement,
while its essential characteristics and their relevance to the basic
objectives of the prohibition are overlooked. In that instance a
membership corporation composed of charitable hospitals employed attorneys to represent individual member hospitals in
the collection of unpaid bills. Each member hospital paid fees to

the organization for whatever services were performed for it by the salaried lawyers, but these fees were set so as to cover only the cost of furnishing the service, with no profit accruing to the organization. The court held this to be the unauthorized practice of law under the New York statute, saying:

> I think it should be said in fairness to plaintiff and to the numerous public-spirited citizens who, actuated by the best of motives, have interested themselves in this case and who have submitted affidavits commending the activities of plaintiff and showing how helpful it is to the hospitals it serves, that the plaintiff was organized with the best of intentions and that it is sponsored by the Greater New York Hospital Association and by the New York Hospital Fund. Undoubtedly plaintiff saves money for the charitable hospitals it serves; those institutions find it less expensive than any other method of collecting their outstanding bills. The officers and trustees of the various hospitals strongly approve of plaintiff; the people who conduct the business of plaintiff, that is, its officials and employees, are apparently honest and efficient. Nevertheless, although the motives of the people who organized the plaintiff are commendable, and although the many persons who have come to its aid merit the respect of this court, the plaintiff must nevertheless yield to the public policy which interdicts the practice of law by lay agencies. That policy springs from a vital public necessity. Balancing the conveniences, and weighing the respective public interests involved, I am constrained to the conclusion that to tolerate the practice of law by this plaintiff—and plaintiff is undoubtedly practicing law—is to set a most dangerous precedent and to sanction a clear, though well-intentioned, violation of statutes which are as specific as they could have been made (384:818).

Thus, the New York Court, in characterizing the activities of the organization as "the practice of law by a corporation," prohibited an apparently benign and useful arrangement, choosing to ignore those essential characteristics of the arrangement that are most relevant to the public interest.

A pair of opinions by the ABA Ethics Committee—Opinions 96 and 198—illustrate how the determinative facts are sometimes presumed in the application of restrictions to intermediary arrangements. These opinions involved an arrangement whereby a corporation, engaged in the business of investigating and adjusting insurance claims, employed lawyers on a case-by-case basis to act for individual insurance companies in the investigation and adjustment of claims *and to represent them in litigation.* In Opinion 96, the ABA Ethics Committee held that lawyer participation in such an arrangement was not improper, apparently on the ground that the services provided were not professional services (despite the fact that the lawyers did represent individual insurance companies in litigation). Opinion 198 was later given to clarify Opinion 96. It characterized the relationship between the individual insurance companies and the corporations furnishing lawyers to them as an agency relationship, with the lay claims adjustment corporation acting as the agent of the individual insurance companies in selecting lawyers to handle particular claims. It went on to state:

> If the activities of the adjustment corporation do not constitute the unauthorized practice of law [under applicable state law], the mere fact that it solicits business does not make it improper for the lawyer to accept employment to represent the insurance company. Of course it is assumed that the adjustment corporation does not exploit the services of lawyers and that there is no connection between the agency and the lawyer which would make its solicitation an indirect solicitation for the lawyer.
>
> The terms of the employment of the lawyer, as well as the actual practice in handling the claims, must conform to the requirements of Canon 35. The lawyer must represent the insurance company and not the lay adjuster. At most the adjuster is merely the means through which the insurance company employs the lawyer. The responsibility of the lawyer must be to the principal and he must look to the principal for his compensation. His services must be free from the control of the lay adjuster. He must be allowed to communicate directly with, and obtain his instructions directly from, the insurance company when he so desires. Generally speaking, copies of all correspondence with the lay adjuster should be forwarded to the insurance company.

The Ethics Committee has thus presumed the absence of any interference with or control over the lawyers by the lay corporation employing them, apparently also presuming the existence of facts to support this presumption. No such facts are described in either opinion.

These opinions raise some interesting questions. If a profit-making lay adjustment corporation may properly be viewed simply as an agent in selecting and employing lawyers to represent individual insurance companies in the litigation of insurance claims, does there appear to be any good reason why a nonprofit labor union might not, with equal propriety, be regarded as an agent in selecting and employing lawyers to represent individual union members in the litigation of unemployment compensation claims? Furthermore, if it may be assumed "that the adjustment corporation does not exploit the services of lawyers and that there is no connection between the agency and the lawyer which would make its solicitation an indirect solicitation for the lawyer," might not the same assumptions be made in the labor union situation? And is there any reason to expect that the conditions imposed in Opinion 198 with respect to the terms of the lawyers' employment and the actual handling of claims would be any less effective in one situation than in the other?

By applying restrictions to intermediary arrangements in this manner, the legal profession is placed in the awkward position of having to justify or explain discriminations among arrangements whose essential differences sometimes lie mainly in their historical origins, their present entrenchment, or the political or social respectability of their participants. For example, lay collection agencies may refer collection cases to preselected lawyers, and lawyers may accept the resulting employment;[64] until the decision in *BRT* however, it was generally held to be improper for a labor union to refer industrial accident cases to preselected lawyers and for lawyers to accept the resulting employment. But the agency theory which supports the collection agency practice might just as easily support the labor union arrangement, and there appears to be no really satisfactory ground upon which to distinguish the two.

64. The referral of collection matters to preselected attorneys by lay collection agencies is permitted, subject to certain restrictions, on the ground that the lay collector acts as an agent of the creditor in selecting a lawyer to institute legal action on his behalf. *ABA Eth. Ops.*, No. 295. See also Wisconsin *ex rel.* State Bar of Wisconsin v. Bonded Collections, Inc. (411), which stated:

> The Court finds nothing inherently wrong in the creditor engaging an agent for the purpose of selecting an attorney for him. Various rules have been propounded from time to time to control this arrangement and it is not here intended to adopt any such set of rules, beyond the conclusion that an agent, to lawfully engage an attorney for a principal, must be acting with the specific authority of his principal, and in the process of engaging such an attorney must be certain that he sets up a true attorney-client relationship between the attorney selected and the creditor. It would also preclude the collector from the management of the litigation and decisions necessary thereto. As a matter of ethics, the fee of the collector should be paid by the creditor and the collector should not share the attorney fee.
>
> The purport of the statement of the above ground rules is to limit the scope of this decision by excepting therefrom what the Court considers *a lawful proceeding* in engaging an attorney. (Emphasis added.)

It seems, then, that the essential problem with respect to intermediary arrangements is the failure of present restrictions to relate adequately and consistently to the fundamental public interest objective of preserving independence of professional judgment and action.

C
A Possible Rationale
for the Regulation of
Intermediary Arrangements

From the standpoint of public interest, then, independence of professional judgment and action is the fundamental value involved in intermediary arrangements. The essential problem with the legal profession's past efforts to regulate such arrangements has been the absence of any consistent relationship between the restrictions imposed and this basic value. The need now is for a consistent rationale for regulation, having as its prime objective the preservation of the lawyer's independence of professional judgment and action. Such a theory may both permit the drawing of sound distinctions among intermediary arrangements and support cogent explanations of the distinctions drawn.

The intermediary arrangements already described at length are similar to one another in a number of ways. Most importantly, they are all devoted essentially to the same activity — enabling individual members of a group to obtain legal services from lawyers who are furnished, secured, recommended, or otherwise selected by someone other than the individual who receives the services. That the arrangement may be called a "legal aid society," a "casualty insurance contract," a "group legal service," or the "unauthorized practice of law by a corporation" should not obscure the fact that in this respect they are all performing essentially the same function.

There are also differences among the various intermediary arrangements. They differ in organization, in the method by which the lawyer is provided or selected, in the relationship between the lawyer and the group, in the kinds of services offered, and in many other ways. The differences that appear particularly significant as grounds upon which to differentiate among them for purposes of regulation fall into three main classes. They relate to: (1) the extent to which a possibility exists for serious conflict of interest between the agency furnishing the lawyer and the individuals who are to receive services; (2) the extent to which the agency may have the opportunity and power to exert control or influence over the lawyer; and (3) the value of the program to society. The first two of these pertain directly to the basic value involved — the lawyer's independence of professional judgment and action. The third concerns what is obviously an important element. Together, the three may provide the foundation for a coherent rationale for the regulation of intermediary arrangements.

A program for providing lawyers' service to individuals through an intermediary arrangement would be clearly in the public interest if the potential conflict of interest and the opportunity for group control over the lawyer's professional judgment were slight and the program's social value large. Perhaps the best example is the legal aid society, providing the services of volunteer private lawyers to indigent clients without charge. At the other end of the scale, an intermediary program would clearly not be in the public interest if it offered great potential for conflict of interest, as well as significant opportunity for control by the organization, but little value to society. An example might be a purely commercial scheme in which a profit-making lay organization, engaged in no other activities, seeks to market the professional services of salaried lawyers to the general public. The value to society of this kind of program would appear to be slight in comparison with the danger that independence of professional judgment might become subverted to the organization's profit motive, to the detriment of individual clients.

In both of these clear cases, the results of this approach correspond to present restrictions as they are now being applied. It is in the area between these two, however, where present grounds of distinction among various arrangements tend to become ambiguous and at times unintelligible. For example, acceptance of the arrangement by which liability insurance company lawyers represent insureds (*ABA Eth. Ops.*, No. 282) is difficult to reconcile with rejection of the arrangement by which a labor union seeks to provide the services of salaried lawyers to represent members in workmen's compensation matters (**409**:217). Perhaps a detailed comparison of the two would serve to illustrate this difficulty as well as to demonstrate a rationale based upon the questions of potential conflict of interest, possibility of control, and social value. It should be pointed out, however, that this comparison is only an example, and the analysis in no way rests on this example alone. Similar comparisons might be made with respect to any number of other arrangements, including the legal aid society, the military legal assistance programs, and the claims adjustment corporation arrangement described earlier.

The community of interest between the union and its members is substantial — a legitimate interest in the welfare of individual union members with respect to employment-connected matters, and, in particular, an interest in seeing to it that members injured in industrial accidents obtain the maximum compensation to which they are entitled by law. It is a community of interest as close as that between the liability insurance and the insured. Spokesmen for the insurance industry do contend, of course, that in defending a suit under provisions of a liability policy the company is really defending its own interests, and that its incidental defense of the insured is permissible because the interests of insured and insurer are identical up to the policy limits or to the point where a conflict develops. This position has been argued most eloquently,[65] but it remains unconvincing. Except in those few states where an action may be brought directly against the insurer, the insured is still the nominal party in interest, and his interest in the litigation is by no means limited to his liability for a money judgment or to the limits of the insurance contract. Nor is the community of interest between the insurer and the insured markedly different from that in other intermediary arrangements. Not all are pecuniary interests, of course, but pecuniary interests are not the only compelling ones. Indeed, the interest of the labor union in the welfare — economic and otherwise — of its members is a most compelling one, and it is substantially identical with the interests of the individuals themselves.

65. E.g., the memoranda of February 14, 1960, and April 24, 1961, submitted to the ABA Committee on Professional Ethics and Unauthorized Practice of Law by the firm of Sullivan and Cromwell on behalf of the American Mutual Insurance Alliance, the Association of Casualty and Surety Companies, and the National Association of Independent Insurers. See also **345**:5-35.

   Moreover, the problem of interference with the lawyer's independence is not disposed of by the simple assertion that the interests of the insurer and the insured are identical up to the point where a conflict arises. As much could be said of any arrangement. The important issues are the potential for conflict of interest and the situation with respect to the power of control when conflict does arise.

   The potential for conflict of interest appears at least as great in the insurance arrangement as in the union program. The possibility that a serious labor union interest would conflict significantly with the interests of its members in obtaining adequate compensation for their injuries is slight.[66] But a considerable possibility for serious conflict of interest exists in the insurance arrangement by virtue of its very nature. One example is the situation where a plaintiff in a personal injury action offers to settle with an insured defendant for an amount within the limits of coverage under a liability insurance policy. Such a

66. A number of possible conflicts have been suggested (see **242**:1344; **330**:1698; **293**:396-97; **215**). They include the possibility that in order to retain the confidence of members or to attract new ones, it may be in the interest of a union to settle all cases but those promising extraordinary recoveries and favorable publicity; that the union may favor out-of-court settlements in order to improve employee relations; that the union might encourage the "package" settlement of multiple claims or the "trading off" of one claim against another, settling some claims for less than full value so that all claimants might receive something; that the union may use the claims of injured members in the collective bargaining process, bargaining away such claims to secure other advantages for its members; that the union may have an interest in the substantive or procedural law involved that is inconsistent with the immediate interests of an individual claimant; or that the union may have an interest in preventing litigation or in interfering with litigation in order to protect fellow employees against employer reprisals as a result of their appearing as witnesses. Most of these suggested conflicts are so insubstantial or improbable as to offer no serious reason for concern. For example, the first suggestion—that the union might seek to induce the lawyer to settle all cases but those promising spectacular recoveries—makes no sense at all unless it is assumed that the union's legal services program is inadequate to handle all cases properly. Without such an assumption it is difficult to see how the handling of the less promising cases would in any way affect either the obtaining of extraordinary recoveries or their publicity value when they are obtained. Presumably, the big recoveries would come in appropriate cases regardless of how the less promising cases were handled. And an accompanying record of modest recoveries in the less promising cases would be unlikely to impair the lustre of the big cases any more than would an accompanying record of settlements.
   Perhaps the most serious of these possible conflicts is the possible "package" settlement of multiple cases or the "trading-off" of one case against another. (Incidentally, this problem is not limited to the field of intermediary arrangements. It may arise even with so-called independent practitioners if they handle a substantial volume of cases involving claims against a relatively few insurance companies.) But even here, a union leader who is even modestly astute cannot help but see that the interests of the members as well as those of the organization itself will, in the long run, be best served through the fair and impartial assertion of members' claims by a competent lawyer exercising his best professional judgment. It seems reasonable to conclude that the incidence of conflicts of interest between the union and its injured members with respect to the assertion of industrial accident claims is small indeed.

settlement may be in the interest of the insured, as payment would be made by the insurance company and the insured would suffer no loss; but it may be contrary to the interests of the insurance company, which may feel that in defending the case it might avoid liability altogether. In rejecting a settlement and electing to defend, however, the company may subject the insured to the risk of a judgment in excess of the policy limits, which excess the insured would have to pay out of his own pocket. This is a fairly common and reasonably serious conflict between the interests of the insured and those of the company. It is sometimes asserted that this conflict is eliminated by the insurer's possible liability for a judgment in excess of the policy limits if it has failed to adhere to a proper standard of care with respect to settlement or defense of the suit.[67] But a cause of action against the insurer is hardly to be equated with the right to be represented in the first instance by a lawyer independent of outside control. And the insured may have a legitimate interest in avoiding litigation, quite apart from the risk of a judgment in excess of policy limits.

When a conflict of interest does arise, the insured may be in a most difficult position. The lawyer provided by the insurance company will customarily advise the insured that a conflict exists and that he has a right to have counsel of his own choosing to look after his individual interests. There may be some question about the real value of this "right," however. Aside from the possible difficulty involved in the new lawyer's acquainting himself with the case on short notice, there is really very little that he can do on behalf of the insured. He cannot elect to settle independently without relieving the insurer of liability, and if he does not settle independently, the insurer will insist on conducting the defense. About the best that he can do is to look on as an interested observer in the hope that an occasional suggestion might be accepted by the insurance company lawyer, or, in the event of an adverse judgment in excess of the policy limits, the hope that he may be able to spot some blunder in the conduct of the case that will serve to stick the insurer with the whole judgment. Thus, the insured is put in such a difficult

67. In at least one state, the insurer has been held to assume a responsibility very near to strict liability for the consequences if it wrongfully denies coverage and refuses a reasonable offer of settlement within the policy limits. Comunale v. Traders & General Ins. Co. (373).

position that, as a practical matter, the power of control over the litigation will remain with the insurer even after a conflict has arisen.

In contrast to the anomalous position of the lawyer provided by an insurance company to defend insureds under liability policies, the position of the lawyer provided by the union to represent injured members in workmen's compensation cases is relatively simple and clear. He has been employed to represent the interests of the individual injured members and not any independent interest of the union. Though a potential for control theorética lly exists, by virtue of the lawyer's position as a salaried employee of the union, the exertion by the union of actual influence or control over the lawyer's activities – if, indeed, any is exerted – is likely to be for the purpose of making sure that he is competent and faithful in representing those individual interests.

Thus, in the insurance setting, the insured must accept the insurer's counsel unless he is willing to give up his insurance protection as well as the legal services supplied by the insurer. In the union setting, however, the union member may choose outside counsel with no more loss than his right to the union-supplied legal services.

One aspect of control deserves special attention. It has been suggested that the line between permissible and impermissible intermediary arrangements should be determined by the form of the lawyer's employment; those arrangements in which the lawyers were either on retainer or employed on an ad hoc basis would be approved, while those in which the lawyers were employed on a salary basis would be disapproved. This distinction, now being urged in the field of union legal service arrangements as well as in the liability insurance field, is at least partly responsive to the problem of control over the lawyer. There is no doubt some validity in the contention that the power and inclination of the employer to exert influence or control over the lawyer, and the lawyer's susceptibility to such control, are greater when the lawyer is employed on a salary basis than when he is on retainer or employed ad hoc. It is doubtful, however, that the form of the lawyer's employment should be the sole basis for distinction.

To begin with, there appears to be a direct relationship between the utility of an intermediary arrangement and the potential for control over the lawyer. From the standpoint of the group, the most useful arrangement in terms of quality, accessibility, and cost of services rendered is generally the one in which the lawyer is employed to devote his whole attention to the particular problems covered by the program. Conversely, an arrangement that would completely eliminate the possibility of control would probably have but modest utility. The only arrangement that might conceivably eliminate all possibility of control is one in which the individual member of the group is given a cash indemnity with which to purchase whatever legal services he requires wherever he can get them. Although this arrangement may possess some utility with respect to cost—as witness its present use by automobile clubs in lieu of the more direct services they have been prohibited from offering—it is not nearly so useful with respect to quality and accessibility as the arrangements in which the organization takes a more active part in securing legal services for individual members and in which the opportunities for control over the lawyer are correspondingly increased. Thus, the element of utility tends to support the use of salaried lawyers in intermediary arrangements, even though the opportunity for control may theoretically be greater.

Next, some reason may exist to doubt that the opportunity for control and the susceptibility to control are significantly greater where the lawyer is a salaried employee than where his services are secured on some other basis. Certainly there is little to choose between the salaried lawyer and the private lawyer who is on what amounts to a full-time retainer. And even where no financial connection has been established between the organization and the lawyer—as when the individual members of the group are simply referred to preselected lawyers—there may still be opportunity for control and susceptibility to control because the organization has the power to cut off the flow of referred clients at any time. This is not to say that there is no difference, of course, but only that the difference is not so great as it is sometimes thought to be. In any event, it is not clear why *every* salary arrangement is more vulnerable to abuse than is *any* fee arrangement.

And finally, even where there may theoretically be a possibility of control over the lawyer, the probability that control will actually be exercised depends in large part upon the extent and nature of possible conflicts of interest between the individual member of the group and the agency providing the service. Given no serious conflict of interest, actual exercise of control is not likely even where the opportunity to do so is extensive. And where serious conflict exists, the agency providing the services may be expected to do so, in almost any kind of arrangement.

The point, of course, is that the form of the arrangement between the organization providing the services and the lawyers rendering them is not, by itself, an adequate criterion for determining whether a given intermediary arrangement is in the public interest. The form of the lawyer's employment may have some bearing upon the question of control over the lawyer, but alone it means little as a basis of distinction.

There appears little to choose between the union program and the insurance arrangement with respect to social value. An arrangement by which a liability insurer can protect its legitimate interests in the litigation of claims is perhaps essential to the existence of liability insurance, and defending claims against insureds may be the only satisfactory method of providing such protection. The arrangement might therefore be viewed as a necessary expedient of considerable value to society. But providing injured workmen with competent counsel to assist them in the obtaining of adequate compensation for their injuries — particularly for small claims that might not be asserted otherwise — is certainly no less valuable to society. And in both instances it is probably significant that these arrangements appear to be what the potential clients themselves want.

The foregoing comparison was not intended as a simple analogy, to argue that because intermediary arrangements were tolerated in the context of casualty insurance, they should therefore also be permitted in union and other contexts. Rather, its purpose has been to suggest that little rational ground appears upon which to distinguish these two intermediary arrangements, nor is there any justification for applying one set of rules to the one and a different set of rules to the other. And, of course, the comparison demonstrates principles by which all intermediary arrangements might be tested.

It is submitted, then, that a sound evaluation of any arrangement for providing lawyers' services to individuals on a group basis must include all three elements — potential conflict of interest, opportunity for control over the lawyer, and social value. This being so, how should these elements be applied?

Perhaps, as a general guide, reference should be made to certain points made earlier. This discussion has dealt only with arrangements in which legal services are rendered directly to clients by lawyers. The conclusions reached are therefore directed primarily toward the question of the permissible conduct of lawyers: In which kinds of intermediary programs may lawyers properly participate? Another point that deserves repeating is that the burden of proof rests on those who would restrict enterprise in the name of the public good. Indeed, it may not be amiss to indulge a presumption that an apparently useful arrangement for obtaining lawyers' services is in the public interest unless it can be demonstrated to be otherwise. In this spirit, the application of these criteria might follow a simple pattern.

First, there is no real reason to prohibit the participation of lawyers in an apparently useful intermediary program in which there is but slight chance of serious conflict of interest between the organization providing the service and the individual members of the group, whether or not an apparent opportunity exists for the exercise of control over the lawyer. The first step, then, is to determine the potential for conflict of interest by examining the respective interests of the organization and the individual members of the group in the particular claims or rights sought to be asserted through the program. Where the organization has no substantial interest in the claims or rights adverse to the interests of individual members of the group, or where such claims or rights are not substantially related in an adverse way to other interests of the organization, there is no reason for the organization to exercise control over the lawyer. Thus, the fact that the organization may have the opportunity or power to exercise control has little bearing on the issue.

Second, where there may be some significant possibility of conflict of interest, determination of the extent to which the arrangement poses a *genuine* threat to the lawyer's professional independence, and thus to the interests of individual members of the group being served, requires an inquiry into both the conflict of interest and the opportunity for control. Where the services to be rendered involve matters in which the organization—or perhaps the majority of individual members—has substantial interests seriously in conflict with interests of any individual member, and where the organization has some reasonable opportunity to exercise control over the lawyers rendering the services, lawyers might appropriately be prohibited from participating, even though the program appeared otherwise useful and beneficial to members of the group. Even so, prohibition of lawyer participation would be justifiable only if the conflict of interests or the threat of control could not be eliminated or brought within acceptable limits by measures short of outright prohibition.

And third, even where an intermediary arrangement might be subject to disapproval under the foregoing tests, other public-interest considerations — such as the importance of the individual rights being asserted or the practical unavailability of other sources of legal assistance — may nevertheless demand that it be permitted to exist.[68]

Perhaps the application of these tests to a few typical intermediary arrangements would serve to illustrate more clearly how they might operate. The plan at issue in *Button* involved the representation of members and others by lawyers employed (regularly but on a per diem basis) by the association. Here, the community of interest between the association and the group of recipients is great; but so, also, may be the potential for conflict of interest. The chance of such conflict is almost implicit in any legal service program based on political action or ideology, the danger being that the interests of the "cause" may become predominant over the interests of any one individual. The plan also offers considerable opportunity for the association to exercise control over the lawyers. Nevertheless, it would appear to be in the public interest because of the overwhelming social

68. These tests may have been the *real*—but unarticulated and perhaps not even consciously thought out—bases of ABA *Eth. Ops.*, Nos. 96 and 198, criticized *supra* at 266–68. Although the Ethics Committee justified its approval primarily in terms of agency (a completely unsatisfactory justification), it *really* may have been resting its decision—perhaps without knowing it—on the idea that: (1) An arrangement by which a lay adjustment corporation employs lawyers to represent individual insurance companies in investigating, adjusting, and litigating insurance claims is useful and beneficial to the segment of the public involved; and (2) On the basis of the Committee's experience, neither (*a*) the potential for conflict of interest between the lay adjustment corporation and the individual insurance companies, nor (*b*) the opportunity or power of the lay corporation to control the professional activities of the lawyer, appears so great as to constitute a serious threat to the lawyer's independence in the exercise of his professional judgment and the discharge of his professional responsibilities to his clients; and (3) Whatever threat the arrangement may pose to the lawyer's independence can be eliminated or substantially mitigated by requiring participating lawyers to adhere to the basic professional standards expressed in the first paragraph of Canon 35.

If this was the real basis of the Committee's approval of the arrangement, it is indeed unfortunate that it was not arrived at consciously, thereby permitting a deliberate examination of the facts relevant to the issues of conflict of interest and potential for control.

value of its objectives—the protection of the constitutional rights of individual members of a disadvantaged and oppressed minority. Any risks to the interests of individual clients are modest and quite acceptable in relation to the goals to be gained. And, of course, the risk involved in any intermediary arrangement may be somewhat reduced by the power of the courts to supervise the conduct of lawyers in litigation.

One form of traditional legal aid involves the rendering of legal services to the poor by lawyers in the salaried employ of a charitable organization. Here again, while the community of interest is great, there is also some potential for conflict of interest. Conflict can arise because the governing body of the legal aid society may take upon itself the right to decide on the social desirability of certain legal remedies—divorce, for example. More importantly, conflict can arise from the fact that available resources are insufficient to cope with an overwhelming case load, so that the time and attention to be given to any individual must be curtailed. Opportunity for control also exists. But again, the social value of this program far outweighs any potential harm to the interests of individual clients.

In the military legal assistance programs, the opportunity and power of the military organization to exercise control over a legal assistance officer may be great. But because of the substantial community of interest between the military service and the individual soldier with respect to individual legal problems (the legal assistance program is limited to civil matters) and the slight chance of any serious conflict, the actual threat to the professional independence of the lawyer is small. The benefits offered to servicemen through the program are thus vastly in excess of any conceivable detriment to an individual by reason of conflict of interest and control over the lawyer.

The *BRT* case dealt with a program involving a strong community of interest and a slight probability of serious conflict. Again, it is difficult to imagine any significant interest of the union that would be genuinely at odds with the interest of the individual member in obtaining the largest possible compensation for his injuries. Thus, although theoretically there may be some opportunity for the exercise of control over the lawyers to whom cases are sent, the actual threat to their professional independence is small.

Much the same can be said of the union plan in which a

lawyer is employed on a salary basis to represent individual
members in workmen's compensation cases, and of the hospital
association plan, in which lawyers employed by the association
on a salary basis engage in the collection of debts on behalf of
member hospitals.

Intermediary arrangements utilized solely for commercial purposes—such as the Estate Organization Service described earlier[69]—would, under this analysis, be regarded as contrary to the
public interest. There is no real community of interest between
the agency seeking to sell legal services and the prospective
recipients; there is considerable prospect that the agency's interest in making a profit may conflict with the interests of individual clients, if only to the extent that costs and profits may
curtail the amount of time a lawyer spends on a particular
client's problem or may encourage the professionally unwarranted substitution of "ready-made" solutions for individual service; and there is opportunity and power in the agency to control
the lawyers who are to render the services. Such plans offer far
too great a threat to the professional independence of the lawyer
in relation to whatever modest social value they may have. It
may be conceivable that the need of some segment of the public
for services in some narrow field of law or practice is so great,
and the prospect of that need being filled in some more traditional manner so remote, that a commercial program would be
justifiable. No illustrative example comes readily to mind, however, and it may be seriously doubted that any such circumstances actually exist. The commercial marketing of lawyers'
services would appear, then, to be generally against the public
interest and properly prohibited.

In a great many instances between these relatively clear examples, the issues will be much closer, but in every instance,
the questions will be the same: To what extent is there a potential conflict of interest between the organization and the individual member with respect to the matters for which lawyers'
services are to be provided? To what extent does the organization have the opportunity and the power to exert influence or
control over the lawyer's discharge of his professional responsibilities? May either conflict or control be prevented by measures short of outright prohibition of the entire program? Does
the program's social value nevertheless justify its existence?

69. See text at note 45 *supra*.

It has been suggested that, while case-by-case application of fundamental principles may provide flexibility in determining the propriety of lawyer participation in intermediary arrangements and may provide the greatest possible assurance of sound decisions in individual cases, criteria or guidelines of a more specific nature might be desirable for predictability and ease of application. It has been proposed, for example, that a specific description might be formulated setting forth the kinds of organizations with which lawyers might be permitted to participate in the providing of legal services on a group basis. One such formulation would allow lawyers to participate in any intermediary arrangement conducted by a group or organization that (1) is primarily engaged in activities other than the providing of lawyers' services, but only if the lawyers' services it provides bear some reasonable relation to its primary activities; or (2) is organized, owned, and managed by lawyers amenable to the Canons of Ethics; or (3) qualifies for tax exemption under the provisions of the Internal Revenue Code dealing with charitable, educational, and eleemosynary organizations. This is the approach taken in the California State Bar's proposed amendments to the California Rules of Professional Conduct.[70] It is also the approach taken by the new American Bar Association Code of Professional Responsibility, although the ABA Code provisions are considerably more restrictive than the proposed California Rules.[71]

70. New Rules 20 and 21 have been approved by the Board of Governors of the State Bar of California (see 172). The new rules are to be distributed to the members of the State Bar and ultimately submitted to the state Supreme Court for adoption. As the rules now stand, they permit lawyers to participate, subject to specified safeguards, in group legal service arrangements conducted by professional associations, trade associations, labor unions, or other nonprofit organizations or combinations of persons having primary purposes and activities other than the rendering of legal services. The rules do not require that the legal services rendered be related to the primary purpose, however.

71. The new Code of Professional Responsibility provides:
A lawyer shall not knowingly assist a person or organization that recommends, furnishes, or pays for legal services to promote the use of his services or those of his partners or associates. However, he may cooperate in a dignified manner with the legal service activities of any of the following, provided that his independent professional judgment is exercised in behalf of his client without interference of control by any organization or other person:
(1) A legal aid office or public defender office:
    (a) Operated or sponsored by a duly accredited law school.
    (b) Operated or sponsored by a bona fide non-profit community organization.
    (c) Operated or sponsored by a governmental agency.
    (d) Operated, sponsored, or approved by a bar association representative of the general bar of the geographical area in which the association exists.

This approach, essentially a specific formulation based on the nature of the group or organization involved, does deserve consideration as a possible alternative to the case-by-case application of fundamental principles. It has at least two inherent problems, however, which prompt the exercise of caution.

First, any attempt to formulate generic categories in advance is likely to be speculative at best and thus probably not completely responsive to the basic issue of independence of professional judgment. Some arrangements that are in fact useful and harmless may nevertheless be prohibited, while others that do pose a significant threat to professional independence may be permitted. Indeed, the formulation suggested above appears to do both. Similarly, the exemption presently granted by Canon 35 to "charitable societies rendering aid to the indigent" may actually permit some arrangements that would unjustifiably threaten the professional independence of participating lawyers.

Second, there is the very real danger that any ready-made formulation will lend itself too easily to mechanical application without adequate attention to the basic issues involved—the very criticism expressed earlier in this chapter with respect to

---

    (2) A military legal assistance office.

    (3) A lawyer referral service operated, sponsored, or approved by a bar association representative of the general bar of the geographical area in which the association exists.

    (4) A bar association representative of the general bar of the geographical area in which the association exists.

    (5) Any other non-profit organization that recommends, furnishes, or pays for legal services to its members or beneficiaries, but only in those instances and to the extent that controlling constitutional interpretation at the time of the rendition of the services requires the allowance of such legal service activities, and only if the following conditions, unless prohibited by such interpretation, are met:

        (a) The primary purposes of such organization do not include the rendition of legal services.

        (b) The recommending, furnishing, or paying for legal services to its members is incidental and reasonably related to the primary purposes of such organization.

        (c) Such organization does not derive a financial benefit from the rendition of legal services by the lawyer.

        (d) The member or beneficiary for whom the legal services are rendered, and not such organization, is recognized as the client of the lawyer in that matter [7: Disciplinary Rule 2-103(d)].

See also Disciplinary Rule 2-104, which applies the same restrictions to the suggestion or volunteering of needed legal services. In essence, the ABA provision accepts intermediary arrangements of the type usually called "group legal services" only when operated by nonprofit organizations having a primary purpose other than the rendition of legal services, to which purpose the legal services must be incidental and reasonably related—and then only to the extent that such recognition is specifically required by decisions of the U.S. Supreme Court.

the application of present restrictions. Indeed, the formulation in advance of the generic categories, in which intermediary arrangements are to be permitted, is really nothing more than an attempt to prejudge specific situations without access to the relevant facts. It would appear, then, that case-by-case application of the basic principles discussed above is probably the best method of determining whether lawyers may participate in intermediary arrangements.

The Report of the ABA Special Committee on Availability of Legal Services took essentially this position (29:518, 526). It acknowledged that group legal services "may substantially enhance the availability to the public of competent legal services" and advocated that "such arrangements should be permitted if there is no substantial danger of a serious conflict of interest among the members of the group or between the members and the group itself or the entity providing the lawyer's services." The report then recommended the adoption of a system of safeguards "to protect the legitimate interests of the public and the state in preserving the independent exercise of the lawyer's professional judgment and preventing the exploitation of his services." In addition to provisions designed mainly to bring the details of intermediary programs to the attention of the state regulatory authority, these safeguards included the following general principles:

> 3. The group or entity may provide for its members any legal services which do not involve a conflict of interest among members of the group or between the members and the group itself or the entity providing the legal services; . . .

> 5. The terms of such agreement [between the group or organization and the lawyer] shall affirmatively provide: that the lawyer (despite his relationship to the group or organization) is in all events unqualifiedly independent of all professional obligations to anyone other than the individual member of the group whom he serves; that his obligations are in all events directly to and solely to the individual member, that neither the group nor any other member thereof shall interfere or attempt to interfere with the lawyer's independent exercise of his professional judgment; and that the lawyer, in his relations with the individual members and the group must at all times strictly comply with all provisions of the Canons of Ethics of the profession; . . .

> 8. Although the organization may itself pay the attorney's compensation, the organization must not utilize such pay-

ment as a means for directing or controlling the attorney in his exercise of judgment in representing any member. Where the attorney represents a member and by agreement is paid directly by the member on any basis, there must be no division of the attorney's compensation between the attorney and the organization or between the attorney and any person not licensed to practice law;

9. There must be a true attorney-client relationship between the attorney and the member being represented by him;

10. Any violation by the group or entity of the terms of the agreement between it and the lawyer shall be grounds for the termination of the agreement; and any violation by the attorney of the appropriate Canons of Ethics or rules of court, shall be grounds for the discipline of the attorney.

This seems to be a sound and sensible approach to regulation, as it focuses squarely on the basic value involved in intermediary arrangements—the lawyer's independence of professional judgment. At the same time it allows the flexibility necessary for growth and development in an important new area of law practice. This approach has now been rejected by the ABA House of Delegates, however, in favor of the more restrictive provision of the new Code of Professional Responsibility (see 58). Time alone will show what the end result will be.

D
The Interests
of the Legal Profession

The foregoing discussion has dealt almost exclusively with questions relating to the direct public interest. This is because the public interest must be the controlling factor in the legal profession's decision about intermediary arrangements. The interests of the profession itself are also important, however, and should be considered.

Intermediary arrangements might be said to involve three of the profession's primary interests. First, they are pertinent to the profession's interest in preserving the private practice of law. Second, they relate to a similar interest in the preservation of the practice of law as a profession. And third, they are relevant to the profession's interest in preserving lawyers as vital and effective elements in society.

1
Preserving
the Private Practice of Law

Some lawyers fear that if intermediary arrangements are permitted to operate any more extensively than at present, they will encroach seriously upon the private practice of law. Indeed, these arrangements are sometimes viewed as a threat to the existence of at least the general practice of law (132:18-30). This apprehension is understandable, although such a prediction of the future, like any social prediction, is at best an exercise in conjecture. There is reason to believe that this fear of encroachment may be somewhat exaggerated.

Present and proposed intermediary arrangements do compete with private law practice in limited areas, but many of the people who are or who would be served by such programs are not now clients, or even potential clients, of private practitioners. Many of the matters sought to be handled through intermediary arrangements are not presently attractive to private lawyers, primarily because they are too small to be handled economically in traditional private practice. Many of the services rendered or proposed to be rendered by lawyers through intermediary programs are thus "new" services rendered to "new" clients who can obtain such services from lawyers only through such programs. Thus, intermediary arrangements may actually mean more clients for the legal profession and more employment for lawyers—albeit through the intermediary arrangements.

It is true, of course, that some of the services provided or proposed to be provided by lawyers through intermediary arrangements do overlap those services that are, or might be, rendered by lawyers in traditional private practice. Thus, such programs do compete with lawyers in private practice for some of the same clients. To the extent that this is so, intermediary arrangements may indeed displace some traditional private practice relationships, but serious encroachment on the private practice of law is not the inevitable result.

Society is becoming more group oriented, and the utility and therefore the scope of intermediary programs may be expected to grow in the future. It is not a foregone conclusion, however, that private lawyers will be unable to compete with such programs in serving the vast majority of individual clients and in handling the major portion of the public's law business. Specialization and practice in larger firms, improved office and practice management, delegation of routine functions to nonlawyer technicians, and other methods of increasing lawyers' effectiveness may enable private lawyers to enhance the utility of private law practice substantially. By thus making higher quality legal services more readily available at lower cost, private lawyers may yet remain the primary source of legal services for most Americans. Indeed, it is not at all clear why private law firms — perhaps larger in size, more efficiently organized, and more specialized in function than most present firms — cannot be the agencies that will in the future provide lawyers' services to individuals even through intermediary programs. Furthermore, the areas in which intermediary programs compete with private lawyers are presently insignificant compared with the whole of law practice. Thus, although intermediary arrangements in these areas might encroach to some extent upon the practices of some lawyers, they would probably make a fairly small impression on the entire practice of law.

One other aspect of the private practice of law deserves attention. The observation was made previously that lawyers who are permitted to receive clients through intermediary arrangements may enjoy a competitive advantage over others practicing in the same fields. The fact that one lawyer might have a competitive advantage over another is of concern mainly to lawyers, however. And, even among lawyers, the interests of the profession as a whole are not necessarily the same as those of the particular lawyers involved.

The profession as a whole should be concerned with the matter of competitive advantage primarily for its possible effect on the public interest, on the professional nature of the practice of law, or on the position of lawyers generally as effective elements in society. Indeed, the interests of the public and the profession even now often require measures that result in competitive advantage to some lawyers and disadvantage to others. Present ethical restrictions on law practice give certain segments of the bar competitive advantage over others. The established large firm has an advantage over the individual practitioner just getting started in practice, for example. The established firm has the opportunity as well as the ability — through existing associations with the business community and desirable business clients — to attract an ever-increasing number of desirable clients. The solo practitioner just getting started in practice has neither the opportunity nor the ability to attract such clients. Furthermore, the Canons of Ethics deny him the privilege of advertising and soliciting business — methods that might possibly put him on a competitive par with the established firms, or at least reduce his disadvantage. Such competitive advantage is usually justified on grounds that the restrictions which produce it are necessary to protect the public and to preserve the professional nature of the practice of law. Consequently, the profession as a whole is relatively unconcerned that one result may be greater prosperity for some lawyers than for others. Similarly, the bar seems satisfied with the law list exception to the rules against advertising, though the end result is competitive advantage to some lawyers and disadvantage to others. Why, then, should the profession be unduly disturbed if an intermediary arrangement that otherwise served the interests of the public and profession were to cause some slight redistribution of competitive advantage among lawyers? The bar would be on shaky ground indeed if this were the only objection it could offer.

2
Preserving
the Practice of Law
as a Profession

This interest of the profession is at the same time a public interest. It has two facets that relate to intermediary arrangements. The first is the matter of the participating lawyer's independence of professional judgment and action. The second is the so-called "commercialization of the legal profession." Professional independence, as it relates to the public interest, has already been discussed at length. Because the interests of the profession coincide substantially with those of the public, the subject will not be discussed further here. It may be well to repeat, however, that the interests of neither the profession nor the public are served by the prohibition of intermediary arrangements that pose no genuine threat to the lawyer's independence of professional judgment and action.

Used in relation to intermediary arrangements, the rather vague but often-used term "commercialization of the legal profession" appears to mean: (1) the obtaining of benefit — especially economic — from a lawyer's professional activities by laymen or lay organizations other than clients; (2) the bringing of discredit upon the profession through commercial forms of advertising and improper solicitation of business; or (3) the use of the intermediary device by unscrupulous lawyers as a cover for improper solicitation schemes. All are legitimate concerns of the legal profession, but none would appear to require prohibition of otherwise acceptable intermediary arrangements.

The law is a proud profession, and it is natural that lawyers should resist any scheme that threatens to "use" or "exploit" them for the benefit of laymen or lay organizations, particularly on a commercial basis. Some of the arrangements described earlier in this paper do threaten such exploitation and thus they may properly be said to threaten the "commercialization of the legal profession." It should be pointed out, however, that those arrangements that genuinely threaten exploitation are also subject to condemnation on the far more fundamental ground that they threaten the independence of professional judgment and action of the participating lawyers.

Many intermediary arrangements, however, do not involve any significant risk that the participating lawyers will be exploited for the commercial benefit of lay agencies. Indeed, in most instances the benefit to the lay agency is quite incidental and often not at all economic in nature. And it is hard to see why an intermediary arrangement that is otherwise in the public interest and that poses no threat to professional independence should be struck down merely because some incidental benefit accrues to the lay agency involved.

It has already been suggested that some restrictions might be imposed on advertising and solicitation by organizations operating intermediary arrangements to protect the public against misrepresentation. Restrictions aimed at preserving the bar's image as a profession are more difficult to justify, however, although such restrictions might be preferable to the complete prohibition of otherwise acceptable intermediary arrangements. But is the problem really as big as it is sometimes thought to be? In all the literature on group legal services, it is difficult to find an instance of group advertising that reflects adversely upon the legal profession. And those relatively few instances of group solicitation that might harm the profession's image would seem to be controllable by means of appropriate restrictions on such activities.

Much the same thing might be said about the possible use of intermediary device by unscrupulous lawyers as a cover for improper solicitation schemes. Surely any possible abuse can be adequately curbed without resorting to the complete prohibition of all intermediary arrangements. It should not be unduly difficult to discern the differences between a genuine intermediary arrangement and a mere sham. For example, they might be distinguished on the basis of such indicia as the nature of the group, the role actually played by the lawyer in the formation of either the group or its legal service program, and the methods used in promoting the program. By examining such readily discoverable characteristics, a bar association disciplinary body should be able to tell the difference between a genuine intermediary arrangement and a mere solicitation scheme for a lawyer. Whatever the problems of professional discipline, it is inconceivable that the number of dishonorable lawyers is so great or the problem of their possible misuse of the intermediary device so impossible of solution as to require that honorable lawyers be prohibited from serving the public through legitimate and beneficial intermediary arrangements.

In discussing the bar's interest in preserving the practice of law as a profession, perhaps it would be well to comment briefly upon certain implications that arise from opposition to lawyer participation in socially useful intermediary arrangements. It seems ironic that, while there is great concern that such arrangements might tarnish the profession's image, restrictions that, without justification, prevent lawyers from participating in socially useful arrangements defame the bar far more than anything lay agencies might do or say.

To begin with, such restrictions demonstrate what surely must appear to the public to be complete disregard for the public interest in favor of selfish interest. It makes little difference that the restrictions may actually be based on the profession's view of what constitutes public interest; the public will not, and cannot be expected to, differentiate between selfish interest and what it no doubt deems a mistaken notion as to public interest. The fact is that the profession appears in the worst possible light

when it cannot offer compelling reasons to justify the rejection of
what appear to the public to be innocuous and socially useful
arrangements.

In addition, when lawyers are prohibited from participating in
useful intermediary arrangements that pose no significant threat
to their independence of professional judgment and action, the
inescapable inference to be drawn is that lawyers cannot be
trusted to conform to the ethical standards of their own profession. Indeed, it appears as if the bar were declaring publicly that
lawyers cannot be trusted to discharge faithfully what is really
their most basic obligation as lawyers — complete fidelity to the
interests of the client. Manifestly, this is not so. Daily, and
almost as a matter of course, lawyers act with honor in situations
that test honesty and fidelity to the utmost. The practice of law
would be impossible otherwise. To suggest, even by implication, that they cannot be trusted to do so in the context of
intermediary arrangements posing little or no threat to professional independence is the worst kind of slander on the profession.

This apparent lack of faith in the integrity of the profession
probably stems from an attitude that seems to be fairly common
among some lawyers: The notion that the lawyer who is not in
private practice — preferably alone or as a member of a small firm
engaged in general practice — is not really a lawyer.[72] It denies
full professional status to corporation and association counsel, to
lawyers in government, to law teachers, and to others. It is an
affront to better than one-fourth of the members of the bar. This
attitude mistakes a particular arrangement by which legal services may be rendered — private practice — for professionalism.
The essence of professionalism, however, is commitment to the
public interest, and private practitioners have no monopoly. The
lawyer in government, the lawyer in the corporate legal department, and the lawyer in the intermediary arrangement can all be
professionals in the best sense.

The foregoing suggests that neither the professional image
nor the fact of incidental benefit to lay agencies through in-

---

72. Lest it be thought that this notion is too frivolous to deserve mention, see Application of Hunt (354), in which a bar committee urged that the temporary license of a
full-time salaried lawyer for a corporation not be made permanent, on the ground that his
activities as corporation counsel during the year covered by his temporary license did not
constitute "the practice of law."

termediary arrangements has any real relevance to the question of preserving the practice of law as a profession. True professionalism is not an image nor a particular way of practicing law. It is genuine devotion to the public interest. How can this kind of professionalism be in any way diminished by permitting lawyers—retaining their independence of professional judgment and action—to provide quality services at reasonable cost to people who need them?

3
Preserving Lawyers
as Effective Elements
in Society

The lawyer plays an important role in society, a role for which he is uniquely qualified. It includes not only the counseling, advocacy, and other functions performed directly for clients, but also important functions of community leadership and service. There are those who see this multifaceted role as inextricably bound to traditional private practice. Thus, protective measures are thought to be necessary to prevent encroachment on private law practice and any possible resultant impairment of the lawyer's ability to play this important role.

The lawyer's usefulness to society is not tied to traditional private practice, however. And regardless of the self-protective walls erected by the profession, the only sure way to preserve lawyers as effective elements in society is to see that they remain responsive to society's needs and demands. Therefore, the interests of the profession, no less than the interests of the public, would seem to be best served by extending and expanding the capacity of lawyers to serve the public and by increasing the public's use of lawyers' services. The future vitality of the legal profession lies not in its ability to resist encroachment by other socially useful institutions but in its own ability to change and adapt to today's needs.

Some Concluding Thoughts

One of the main impressions gained from involvement in this study has been a sense of the importance of time. Events, many of them producing pervasive changes in society, are moving at an almost incredibly rapid pace. Obsolescence is now computed in many fields in terms not of generations but of decades or less, and the so-called generation gap — often vast in terms of knowledge or understanding — now seems at some points to be no wider in time than a year or two.

The social upheaval now taking place involves questions of vital concern to the legal profession. Among the most immediate and pressing are questions about how society is to be ordered, how differences are to be resolved, and who is to have a part in those processes. Such questions are going to be answered, one way or another, and soon. Many of them are even now being answered. And it is far from certain that the old order — the law, the legal system, and the functions of lawyers — will survive entirely unchanged. If the legal profession is to have any positive or creative part in determining what the legal order of the future is to be and what part lawyers are to have in it, then prompt and rational consideration must be given to these problems. In no other way can lawyers hope to contribute meaningful answers or preserve important public and professional values.

Another observation should perhaps be made, even though it is somewhat incidental and ought to be unnecessary. In the dialogue that has developed over the issues discussed in this report, there seems to have been a tendency on the part of those who take traditional positions to assume that they alone care about the legal profession. But the answers to the questions raised here are not so clear or obvious as to preclude honest differences of opinion among men of good will, and no one point of view has a monopoly on virtue or good intentions. Indeed, the man who advocates a change in the litany may be as devout as the one who defends it against change. And the lawyer who seeks rational responses and accommodations to social change in order to preserve legitimate public and professional values may be more entitled to the name "conservative" than he who would attempt to stop change.

Before going on to a summing up of this study, it might be well to repeat a description of the limits within which it was pursued. It has been primarily concerned with civil legal services provided by lawyers to people of moderate means in the urban or metropolitan situation. The discussion was not meant to deal — except, perhaps, incidentally — with the providing of services to the poor or to business or property clients, nor with the practice of law in rural or small town situations. Moreover, while some consideration has been given to the interests of the profession as a whole and lawyers individually, the primary concern throughout has been the public interest. The pervading question has been, "How will the idea, arrangement, institution, rule, or process under consideration help — or hurt — the public?"

The study has been both analytical and argumentative, of course. As analysis, it has sought to illuminate some of the basic issues involved in the problems considered. If it has been successful in this regard, replication of the analysis at this point would be redundant; if it has not, repetition would probably be futile. As argument, however, it seeks to move the legal profession to action along four somewhat different planes, and a review of this four-fold call to action may be useful.

A
Specific Possibilities
for Change

Several specific suggestions for making lawyers' services more readily available to people of moderate means have been offered. These possibilities include: a more efficient law practice; larger practice units; specialization; more effective use of nonprofessional personnel; recovery of lawyers' fees by successful litigants; legal service financing plans; legal service insurance; subsidies; better lawyer referral services; modified restrictions on business-getting activities by lawyers; special law offices for people of moderate means; and group legal services.

Obviously, not all of these possibilities are of equal merit. Some are alternative approaches to the same problem, and the adoption of one may preclude or obviate the others. But all would appear to possess sufficient merit to deserve the thoughtful consideration that this study has sought to stimulate.

B
A Point of View

While the specific suggestions have drawn most of the attention and generated most of the controversy, they are far from being the most important aspect of the study. Of greater importance is its largely implicit call for perspective in dealing with the problems of the profession and of the legal system. It is, above all, a way of looking at a set of problems. Admittedly, it is not the only way of looking at them, and it may not even be the best way. But it is a way, and one that seems to make some sense.

Heretofore, the problems discussed in this report have been viewed and dealt with largely from the standpoint of tradition—often merely for the sake of tradition. But valuable as tradition may be, tradition for tradition's sake may not always produce adequate answers to today's serious problems. This study was thus an attempt to view these problems from a different and possibly more responsive perspective. It sought to look at the issues from an economic viewpoint and deal with the problems of availability of legal services as problems of producing and distributing services. It is submitted that the economic view is reasonable and useful and that it deserves the consideration of the profession.

There are those, of course, who dislike this way of looking at the matter. In most instances, however, it is not the economic viewpoint that has been consciously considered and rejected, but the results it produces or may produce. And the results are rejected mainly because they conflict with some traditional idea or attitude. To such critics this study should offer a challenge—a challenge to do more than simply condemn the point of view or the possibilities for change that it suggests, but to offer instead a more meaningful perspective.

C
The Law
and the Legal System

The point was made at the beginning of this report that definitive answers to the problems of availability of legal services are likely to be those produced by examination of the legal system itself. While lawyers are adept at finding new remedies and new ways of solving problems within the context of existing law, institutions, and procedures, the fact remains that what the lawyer can offer in the way of solutions to problems is somewhat limited by what the legal system itself offers. He can sell only the merchandise that is in the store, as it were.

This is an age in which the quality of the life enjoyed by the individual is seriously threatened by the size and complexity of institutions. Big government, big business, and big institutions of all kinds are coming more and more to dominate the lives of individuals, and individuals are coming to be ever less able to make themselves heard and to cause their interests to be considered by the decision-makers. Maintenance of the quality of individual life will therefore increasingly require laws and legal processes more responsive to the needs and problems of individuals. Thus, while the legal profession considers methods of making lawyers' services more readily available to the public, it must also give serious attention to the adequacy of existing law and legal institutions.

This law reform aspect of the lawyer's function is perhaps best illustrated by the efforts of some of the legal services programs being operated under the auspices of the federal Office of Economic Opportunity. Many of the able and dedicated lawyers in these programs are doing much to reform welfare law, landlord-tenant law, and other fields of law important to poor people. Similar efforts on a broad front by the entire legal profession will be required if the law and the legal system are to be made genuinely responsive to the needs and problems of all members of our complex society in the years ahead.

D
Research

This report has demonstrated one fact conclusively: No one really knows very much about lawyers and the legal profession. For this reason, the foregoing analysis, which challenged many widely held assumptions about lawyers and the profession, itself had to be based largely on assumption. It is hoped that the assumptions indulged here may be somewhat more reasonable than the ones they are meant to supplant, but they are assumptions nevertheless.

Clearly, there is a pressing need for data about lawyers and the legal profession, from which to develop more complete and definitive solutions to the problems with which this report has been concerned. The profession must undertake comprehensive empirical studies in order to obtain increased knowledge about the profession — where lawyers are, what they do, how they do it, and why. This examination of the problems of availability of legal services might be seen as a predicate for such studies, and if it has done no more than point up the need for them and their value, it may have been worthwhile.

Unfortunately, problems will not always wait for thorough empirical study. It may thus be necessary to continue to seek solutions to many problems analytically, making assumptions where the facts are unknown, even while more definitive answers are sought empirically. As long as this is so, it will always be in order for the profession to take the kind of long hard look at itself that has been attempted here.

Works Cited

Books and Articles

1. Abrahams, R. "Law Offices to Serve Householders in the Lower Income Groups," 42 *Dick. L. Rev.* 133 (1938).
2. _____. "The Neighborhood Law Office Experiment," 9 *U. Chi. L. Rev.* 406 (1942).
3. _____. "Twenty-five Years of Service: Philadelphia's Neighborhood Law Office Plan," 50 *A.B.A.J.* 728 (1964).
4. Adler, M. "Are Real Estate Agents Entitled to Practice a Little Law?" 4 *Ariz. L. Rev.* 188 (1963).
5. American Assembly. *Report on Law and the Changing Society* (1968).
6. American Bar Association. *Canons of Professional Ethics* (1967).
7. _____. *Code of Professional Responsibility* (Final Draft, July 1, 1969).
8. _____. *Coordinator* (Dec. 1965) at 1, col. 2.
9. _____. 17 *Coordinator* (No. 4, Apr. 1969).
10. 23 *A.B.A.J.* 899 (1937).
11. American Bar Association. *Lawyers and the Poor* (undated pamphlet).
12. _____. *Opinions of the Committee on Professional Ethics* (Supp. 1968).
13. _____. *Opinions of the Committee on Professional Ethics with the Canons of Professional Ethics Annotated and Canons of Judicial Ethics Annotated* (1967).
14. 53 *A.B.A. Rep.* (1928).
15. 60 *A.B.A. Rep.* (1935).
16. 61 *A.B.A. Rep.* (1936).
17. 62 *A.B.A. Rep.* (1937).
18. 65 *A.B.A. Rep.* (1940).
19. 66 *A.B.A. Rep.* (1941).
20. 67 *A.B.A. Rep.* (1942).
21. 69 *A.B.A. Rep.* (1944).
22. 71 *A.B.A. Rep.* (1946).
23. 72 *A.B.A. Rep.* (1947).

24. 75 *A.B.A. Rep.* (1950).

25. 76 *A.B.A. Rep.* (1951).

26. 88 *A.B.A. Rep.* (1963).

27. 90 *A.B.A. Rep.* (1965).

28. 92 *A.B.A. Rep.* (1967).

29. 93 *A.B.A. Rep.* (1968).

30. American Bar Association, Board of Governors Subcommittee Implementing Recommendations of Committee on Specialization and Specialized Legal Education."Report," 79 *A.B.A. Rep.* 403 (1954).

31. American Bar Association, Committee on Availability of Legal Services. "Report," 93 *A.B.A. Rep.* 518, 526, 529 (1968).

32. _____. "Report," *Committee and Section Reports to the House of Delegates*, Rept. No. 33 (Jan. 27-28, 1969).

33. _____. "Report on Specialization," 92 *A.B.A. Rep.* 584 (1967).

34. American Bar Association, Committee on Comparative Law and Practice. "Report," *ABA International and Comparative Law Section Proceedings* 115 (1962).

35. American Bar Association, Committee on Economics of Law Practice. *Minimum Fee Schedules: Manual for Assistance of State and Local Bar Committees* (1963)

36. _____. *Proceedings of National Conference on Law Office Economics and Management* (1965 and 1967).

37. American Bar Association, Committee on Evaluation of Disciplinary Enforcement. "Report," *Committee and Section Reports to the House of Delegates*, Rept. No. 40 (Aug. 5-9, 1968).

38. American Bar Association, Committee on Law Lists. *Mimeographed Compilation of Rules and Standards as to Law Lists* (undated).

39. _____. *Third Report on Branches of the Profession Practiced* (mimeo., undated).

40. American Bar Association, Committee on Lawyer Referral Service. *1967 Annual Survey of Lawyer Referral Services.*

41. _____. *Handbook on the Lawyer Referral Service* (5th ed., 1965).

42. _____. *Lawyer Referral Bull.* (May 1955).

42A. _____. *Lawyer Referral Bull.* (Oct. 1962).

43. _____. *Lawyer Referral Bull.* (Apr. 1964).

43A. _____. *Lawyer Referral Bull.* (Oct. 1964).

44. _____. *Lawyer Referral Bull.* (Oct. 1965).

44A. _____. *Lawyer Referral Bull.* (Jan. 1965).

45. _____. *Lawyer Referral Bull.* (Jan. 1968).

46. _____. *Lawyer Referral Bull.* (July-Oct. 1968).

47. _____. "Report," 92 *A.B.A. Rep.* 464 (1967).

48. American Bar Association, Committee on Legal Aid and Indigent Defendants. "Report to House of Delegates," 93 *A.B.A. Rep.* 440 (1969).

49. American Bar Association, Committee on Recognition and Regulation of Specialization in Law Practice. "Report," 87 *A.B.A. Rep.* 361 (1962).

50. American Bar Association, Committee on Specialization. "Report," 93 *A.B.A. Rep.* 261 (1969).

51. _____. "Report," *Committee and Section Reports to the House of Delegates,* Rept. No. 33 (Jan. 27-28, 1969).

52. American Bar Association, Committee on Specialization and Specialized Legal Education. "Report," 79 *A.B.A. Rep.* 582 (1954).

53. American Bar Association, Committee on Unauthorized Practice of Law. *Informative Opinions* (1967).

54. _____. "Statement on Specialization and Specialized Legal Education," 20 *Unauthorized Prac. News* 4 (Dec. 1954).

55. American Bar Association, Section of Legal Education and Admissions to the Bar. *Review of Legal Education* (Fall 1968).

56. American Bar Association, Special Committee on Law Lists. "Report," 63 *A.B.A. Rep.* 442 (1938).

57. American Bar Foundation, *The 1967 Lawyer Statistical Report* (1968).

58. 14 *Am. Bar News* 1 (No. 9, Sept. 1969).

59. American Dental Association. *Principles of Ethics,* § 12 (June 1967).

60. American Institute of Architects. *The Standards of Professional Practice,* § § 1.4, 1.5, 3.7 (1967).

61. American Institute of Certified Public Accountants. *Code of Professional Ethics and Numbered Opinions,* art. 3 (undated).

62. American Medical Association. *Principles of Medical Ethics,* § 5 (1966).

63. 12 *Am. U.L. Rev.* 184 (1963).

64. Association of American Law Schools. "A Letter to a Member of a Grievance Committee," *Selected Readings on the Legal Profession* 130 (1962).

65. Baeck, P. "Imposition of Fees of Attorneys of Prevailing Party upon the Losing Party Under the Laws of Austria," *ABA International and Comparative Law Section Proceedings* 119 (1962).

66. _____. "Imposition of Legal Fees and Disbursements of Prevailing Party upon the Losing Party — Under the Laws of Switzerland," *ABA International and Comparative Law Section Proceedings* 124 (1962).

67. Baerncopf, D. A., and Dole, D. A. *Survey of the Economics of Law Practice in Oregon, 1961* (1963).

68. Baldwin, J. G. *Sketches of the Flush Times of Alabama* 47 (1858), as quoted in Haar, *The Golden Age of American Law* 37-39 (1965).

69. Bamberger, C. "Legal Aid: An Opportunity for the American Bar," 42 *Notre D. L. Rev.* 287 (1966).

70. Bass, S. *Unauthorized Practice Source Book* (rev. ed., 1965)

71. Bernstein, C. C. "The Arizona Realtors and the 1962 Arizona Constitutional Amendment," 29 *Unauthorized Prac. News* 169 (Summer 1963).

72. Blakslee, J. "Legal Aid Offices and Advertising," 53 *A.B.A.J.* 1148 (1967).

73. Blaustein, A., and Porter, C. O. *The American Lawyer* (1954).
74. Bodle, G. "Group Legal Services: The Case for BRT," 12 *U.C.L.A.L. Rev.* 306 (1965).
75. "The Boston Story of Lawyer Reference Service," *Lawyer Referral Bull.* 2 (Oct. 1961).
76. Bracken, J. P. "Specialization in the Law: A Fact and Not a Theory," 53 *A.B.A.J.* 325 (1967).
77. Brennan, W. J. "The Responsibilities of the Legal Profession," 54 *A.B.A.J.* 121 (1968).
78. Brenneman, H. "Annual Legal Check-up," 34 *Mich. St. B.J.* 33 (1955).
79. 29 *Bklyn. L. Rev.* 318 (1963).
80. Brown, L. M. "Law Offices for Middle-Income Clients," 40 *J. St. Bar Cal.* 720 (1965).
81. _____. "The Lawyer's Prescription," 38 *J. St. Bar Cal.* 388 (1963).
82. _____. "Legal-Cost Insurance," 1952 *Ins. L.J.* 475.
83. Brownell, E. *Legal Aid in the United States* (1951).
84. _____. *Legal Aid in the United States* (Supp. 1961).
85. By-Laws, Art. X, § 7 (q) 88 *A.B.A. Rep.*, Appendix, p. 33 (1964).
86. Cahn, E., and Cahn, J. C. "What Price Justice: The Civilian Perspective Revisited," 41 *Notre D. Law.* 927 (1966).
87. California, State Bar of, Committee on Specialization. "Final Report," 44 *J. St. Bar Cal.* 493 (1969).
88. _____. "Preliminary Report: Results of Survey on Certification of Specialists," 44 *J. St. Bar Cal.* 140 (1969).
89. California, State Bar of, Group Legal Services Committee, "1964 Progress Report," 39 *J. St. Bar Cal.* 639 (1964).
90. Cantrall, A. "A Country Lawyer Looks at Specialization," 48 *A.B.A.J.* 423 (1962).
91. Carlin, J. *Lawyers' Ethics* (1966).
92. _____. *Lawyers on Their Own* (1962).
93. Carrington, P. "Lawyer Referral as Correlated with Other Bar Services," 45 *J. Am. Jud. Soc'y* 317 (1962).
94. Case Comment. "Constitutional Law — Solicitation — Labor Unions," 16 *S.C.L. Rev.* 528 (1964).
95. 12 *Cath. U. L. Rev.* 142 (1963).
96. Cedarquist, W. "Lawyers at the Crossroads — Profession or Trade?" 31 *Unauthorized Prac. News* 79 (Fall-Winter 1965–66).
97. Cheatham, E. E. "Availability of Legal Services: The Responsibility of the Individual Lawyer and of the Organized Bar," 12 *U.C.L.A. L. Rev.* 438 (1965).
98. _____. "The Growing Need for Specialized Legal Services," 16 *Vand. L. Rev.* 497 (1963).
99. _____. *A Lawyer When Needed* (1963).
100. _____. "A Lawyer When Needed: Legal Services for the Middle Classes," 63 *Colum. L. Rev.* 973 (1963).
101. Christensen, B. "The Cost of Legal Services," *Lawyer Referral Bull.* 1 (1965).

102. ———. "Lawyer Referral Service: An Alternative to Lay-Group Legal Services?" 12 *U.C.L.A. L. Rev.* 341 (1965).

103. ———. "Regulating Group Legal Services: Who Is Being Protected—Against What—and Why?" 11 *Ariz. L. Rev.* 229 (1969).

104. ———. "Where Are We Going? And Why?" *Lawyer Referral Bull.* (Jan. 1965).

105. Chroust, A. 2 *The Rise of the Legal Profession in America* (1965).

106. Citizens Commission on Graduate Medical Education. *The Graduate Education of Physicians* (1966).

107. "Cleveland Bar Opposes Public Defender Plan," 17 *A.B.A.J.* 141 (1931).

108. Clifton, N. S., and Smith, C. "Income of Lawyers, 1965," 55 *A.B.A.J.* 562 (1969).

109. Collins, C. C. "Automobile Club Activities: The Problem from the Standpoint of the Clubs," 5 *Law & Contemp. Prob.* 3 (1938).

110. *Columbia Law School News*, Apr. 21, 1969, at 3, col. 1.

111. Columbia University, School of Law. *Bulletin: 1959–1960*, Series 59, No. 9 (Feb. 1959).

112. Comment. "Computer Retrieval of the Law: A Challenge to the Concept of Unauthorized Practice?" 116 *U. Pa. L. Rev.* 1261 (1968).

113. ———. "A Critical Analysis of Rules Against Solicitation by Lawyers," 25 *U. Chi. L. Rev.* 674 (1958).

114. ———. "Group Legal Services: Button & Brotherhood," 18 *Baylor L. Rev.* 394 (1966).

115. ———. "Membership Associations as Attorney-Client Intermediaries," 1968 *U. Ill. L.F.*

116. ———. "The Unauthorized Practice of Law by Laymen and Lay Associations," 54 *Cal. L. Rev.* 1331 (1966).

117. ———. "Union's Attorney Solicitation Program Unethical," 11 *Stan. L. Rev.* 394 (1959).

118. Committee Report. "The Neighborhood Law Office Plan," 2 *Nat'l Law. Guild Q.* 140 (July 1939).

119. Crabites, P. "Our Maleficent Legal Ethics," 1 *Nat'l Law. Guild Q.* 186 (1938).

120. Dean, A. *William Nelson Cromwell* (1957).

121. DeForest, S. "Do Doctors Have the Answers to Lawyers' Economic Problems?" 48 *A.B.A.J.* 442 (1962).

122. Drinker, H. *Legal Ethics* (1953).

123. ———. "Legal Specialists: Specialized Legal Service," 41 *A.B.A.J.* 690 (1955).

124. 1963 *Duke L. J.* 545.

125. Ehrenzweig, A. "Reimbursement of Counsel Fees and the Great Society," 54 *Cal. L. Rev.* 792 (1966).

126. ———. "Shall Counsel Fees Be Allowed?" 26 *J. St. Bar Cal.* 107 (1951).

127. Enersen, B. "Group Legal Services," 35 *J. St. Bar Cal.* 11 (1960).

128. England, G. "How Can Lawyer Referral Reach More People?" *Lawyer Referral Bull.* 1 (Jan. 1966).
129. Erie County, Bar Association of. "Legal Service Financing Plan," ABA Award of Merit, *Summary* 10 (1965).
130. Ernst and Ernst. *The Columbus Bar Association: Economic Survey* 2 (Dec. 1968).
131. Feldman, J. "The Dissemination of Health Information," 103 (1965) (unpublished Ph.D. dissertation, Univ. of Chicago, Dep't of Sociology).
132. Fendler, O. "Are We Hearing the Death Knell of the General Practice of Law?" 33 *Unauthorized Prac. News* 18 (No. 1-2, Spring-Summer 1967).
133. Frank, J. *Courts on Trial* (1949).
134. Frankel, M. "Experiments in Serving the Indigent," 51 *A.B.A.J.* 460 (1965).
135. Freed, R. "Computer Law Searching—a Potential Barrier to the Layman's Direct Access to the Law Books," 34 *Unauthorized Prac. News* 6 (Spring 1968).
136. Freed, S. "Payment of Court Costs by the Losing Party Under the Laws of Hungary," *ABA International and Comparative Law Section Proceedings* 131 (1962).
137. Gallantz, G. G. "Lawyer Referral—a Brief History," 45 *J. Am. Jud. Soc'y* 306 (1962).
138. Gardner, D. "Quick Legal Advice at $1 a Question," Post-Dispatch (St. Louis), Nov. 29, 1963, at 3D, col. 3-8.
139. Goebel, J. *A History of the School of Law—Columbia University* (1955).
140. Gottman, J. *Megalopolis, the Urbanized Northeastern Seaboard of the United States* (1961).
141. Graham, F. "Union Attacked on Legal Clinics," New York Times, May 9, 1965, at 84, col. 1.
142. _____. "Union Offers Legal Aid at Clinics," New York Times, Apr. 10, 1965, at 31, col. 2.
143. Greenville (South Carolina) Daily News, Dec. 7, 1889, at 2, col. 5.
144. Greenwood, G., and Frederickson, R. F. *Specialization in the Medical and Legal Professions* (1964).
145. Haar, C. M. *The Golden Age of American Law* (1965).
146. Hagstrom, W. *The Scientific Community* (1965).
147. Handler, J. *The Lawyer and His Community* (1967).
148. Harnsberger, R. S. "Publication of Specialties and Legal Ability Ratings in Law Lists," 49 *A.B.A.J.* 33 (1963).
149. Harrington, C., and Getty, G. "The Public Defender: A Progressive Step Towards Justice," 42 *A.B.A.J.* 1139 (1956).
150. 77 *Harv. L. Rev.* 122 (1963).
151. Hazard, G. "Rationing Justice," 8 *J. Law & Econ.* 1 (Oct. 1965).
152. _____. "Reflections on Four Studies of the Legal Profession," *Social Problems* 46 (Supp. on Law and Society, Summer 1965).

153. Hervey, J. "Law School Registration, 1965" 18 *J. Legal Ed.* 197 (1965).

154. Hicks, F., and Katz, E. "The Practice of Law by Laymen and Lay Agencies," 41 *Yale L. J.* 69 (Nov. 1931).

155. Holman, F. E. *The Life and Career of a Western Lawyer, 1886-1961* (1963).

156. Holmes, O. W. "Law in Science—Science in Law," 12 *Harv. L. Rev.* 443 (Feb. 1899).

157. Honnold, J. "The Bourgeois Bar and the Mississippi Movement," 52 *A.B.A.J.* 228 (1966).

158. "How Chicago Bar Association Conducts Its Plan," *Lawyer Referral Bull.* 1 (May 1960).

159. 11 *How. L.J.* 242 (1965).

160. Hurst, J. W. *The Growth of American Law* (1950).

161. Iowa State Bar Association. "Lay Opinion of Iowa Lawyers, Courts and Laws" 18 (Apr. 1949).

162. Janopaul, R. "Specialization in the Practice of Law—Canons of Professional Ethics and Opinions of the Committee on Professional Ethics and Grievances," American Bar Foundation Research Memorandum, No. 22 (1960).

163. Johnson, E. "An Analysis of the OEO Legal Services Program," 38 *Miss. L.J.* 419 (1967).

164. _____. "Introductory Address," *Proceedings of the Harvard Conference on Law and Poverty* (Mar. 17-19, 1967).

165. _____. "The O.E.O. Legal Services Program," 14 *Cath. L.* 99 (1968).

166. Johnstone, Q., and Hopson, D. *Lawyers and Their Work* (1967).

167. Joiner, C. "Specialization in the Law: Control It or It Will Destroy the Profession," 41 *A.B.A.J.* 1105 (1955).

168. _____. "Specialization in the Law? The Medical Profession Shows the Way," 39 *A.B.A.J.* 539 (1953).

169. Joost, R. H. "Consolidation of Law Offices," 53 *A.B.A.J.* 429 (1967).

170. 40 *J. St. Bar Cal.* 442 (1965).

171. 42 *J. St. Bar Cal.* 478 (1967).

172. 44 *J. St. Bar Cal.* 471 (1969).

173. Kansas, Bar Association of the State of. *Survey of the Economics of Law Practice* (1964).

174. Katz, S. "Looking Backward: The Early History of American Law," 33 *U. Chi. L. Rev.* 867 (Summer 1966).

175. Katzenbach, N. "Luncheon Address," *National Conference on Law and Poverty, Conference Proceedings* 61 (June 23-25, 1965).

176. Katzman, M. "There Is a Shortage of Lawyers," 21 *J. Legal Ed.* 169 (1968).

177. Koos, E. *The Family and the Law* (1949).

178. Kuenzel, C. "The Attorney's Fee: Why not a Cost of Litigation?" 49 *Iowa L. Rev.* 75 (1963).

179. Kutner, L. *I the Lawyer* (1966).

180. Ladinsky, J. "The Impact of Social Backgrounds of Lawyers on Law Practice and the Law," 16 *J. Legal Ed.* 127 (1963).

181. ———. "The Social Profile of a Metropolitan Bar," 43 *Mich. St. Bar J.* 12 (No. 2, Feb. 1964).

182. Landes, M. "Project: Automated Legal Research," 52 *A.B.A.J.* 730 (1966).

183. Lascoe, D. "One Company's Policy on Wage Attachments," 23 *Legal Aid Briefcase* 264 (1965).

184. Law Society. *Annual Report of the Council and Accounts, 1966–1967.*

185. ———. *Legal Advice and Assistance — Memorandum of the Council of the Law Society* (Feb. 1968).

186. ———. *Legal Aid and Advice — Fourteenth Report of the Law Society and Comments and Recommendations of the Lord Chancellor's Advisory Committee* (1963-64).

187. ———. *Legal Aid and Advice — Sixteenth Report of the Law Society and Comments and Recommendations of the Lord Chancellor's Advisory Committee* (1965-66).

188. "Law Students in Court," 24 *Legal Aid Briefcase* 266 (1966).

189. Lawlor, R. "Forum: Computers and Automation in Law," 40 *J. St. Bar Cal.* 30 (1965).

190. Levitorn, C. "Automobile Club Activities: The Problem from the Standpoint of the Bar," 5 *Law & Contemp. Prob.* 11 (1938).

191. Levy, B. *Corporation Lawyer: Saint or Sinner?* (1961).

192. Lewis, H. H. W. "Corporate Capacity to Practice Law — a Study in Legal Hocus Pocus," 2 *Md. L. Rev.* 342 (1938).

193. Linowitz, S. "Our Changing Society: The Lawyer's Challenge," 54 *A.B.A.J.* 445 (1968).

194. Llewellyn, K. N. "The Bar's Troubles, and Poultices — and Cures?" 5 *Law & Contemp. Prob.* 104 (1938).

195. ———. *Jurisprudence: Realism in Theory and Practice* (1962).

196. ———, and Hoebel, E. *The Cheyenne Way* (1941).

197. Lorinczi, G. "Computers and Unauthorized Practice," 54 *A.B.A.J.* 379 (1968).

198. ———. "When Does the Computer Engage in Unauthorized Practice?" 34 *Unauthorized Prac. News* 14 (Spring 1968).

199. Love, A., and Childers, J. S. *Listen to Leaders in Law* (1963).

200. MacKinnon, F. B. *Contingent Fees for Legal Services* (1964).

201. Madden, F. J. "Procedures and Operations," 45 *J. Am. Jud. Soc'y* 313 (1962).

202. ———, and Christensen, B. "Lawyer Referral Service: A Sensible Approach to a Difficult Problem," 49 *A.B.A.J.* 965 (1963).

203. Mancuso, E. T. "Law Students and Defender Offices," 24 *Legal Aid Briefcase* 242 (1966).

204. Marden, O. "Lawyer Referral Services: They Are Important to Lawyers and the Public," 43 *A.B.A.J.* 517 (1957).
205. Markus, R. M. "Group Representation by Attorneys as Misconduct," 14 *Clev.-Mar. L. Rev.* 1 (1963).
206. Mars, D. "The Problem of the Indigent Accused: Public Defenders in the Federal Courts," 45 *A.B.A.J.* 272 (1959).
207. Marsh, W.D. "Neighborhood Law Offices or Judicare?" 25 *Legal Aid Briefcase* 12 (1966).
208. Martin, G. A. "Legal Aid in Ontario," 10 *Can. B.J.* 473 (1967).
209. *Martindale-Hubbell Law Directory*, 4 vols.
210. Masotti, L., and Corsi, J. "Legal Assistance for the Poor: An Analysis and Evaluation of Two Programs," 44 *J. Urb. L.* 483 (1967).
211. Matthews, E. J. T. "Lawyer Referral – the English Equivalent," *Lawyer Referral Bull.* 2 (Jan. 1963).
212. Mayhew, L. and Reiss, A. J., Jr. "The Social Organization of Legal Contacts," 34 *Am. Soc. Rev.* 309 (1969).
213. McArdle, M. "Law Students' Participation in NDP Projects," 24 *Legal Aid Briefcase* 262 (1966).
214. Megarry, R. E. *Lawyer and Litigant in England* (1962).
215. 65 *Mich. L. Rev.* 805 (1967).
216. Michigan State College, Social Research Service. "Report on a Pilot Study to the State Bar of Michigan" 6 (Sept. 1949).
217. 49 *Minn. L. Rev.* 333 (1964).
218. 34 *Miss. L.J.* 344 (1963).
219. Missouri Bar. *Advisory Opinions.*
220. _____. *Missouri Bar–Prentice-Hall Survey* (1963).
221. Morris, C. "Law Lists and the A.B.A. Standing Committee on Law Lists," 7 *Practical Lawyer* 44 (No. 5, May 1961).
222. Morris, E. "The President's Page," 54 *A.B.A.J.* 419 (1968).
223. Mueller, G. "Pre-Requiem for the Law Faculty," 18 *J. Legal Ed.* 411 (1966).
224. National Legal Aid and Defender Association. *Summary of Conference Proceedings* (1966).
225. National Society of Professional Engineers. *Code of Ethics* § 3 (June 1954).
226. _____. *Opinions of the Board of Ethical Review* (undated).
227. New York, Association of the Bar of the City of, and New York County Lawyers' Ass'n Committee on Professional Ethics. *Opinions* (1956).
228. _____. "Report" (1968).
229. Niles, R., "Ethical Prerequisites to Certification of Special Proficiency," 49 *A.B.A.J.* 83 (1963).
230. Note. "Advertising, Solicitation, and Legal Ethics," 7 *Vand. L. Rev.* 677 (1954).

231. ———. "Attorney's Fees: Where Shall the Ultimate Burden Lie?" 20 *Vand. L. Rev.* 1242 (1967).

232. ———. "Echoes of Antiquity: The Doctrine of Champerty and Maintenance and the Rule of Canon 42," 43 *Notre D.L. Rev.* 533 (1967).

233. ———. "The Emergence of Lay Intermediaries Furnishing Legal Services to Individuals," 1965 *Wash. U.L.Q.* 313.

234. ———. "Group Legal Services," 79 *Harv. L. Rev.* 416 (1965).

235. ———. "Group Legal Services: The Ethical Traditions and the Constitution," 43 *St. John's L. Rev.* 82 (1968).

236. ———. "Group Legal Services and the Right of Association," 63 *Mich. L. Rev.* 1089 (1965).

237. ———. "Legal Aid Programs of a Labor Union and the Unauthorized Practice of Law," 20 *U. Pitt. L. Rev.* 85 (1958).

238. ———. "Legal Ethics — Ambulance Chasing," 20 *N.Y.U.L. Rev.* 182 (1955).

239. ———. "Neighborhood Law Offices: The New Wave in Legal Services for the Poor," 80 *Harv. L. Rev.* 805 (1967).

240. ———. "Providing Legal Services for the Middle Class in Civil Matters: The Problem, the Duty, and a Solution," 26 *U. Pitt. L. Rev.* 811 (1965).

241. ———. "Small Claims Courts as Collection Agencies," 4 *Stan. L. Rev.* 237 (1952).

242. ———. "The Unauthorized Practice of Law by Lay Organizations Providing the Services of Attorneys," 72 *Harv. L. Rev.* 1334 (1959).

243. Onion, J. F. "The Unauthorized Practice of Law," 25 *Unauthorized Prac. News* 271 (No. 4, Winter 1959).

244. 26 *Ore. St. Bar Bull.* 1 (No. 10, July 1966).

245. 27 *Ore. St. Bar Bull.* 1 (No. 1, Oct. 1966).

246. Parker, G. "Legal Aid — Canadian Style," 14 *Wayne L. Rev.* 471 (1968).

247. Parker, R. H. L. "The Development of Legal Aid in England Since 1949," 48 *A.B.A.J.* 1029 (1962).

248. Parsons, B. *Summary Report of the New Mexico Survey of the Economics of Law Practice* (1963).

249. Pelletier, G. A. "English Legal Aid: The Successful Experiment in Judicare," 40 *U. Colo. L. Rev.* 10 (1967).

250. 107 *Pa. L. Rev.* 392 (1959).

251. Philadelphia Bar Association. *Manual of Instructions for Neighborhood Law Offices* (1964).

252. Porter, C. O. "Answers to Objections to the Lawyer Reference Service," 31 *Ore. L. Rev.* 15 (1951-52).

253. Pound, R. *The Lawyer from Antiquity to Modern Times* (1953).

254. Powell, L. F. "The President's Page," 51 *A.B.A.J.* 20 (1965).

255. Preloznik, J. F. "Wisconsin Judicare," 25 *Legal Aid Briefcase* 91 (1967).

256. Prentice-Hall Editorial Staff. 1 *Complete Guide to a Profitable Law Practice* (1965).

257. "Publicity—Does It Pay?" *Lawyer Referral Bull.* 1 (Jan. 1964).

258. "Publicity on a Tight Budget," *Lawyer Referral Bull.* (Apr. 1964).

259. Radin, M. "Maintenance by Champerty," 24 *Cal. L. Rev.* 48 (1935).

260. Redfield, R. *Factors of Growth in a Law Practice* (1962).

261. Reiss, A. *Occupations and Social Status* (1961).

262. Resh, W. "Safeguarding the Administration of Justice from Illegal Practice," 25 *Unauthorized Prac. News* 81 (No. 2, Summer 1959).

263. Riggs, R. E. "Unauthorized Practice and the Public Interest: Arizona's Recent Constitutional Amendment," 37 *So. Cal. L. Rev.* 1 (1964).

264. Robb, J. D. "Alternate Legal Assistance Plans," 14 *Cath. L.* 127 (1968).

265. Roche, M. "Ethical Problems Raised by the Neighborhood Law Office," 41 *Notre D.L.* 961 (1966).

266. Rohner, R. "Jurimetrics, No!" 54 *A.B.A.J.* 896 (1968).

267. Rossman, G., and Stringham, R. *Increasing a Law Practice* (1965).

268. Rowe, C. *How and Where Lawyers Get Practice* (1955).

269. Rubin, A. "Is Any but the Best Good Enough?" *Lawyer Referral Bull.* 1 (Apr. 1966).

270. Sandburg, C. "The Lawyers Know Too Much," in Blaustein and Porter, *The American Lawyer* 33 (1954).

271. Sanders, P. "Foreword," 5 *Law & Contemp. Prob.* 1 (Winter 1938).

272. Satterfield, J. C. "The President's Page," 48 *A.B.A.J.* 99 (1962).

273. Schima, H. "The Treatment of Costs and Fees of Procedure in the Austrian Law," *ABA International and Comparative Law Section Proceedings* 121 (1962).

274. Schlossberg, A., and Weinberg, W. R. "The Role of Judicare in the American Legal System," 54 *A.B.A.J.* 1000 (1968).

275. Schwartz, M. "Foreword: Group Legal Services in Perspective," 12 *U.C.L.A. L. Rev.* 279 (1965).

276. Segal, R. M. "Labor Union Lawyers: Professional Services of Lawyers to Organized Labor," 5 *Ind. & Lab. Rel. Rev.* 343 (1952).

277. Shriver, S. "The OEO and Legal Services," 51 *A.B.A.J.* 1064 (1965).

278. Siddal, R. "Specialization in the Law: A Retort to Professor Joiner's Call for Control," 42 *A.B.A.J.* 625 (1956).

279. Silverstein, L. 1 *Defense of the Poor in Criminal Cases in American State Courts* (1965).

280. _____. "Eligibility for Free Legal Services in Civil Cases," 44 *U. Det. J. Urb. L.* 549 (1967).

281. _____. "The New Ontario Legal Aid System and Its Significance for the United States," 25 *Legal Aid Briefcase* 83 (1967).

282. _____. "Waiver of Court Costs and Appointment of Counsel for Poor Persons in Civil Cases," 2 *Val. L. Rev.* 21 (1967).

283. Simpson, F. "Group Legal Services: The Case for Caution," 12 *U.C.L.A.L. Rev.* 327 (1965).
284. Smigel, E. O. *The Wall Street Lawyer* (1964).
285. Smith, A., and Curran, B. "A Study of the Lawyer-Social Worker Professional Relationship," *Research Contributions of the American Bar Foundation*, 1968, No. 6.
286. Smith, C., and Clifton, N. S. "Income of Lawyers, 1965," 55 *A.B.A.J.* 562 (1969).
287. Smith, R. "Legal Service Offices for Persons of Moderate Means," 31 *J. Am. Jud. Soc'y* 37 (1947).
288. Sonneberg, H. F. "Why Not Blue Scales for Legal Services?" 22 *Milw. Bar Ass'n Gavel* 12 (1961).
289. 15 *S.C.L. Rev.* 845 (1963).
290. Spangenberg, R. L. "The Roxbury Defender Project," 24 *Legal Aid Briefcase* 247 (1966).
291. Sparer, E. "The Role of the Welfare Client's Lawyer," 12 *U.C.L.A. L. Rev.* 361 (1965).
292. Sprecher, R. A. "Ethical Advertising and Solicitation: Law Lists," 53 *A.B.A.J.* 121 (1967).
293. 11 *Stan. L. Rev.* 394 (1959).
294. Recent Developments, "State Statute Barring Solicitation of Legal Work Held to Violate Due Process as Applied to NAACP," 63 *Colum. L. Rev.* 1502 (1963).
295. Stein, J. "Oh, Mr. Martindale—Yes, Mr. Hubbell!" *D.C. Bar J.* 132 (1966).
296. Stevenson, N. *How to Build a More Lucrative Law Practice* (1967).
297. Stoebuck, W. B. "Counsel Fees Included in Costs: A Logical Development," 38 *U. Colo. L. Rev.* 202 (1966).
298. Stoller, B. "Small Claims Courts in Texas: Paradise Lost," 47 *Tex. L. Rev.* 448 (1969).
299. Stolz, P. "Insurance for Legal Services," 35 *U. Chi. L. Rev.* 417 (1968).
300. _____. "The Legal Needs of the Public: A Survey Analysis," *Research Contributions of the American Bar Foundation*, 1968, No. 4.
301. 36 *Survey of Current Business* 33 (No. 12, Dec. 1956).
302. Symposium. "Group Law Practice," 18 *Clev.-Mar. L. Rev.* 1 (1969).
303. 16 *Syr. L. Rev.* 141 (1964).
304. Teschner, P. "Specialisms, Tax Lawyers, the Legal Profession," 21 *Tax Law.* 407 (1968).
305. _____. "Specialists, Experts, and Lawyers: On the Integrity of the Legal Profession," 41 *U. Det. L.J.* 483 (1964).
306. 43 *Tex. L. Rev.* 254 (1964).
307. Texas, State Bar of. "What Texans Think of Lawyers" 24 (1952).
308. Time, Mar. 29, 1968, at 76.
309. Tracy, J. E. *The Successful Practice of Law* (1947).

310. Traycik, L., and McKenzie, R. "Bank Financing of Attorney Fees," 44 *Mich. St. Bar J.* 15 (Dec. 1965).

311. Tucker, E. "Brotherhood of R.R. Trainmen v. Virginia: A Call to Realism in Legal Ethics," 14 *J. Pub. L.* 3 (1965).

312. Tweed, H. *The Changing Practice of Law* (1955).

313. _____. "The Changing Practice of Law: The Question of Specialization," 48 *A.B.A.J.* 117 (1962).

314. _____. "Lawyers' Committee on Civil Rights Under Law Formed at Request of President Kennedy," 49 *A.B.A.J.* 785 (1963).

315. 33 *Unauthorized Prac. News* 73 (Nos. 1-2, Spring-Summer 1967).

316. U.S. Bureau of the Census, *Statistical Abstract of the United States: 1952* (73d ed. 1952).

316A. _____. *Statistical Abstract of the United States: 1966* (87th ed. 1966).

317. _____. *Statistical Abstract of the United States: 1967* (88th ed. 1967).

318. U.S., 77th Cong., 2d Sess. *Hearings on H.R. 7378 (Revenue Revision of 1942) Before the House Committee on Ways and Means* (1942).

319. _____. *Hearings on H.R. 7378 Before the Senate Committee on Finance* (1942).

320. U.S. Dept. of Health, Education, and Welfare, Office of Economic Opportunity, 3 *Law in Action* 7, col. 1 (No. 10, Mar. 1969).

321. _____. *1968 Year-End Report* (Jan. 7, 1969).

322. 32 *U. Cin. L. Rev.* 550 (1963).

323. 37 *U. Colo. L. Rev.* 300 (1965).

324. 40 *U. Det. L.J.* 531 (1963).

325. 1963 *U. Ill. L. F.* 97.

326. 26 *U. Pitt. L. Rev.* 142 (1964).

327. Univ. of Washington, Bureau of Business Research. *How Small Business Firms in the State of Washington Cope with Their Legal Problems* 67 (July 1963).

328. Utton, A. "The British Legal Aid System," 76 *Yale L.J.* 371 (1966).

329. 20 *Vand. L. Rev.* 1216 (1967).

330. 51 *Va. L. Rev.* 1693 (1965).

331. *Vital Statistics of the United States, 1969* (2 vols.).

332. vom Baur, T. "Report of Standing Committee on Unauthorized Practice of Law—American Bar Association—August 1959," 25 *Unauthorized Prac. News* 199 (No. 3, Fall 1959).

333. Voorhees, T. "The Lawyer Referral Service: The Medium Size and Smaller Communities," 40 *A.B.A.J.* 663 (1954).

334. _____. "Legal Advice for Those with Jobs," 40 *A.B.A.J.* 579 (1954).

335. _____. "The OEO Legal Services Program: Should the Bar Support It?" 53 *A.B.A.J.* 23 (1967).

336. _____. "The Outlook for the Lawyer Referral Service," 38 *A.B.A.J.* 193 (1952).

337. Wald, P. *Law and Poverty: 1965* (1965).
338. Warkov, S., and Zelan, J. *Lawyers in the Making* (1965).
339. Weaver, R. C. *The Urban Complex* (1964).
340. *Webster's Seventh New Collegiate Dictionary* (1965).
341. Weihofen, H. "Practice of Law by Motor Clubs — Useful but Forbidden," 3 *U. Chi. L. Rev.* 296 (1936).
342. ———. "Practice of Law by Non-Pecuniary Corporations: A Social Utility," 2 *U. Chi. L. Rev.* 119 (1934).
343. Wham, B. "Specialization in the Law: The Public Need Must Be Better Served," 42 *A.B.A.J.* 39 (1956).
344. "What Minnesota Thinks of Lawyers," 9 *Bench & Bar of Minnesota* 15 (No. 6, May 1952).
345. "Where Does a Defense Attorney's Responsibility Lie?" 4 *Fed'n of Ins. Counsel Q.* 5 (No. 2, Winter 1954).
346. White, R., Stein, J. H., and Fishman, R. *Paraprofessionals in Legal Service Programs: A Feasibility Study* (Dec. 1968).
347. Winkler, C. "Legal Assistance for the Armed Forces," 50 *A.B.A.J.* 451 (1964).
348. Wolfskill, G. *The Revolt of the Conservatives: A History of the American Liberty League, 1934-1940* (1962).
349. 49 *Yale L.J.* 699 (1940).
350. Yegge, R. B. "American Lawyers, 1976: A Clouded Crystal Ball," 52 *A.B.A.J.* 737 (1966).
351. Zimroth, P. "Group Legal Services and the Constitution," 76 *Yale L.J.* 966 (1967).

Cases

352. A.T. & S.F.R. v. Jackson, 235 F.2d 390 (10th circ. 1956).
353. *In re* Ades, 6 F. Supp. 467 (D. Md. 1934).
354. Application of Hunt, 230 A.2d 432 (Conn. 1967).
355. Automobile Club of Mo. v. Hoffmeister, 338 S.W.2d 348 (Mo. App. 1960).
356. Azzarello v. Legal Aid Society, 117 Ohio App. 471,185 N.E.2d 566 (1962).
357. Bar of Fairfield County v. Dacey, 154 Conn. 129, 222 A.2d 339 (1966).
358. Benjamin v. Legal Aid Society, 117 Ohio App. 471, 185 N.E.2d 566 (1962).
359. Berry v. District Court of Third Judicial District, 91 Idaho 600, 428 P.2d 519 (1967).
360. Berry v. Koehler, 84 Idaho 170, 269 P.2d 1010 (1962).
361. Berry v. Koehler, 86 Idaho 225, 384 P.2d 484 (1963).
362. Berry v. Summers, 76 Idaho 446, 283 P.2d 1093 (1955).
363. *In re* Brotherhood of Railroad Trainmen, 13 Ill.2d 391, 150 N.E.2d 163 (1958).

364. Brotherhood of Railroad Trainmen v. Virginia, *ex rel.* Virginia State Bar, 377 U.S. 1 (1964).

365. Brotherhood of Railroad Trainmen v. Virginia, *ex rel.* Virginia State Bar, 377 U.S. 1, *rehearing denied,* 377 U.S. 960 (1964).

366. Brotherhood of Railroad Trainmen v. Virginia, *ex rel.* Virginia State Bar, 207 Va. 182, 149 S.E.2d 265, *cert. denied,* 385 U.S. 1027 (1967).

367. Chicago Bar Ass'n v. Quinlan & Tyson, Inc., 53 Ill. App.2d 388, 203 N.E.2d 131 (1964), *modified,* 34 Ill.2d 116, 214 N.E.2d 771 (1966).

368. *In re* Cohn, 10 Ill.2d 186, 139 N.E.2d 301 (1956).

369. Columbus Bar Ass'n v. Potts, 175 Ohio St. 101, 191 N.E.2d 728 (1963).

370. *In re* Community Action for Legal Services, Inc., 26 App. Div.2d 354, 274 N.Y.S.2d 779 (1966).

371. *In re* Community Legal Services, Inc., 26 App. Div.2d 354, 274 N.Y.S.2d 779 (1966).

372. *In re* Community Legal Services, Inc., Pa. C.P.4, March Term, 1966, No. 4968 (35 U.S.L.W. 2017, June 30, 1966).

373. Comunale v. Traders & General Ins. Co., 50 Cal.2d 654, 328 P.2d 198 (1958).

374. *In re* Co-operative Law Co., 198 N.Y. 479, 92 N.E. 15 (1910).

375. Dorsey v. E.S.C., 355 Mich. 103, 94 N.W.2d 407 (1959), *dismissed,* 360 U.S. 251 (1959).

376. Doughty v. Grills, 37 Tenn. App. 63, 260 S.W.2d 379 (1952).

377. Dworken v. Apt. House Owners Ass'n, 38 Ohio App. 265, 176 N.E. 577 (1931).

378. Escobedo v. Illinois, 378 U.S. 478 (1964).

379. *In re* Gault, 387 U.S. 1 (1967).

380. Gideon v. Wainwright, 372 U.S. 335 (1963).

381. Gunnels v. Atlanta Bar Association, 191 Ga. 366, 12 S.E.2d 602 (1940).

382. Hildebrand v. State Bar, 36 Cal.2d 504, 225 P.2d 508 (1950).

383. Hoffmeister v. Tod, 349 S.W.2d 5 (Mo. 1961).

384. Hospital Credit Exchange, Inc. v. Shapiro, 186 Misc. 658, 59 N.Y.S.2d 812 (1946).

385. Hulse v. Brotherhood of Railroad Trainmen, 340 S.W.2d 404 (Mo. 1960).

386. Jacksonville Bar Ass'n v. Wilson, 102 So.2d 292 (Fla. 1958).

387. Kent v. United States, 383 U.S. 541 (1966).

388. Kentucky Bar Ass'n v. First Federal Savings & Loan, 342 S.W.2d 397 (Ky. 1961).

389. *In re* Maclub of America, Inc., 295 Mass. 45, 3 N.E.2d 272 (1936).

390. Midland Credit Adjustment Co. v. Donnelley, 219 Ill. App. 271 (1921).

391. Miranda v. Arizona, 384 U.S. 436 (1966).

392. National Association for the Advancement of Colored People v. Button, 371 U.S. 415 (1963).

393. *In re* O'Neill, 5 F. Supp. 465 (E.D.N.Y. 1933).

394. People v. Cal. Protective Corp., 76 Cal. App. 354, 244 P. 1089 (1926).

395. People *ex rel.* Chicago Bar Ass'n v. Chicago Motor Club, 362 Ill. 50, 199 N.E. 1 (1935).

396. People *ex rel.* Chicago Bar Association v. Motorists Association, 354 Ill. 595, 188 N.E. 827 (1933).

397. People *ex rel.* Courtney v. Ass'n of Real Estate Taxpayers, 354 Ill. 102, 187 N.E. 823 (1933).

398. People v. Merchants Protective Corp., 189 Cal. 531, 209 P. 363 (1922).

399. Powell v. Alabama, 287 U.S. 45 (1932).

400. Rhode Island Bar Ass'n v. Automobile Service Ass'n, 55 R.I. 122, 179 A. 139 (1935).

401. Ryan v. Penn R., 260 Ill. App. 364 (1932).

402. Stanislaus County Bar Ass'n v. California Rural Legal Assistance, Inc., No. 93302 (Dept. No. 4, Stanislaus County, Cal., October 12, 1966).

403. State *ex rel.* Florida Bar v. Sperry, 140 S.2d 587 (Fla. 1962), *rev'd*, 373 U.S. 379 (1963), *modified*, 159 So.2d 229 (Fla. 1963).

404. State v. Merchants Protective Corp., 105 Wash. 12, 177 P. 694 (1919).

405. State *ex rel.* Seawell v. Carolina Motor Club, 209 N.C. 624, 184 S.E. 540 (1936).

406. State Bar v. Ariz. Land Title & Trust Co., 90 Ariz. 76, 366 P.2d 1 (1961), *modified*, 91 Ariz. 293, 371 P.2d 1020 (1962).

407. *In re* Thibodeau, 295 Mass. 374, 3 N.E.2d 749 (1936).

408. *Re* Unauthorized Practice of Law in Cuyahoga County, 175 Ohio St. 149, 192 N.E.2d 54 (1963), *cert. denied*, 376 U.S. 970 (1964), *rehearing denied*, 377 U.S. 940 (1964).

409. United Mine Workers of America, Dist. 12 v. Illinois State Bar Association, 389 U.S. 217 (1967).

410. Vitaphone Corp. v. Hutchinson Amusement Co., 28 F. Supp. 526 (D. Mass. 1939).

411. Wisconsin *ex rel.* State Bar of Wisconsin v. Bonded Collections, Inc. (Cir. Ct., Eau Claire County, Wis., Feb. 2, 1967).

Other

412. 14 Am. Jur.2d Champerty and Maintenance §§ 1–3, 19 (1964).

413. 19 Am. Jur.2d Corporations § 528 (1965).

414. Annotation, 2 A.L.R.3d 724 (1965).

415. _____, 11 A.L.R.3d 1206 (1967).

416. _____, 45 A.L.R.2d 1243 (1956).

417. _____, 105 A.L.R. 1364 (1936).

418. _____, 106 A.L.R. 548 (1937).

419. _____, 139 A.L.R. 620 (1942).

420. Ariz. Constitution art. 26, § 1.

421. Ill. Rev. Stat., ch. 32, § 411 (1967).

422. _____, ch. 91, § 86–105.3 (1967).

423. Int. Rev. Code of 1954.

424. Legal Aid and Advice Act of 1949, 12 & 13 Geo. 6, ch. 51, § 7(8).

425. _____, 12 & 13 Geo. 6, ch. 51, § 2, *as amended*, Legal Aid Act of 1960, 8 & 9 Eliz. 2, ch. 28, § 1.

426. Stat. Instr. 1959, No. 47, *as amended*, Stat. Instr. 1960, No. 729.

427. Stat. Instr. 1962, No. 148, § 19, Sched. 2.

428. _____, No. 148, *as amended*, Stat. Instr. 1962, No. 1714, and Stat. Instr. 1964, No. 1893.

429. Publ. L. 89–332, § 1, 79 Stat. 1281 (Nov. 8, 1965).

430. 18 U.S.C. § 3006A (1964).